Brother William's War
Illustrated

William J. Watson
Author

Jane Zimmermannn Slaton
and
Maggie Slaton Harshbarger
Illustrators

2011

Brother William's War, second edition: 2010
Brother William's War, third edition, illustrated: 2011

Illustrations by Jane Zimmerman Slaton, great-great niece of William Coleman, and her daughter, Maggie Slaton Harshbarger.

Published by Broken Lance Enterprises, E27 Hillside Court, Stroudsburg, Pa. 18360

ISBN-13: 978-0615452616 (Broken Lance Enterprises)
ISBN-10: 0615452612

William Coleman
6th South Carolina Volunteer Infantry

HANNA

I am an old, tired woman, but not so old and tired that I can't do my duty when it stares me plainly in the face. I don't know why Brother William never told any of us about his journal; maybe he just didn't have time, between walking home from Virginia after Appomattox and then dying, to tell us everything. And I don't know why he gave it to Sarah Wright — well, I do know why, because he tells us in the journal, but my goodness gracious, the woman couldn't read. She never knew what she was hiding. Thank God above that her grandson John had the wit to realize what he'd found when he was cleaning out her belongings after she died.

I look at what Brother William wrote in his journal, and I look at the essay I wrote a few years ago for the schoolchildren of Chester on what the war meant to us all those years ago. I listen to the mockingbird in the tree outside my window, and remember the day Brother William died. I laugh and cry. I didn't know. None of us who stayed at home knew.

Brother William was taken so quickly from us. We'd never talked about the war. He'd written letters — some of them are published as part of this book — but I see now, after reading his journal, that his letters to me and most others were carefully worded. He never lied to those of us back home, but he left a lot out. Like making lace: What's left out gives shape to what's left. He almost spoke truth once, in a letter to Elizabeth, but that's as close as he came. We just never knew — none of the men would ever say afterwards what they'd actually done, not really. What they did say was pretty much like William's letters, full of words that turned out to be not enough. It wasn't until I read his journal that I knew — I knew. Finally. And even William didn't know until the war was over. How very like him, to be so smart and yet so blind, and then to finally put it all together in one blazing insight. What he knew pulled him through the war even though he couldn't explain it until it was over. Brother William.

With John Wright's help, I have put together Brother William's journal, my own essay, which I did have the strength to refrain from editing, and some letters he and I have found. It is quite a saga.

Why now? Why publish this 50 years after it is over? I feel it is right. Brother William could think it through and give you a reason. I can't, not like he could. Others could probably do it, But Lee is dead and Jackson is dead and A.J. Mantour is dead and John Bratton and Wade Hampton — the only one still alive is Longstreet, and no one will listen to him anymore. Well, Tom Wright is still alive, but he is not the man he was when he marched off with the Sixth Regiment.

God took William after he'd finished his journal, and never gave him a chance to change a single word. It's just as he thought and felt while the war was going on. God kept it hidden all these years, and God made it known to me now. We had 12 years of Maine Yankees with bayonets "reconstructing" us depraved Southerners in Chester and 38 more years of hearing "slavery, slavery, slavery" shouted at us, and I was bewildered by it and then saddened by it and then angered by it and now I am going to say "Enough! Here is Brother William's war, and here is mine right alongside it! We were just people like you! I dare you to find shame in us!"

Maybe it's time. The Yankees gave us back our flags a few years ago; maybe they are ready to hear this. And even if they are not, there are Southerners who need to hear it, before it gets swept away forever by time. Brother William found no shame in what he did; neither do I, and neither should you.

I am doing the right thing. Like Brother William, I am satisfied.

Hanna Coleman
Chester, S.C.
Oct. 26, 1911

WILLIAM

I think that if I am going to get involved in this — if I am going to leave a good position in a bank and go gallivanting off with A.J. and his silly militia — I think I will write it all down as it happens, to share it with everyone and make anyone who reads it feel like they were there with me. And it looks like I have no choice about getting involved — that must be the first thing I write.

I think it is all going to amount to nothing. But I will look at it as an adventure. Who knows? Maybe I'll look at this journal as an old man and be amused.

William Coleman
Chester, S.C.
April 8, 1861

CHAPTER ONE

A.J. was strutting again, preening in his blue militia uniform in front of the bank where everyone could see. He did it a lot. The militia began drilling once a week after John Brown's raid, and A.J. often wore the uniform to the bank, claiming it saved him a trip home after work. Most people knew he just liked to be seen wearing the bright blue uniform with the cutaway front and shiny brass palmetto buttons.

"Last chance, Coleman. It's not too late. Come along and kill some Yankees with us."

It is early April but I'm hot and sweating and the high collar of my shirt, proper attire for a bank clerk and something the citizens find reassuringly staid, is chafing my chin. A.J. has been trying to recruit me for his company, the Calhoun Guards, for months now, ever since South Carolina seceded. I have watched them march and drill with their old guns up and down the hilly streets of Chester all winter. It seems to me childish. I am 29 years old – the same as A.J. – and I am a bank clerk. Not a teller; I have left that behind. I am in charge of keeping the ledgers for the entire Farmers and Merchants Bank of Chester. Mr. Thomas Mantour, A.J.'s father and the president of the bank, has hinted that it won't be long before farmers seeking credit to buy seed will have to deal with me, not him. Ever since the railroad went through three years ago, he has been spending more time with strangers looking to buy land and less time with the farmers and small plantation owners who used to make up most of the bank's business.

Chester is growing and I'm going to be part of it, a big part. I see no reason to waste time playing soldier. But A.J. is, after all, Thomas Mantour's son and a vice president of the bank, even if that is a sinecure. One must be cautious.

"Surely you and the Calhoun Guards are enough to defend the state," I suggest, taking off my spectacles and cleaning them. "You don't need a half-blind bank clerk with a history of illness to help when you have all those brave, healthy farm boys taking your orders."

A.J. composes his pudgy face into a look of great solemnity and looks me in the eye. I know from long experience he considers this his most effective tactic for persuasion.

"The Confederacy needs every man," he intones.

I chuckle. Inwardly, anyway.

"Why? So far Abe Lincoln and his Black Republican friends haven't done a thing to stop states from seceding. There will be no fighting."

A.J.'s features contort. He is doing his best to keep from looking like someone who knows a secret, but he's not having much luck. I can see the secret twisting inside him, trying to get out. He loses the battle.

He walks over to the doorway where I have been watching him clank his sword and bow to the giggling young ladies who have been coming daily to the square at the top of the hill to watch Chester's several militia companies parade and drill.

"Coleman," he says quietly. "What if I told you we had to have a fight because we had to have Virginia and the only way to get Virginia is if there's fighting?"

"I would say you need an enemy before you can fight and Abe Lincoln is in Washington," I retort. "Virginia played a key role in establishing the United States and I don't know why everyone is surprised she wants to stay with the Union. Besides, you know all this is going to blow over in a few months. Lincoln will guarantee he won't interfere with slavery and South Carolina will go back in the Union."

A.J. was shaking his head.

"Back in the Union to be subjected to every indignity the North can imagine? Coleman, you're not grasping what's going to take place. We aren't seceding because of slavery – the big plantation owners might think so, and some of the politicians. But it's just the issue that everyone can understand, the issue that will get us out from under the North. We have a right to make our own destiny."

"And we have Mr. Lincoln's army right here in South Carolina," he says. "They are refusing to turn over Fort Sumter, even though Secretary Seward promised it would be turned over to the state months ago."

"I think Secretary Seward spoke before hearing what President Lincoln had to say," I say. "Besides, a few men sweating in a fort in Charleston Harbor is scarcely an invasion of the South, especially when it was a federal fort to begin with."

He gets that secret look again.

"There are some very powerful men who feel Lincoln's refusal to turn over the fort is an aggressive act," he says. "And we have the right to defend ourselves."

A.J. drops these kinds of references into his conversation and makes some people think he's on speaking terms with these "powerful men." Actually, he and his father, for all their money, are still outside the real power structure in the state. They are ambitious men, and I am quite willing to share in the prosperity they seem likely to bring with their bank. But they are not planters, they do not own slaves, and those who do own slaves regard the Mantours as mere upstate merchants, not much better than Yankees. It is no accident that the Mantours established their bank in the northern part of the state, among independent farmers and small plantation owners, rather than in the steaming Low Country with its sprawling rice and indigo plantations. Banking there follows patterns and precedents set decades ago; the Mantours would be shunned as callow newcomers by the old families that dominate the economy and politics of Charleston.

Up here, though, it's different. People are restless and hungry for land and the security it gives them. They are descended, mostly, from Scots-Irish and came into the state by way of Pennsylvania and Virginia, and they seem to pass on, from generation to generation, the memory of being put off the land in Scotland and Ireland. Mostly they raise pigs and some cattle and corn, and they are an independent-minded bunch. There are a few small plantations with cotton and slaves, but not many. And now that the railroad is here, coming up from Columbia and running through little Charlotte and all the way to Richmond and the North, there are more and more people like the Mantours – storekeepers, merchants and such. Old Thomas even had a meeting last year with several men said to be Yankee capitalists interested in starting a factory to produce cloth from cotton. Besides, A.J. knows where his father gets the money for his bank - he borrows it from Yankee banks, then lends it out at higher interest to people around here. A lot of powerful men, it seems to me, have a lot more profitable things to do than get involved in a war.

Then Abe Lincoln got elected, and now I have Andrew Jackson Mantour trying to recruit me for an army that will never fight. His militia company is funded with Mantour money, just as other companies are funded by wealthy men in the district, who then get themselves elected captain. They say Wade Hampton has put together an entire legion, with infantry, cavalry and artillery, and has made himself colonel of it. He is the wealthiest man in the South, with plantations in several states and hundreds of slaves, so he can afford it, but still – he is swept away by secession fever, just like almost everyone else. It is all anyone talks about, and men have been joining and then talking big about whipping Yankees.

A.J. is still looking at me, waiting for me to respond. I tell him I will give his invitation the consideration it deserves; he either misses or ignores the two-edged nature of my remark and tells me not to wait too long, he expects the company to be called to Charleston in a matter of days.

It is now noon, and time for dinner. The entire town shuts down for two hours. I dismiss Michael Moore, a rough farmer wearing what looks to be his best, although not too impressive, suit of clothes. He has come to see about a crop loan. I tell him to come back after dinner. He doesn't look happy, but he leaves.

I am a careful man. After checking my collar, I leave the bank and walk down the street to visit with John McKee. He is a wise old lawyer, who helped my father convince me to take up banking as my life's work.

Mr. McKee no longer practices law; he is retired. He is also bored, so he keeps an office in town, a few doors down from the bank, and can be found there most days, dispensing wisdom and advice to the men who trouble themselves to seek him out. He was one of our district's delegates to the secession convention in Charleston. I find him standing before his office window, clipping a cigar and frowning as A.J. bows to some giggling teenage girls across the street.

I share A.J.'s appraisal of our political situation, without mentioning the source. Mr. McKee knew.

"Young Mantour talks too much," he says. Then he turned.

"A man could do worse than join the military in times like these," he finally says. "An ambitious man could do himself some good with a stint in the militia — all those young boys are going to have families and need jobs or maybe start businesses someday; they'll be looking to borrow money and where better than from a bank where they know one of the officers because they shared a campfire with him?" He lights his cigar and squints at me, waiting to see what I'll say. I say nothing.

"It will amount to nothing," McKee says. "The Yankees won't fight — they wouldn't fight against Mexico, they won't fight us now. Not really; some posturing, some blood spilled to consecrate the new nation, and you'll be back in the bank in three months."

This is not what I expected. I stammer out my thanks for his insight, and take my leave.

I make my way a few blocks to my mother's house, where my baby sister Hanna tells me a package has arrived.

I call her baby sister, but Hanna is 12 years old. She has the red hair that afflicts most of the Coleman family, but she and I share grey eyes instead of the usual blue. She is on the cusp of becoming a young lady, although as the only girl in a family with four brothers, she has always been in danger of being a tomboy. Right now she is all questions and energy, pushing the package at me and begging me to open it. I tell her it can wait until supper, then laugh at the disappointment that settles over her freckled features.

It is a small, soft package, a foot on each side and two or three inches deep, in plain paper with only my name and address on the top, tied up in string. It was delivered, she said, by a young man she never saw before – a common-enough event these days since the United States Post Office shut down when South Carolina voted to secede and everyone reverted to private messengers, railroad agents and stage operators to deliver mail.

I carefully untie the string and unfold the paper, to reveal white cloth. Picking it up, I shake it and it unfolds to become a petticoat. I can feel the heat starting at my scalp and moving down my face and neck.

"However did you come by that?" Hanna asked. Thank goodness she is too innocent to understand.

"It must be a mistake," I tell her, wrapping the garment back in its paper. "This was intended for someone else. I'll take care of it."

I am no longer hungry. I walk down the block to the Widow Gifte's store; Elizabeth sees me coming and is waiting at the door, cool green eyes dancing with excitement unbecoming a widow of just a year. It is my hope we will wed, after a suitable passage of time. Until then, we must observe great decorum. Her husband, Adam, died a year ago of a strange disease that struck him down in a few days. He was a hale, fit man, prosperous owner of a dry goods store, very well regarded in town. His passing left a rent in the fabric of Chester life. It seems not to have left much of a rent in Elizabeth's life. She took over the store immediately, hardly breaking stride to bury her husband.

Elizabeth is stunned when I show her the package, but she swiftly recovers. Swift recoveries are an Elizabeth characteristic, as I well know.

"William, you must realize how it looks," she says. "Most men your age are eager to put on a uniform, yet you hold back."

Her next words make my stomach turn over; I feel like I am falling.

"Perhaps you should join Captain Mantour's little group," Elizabeth tells me, putting a hand on my shoulder.

I walk back to the bank, by way of some back alleys where the petticoat disappears into a pile of trash. I go back to my desk in the empty bank and pull out some bills that have been paid by Thomas Mantour and must now be entered in the bank's own business ledger. The work is soothing, the midday silence is calming, and gradually my thoughts focus. What do I care that mindless "patriots" choose to characterize as cowardice my sensible decision not to put on a toy-soldier uniform and parade like a clown? I have a responsible job in an important business with an employer who trusts me.

Then I come to a bill from a business I don't immediately recognize, Chatsworth and Hardy, tailors, of Charleston. I give it a closer look.

It is a bill for three dozen petticoats, delivered to Thomas Mantour of High Street in Chester a week before.

There is no anger in me, just a huge emptiness and a sense of loss and betrayal. I close the ledger and walk out of the bank, locking the door carefully behind me. I go looking for A.J., to tell him I'll join the Calhoun Guards. Clearly, my future is going to take a detour.

My recollection
of the War of Secession
or the War Between the States

By Miss Hanna H. Coleman

I have concluded to write what I remember of the War between the North and South, from the first war cloud, until the days of reconstruction. I was a young girl then, and, I fear I will write very little history, but much that is worthless and frivolous. The first I remember was, as a school girl, I went home with my Uncle John Kennedy, to central Mississippi - it was in December 1859. John Brown had caused much trouble, by inciting the negroes, to an insurrection at Harpers Ferry, in Virginia. Crowds met our train as we approached Branchville, S.C. a great rock was hurled into the car window, some sympathizer of old John's I suppose, taking spite on the little Gamecock State.

The war clouds grew darker in ' 60, persons commenced wearing the cockade and companies of minute men, were being formed. The South felt as if it was oppressed, and imposed upon, by the North. Gov. Pickens was then Gov. of S. C. There was a mass meeting held in the First Baptist church in Columbia. Then a convention of prominent men From all over the country convened, at Charleston to nominate candidates for the presidency, Beckenridge and Lane were the men selected by the South; while Lincoln and - - were the Northern candidates. Politicians talked over matters, to see, if the state of affairs could be amicably settled, but nothing satisfactory could be reached. South Carolina took the lead, and seceded from the union. The ordinance was passed.. Every district was represented by signers, Mr. Quay Dunovant, Mr. Richard Woods, and Mr. John McKee, were the signers from Chester District. Mr. McKee was the oldest representative from the state. The Ordinance of secession was passed in Institute Hall in Charleston. The Hall was beautifully decorated with palmetto, outside bands of music playing patriotic airs, many ladies witnessed the proceedings - I have a piece of palmetto brought from the hall by one of them.

At this time, Major Anderson, with a squad of United States troops occupied Fort Moultrie, on Sullivans Island, it was feared he would try and get to Fort Sumter, a much stronger, and in fact, some supposed, impregnable fort, and much farther out at sea. Some five or six of the Charleston riflemen, in charge of Major T. L. Mills was sent out each night at 9 o'clock, in a small boat, to reconnoitre and prevent his escape. Major Anderson knew of this, so he anticipated, and one dark drizzly night about dusk, he left Fort

Moultrie and took possession of Sumter; he had little provisions, and so few men, that the U.S. government sent re-enforcements and food on the "Star of the West," the vessel was sighted, and fired into by the Citadel Cadets, and prevented from accomplishing its mission.

Immediately, great preparations were made for the recapture of Fort Sumter, by the South Carolinians; fortifications were thrown up, new forts built and floating batteries made of palmetto logs, Fort Moultrie strengthened, troops from the state ordered to Charleston- and soon after ward, at 3 o'clock in the morning, the first gun went booming out over the water. All day, fast and furious- Fort Moultrie, the Iron Fort, the floating batteries and batteries on the different Islands threw shot and shell, at doomed Ft. Sumter. Crowds of women and children were on the battery watching the bombardment. 3 o'clock in the afternoon the Stars and Stripes were lowered, and the white flag hoisted; it was a bloodless victory, and proud Fort Sumter was a mass of ruins; her sides were all battered, and great holes torn in her strong walls. It was Major Ripley I believe, that went over first to the Fort, and looking through a port hole, with an oath, very blue ordered Major Anderson and his men to vacate. The Calhoun Guards and Catawba Guards from Chester, were selected to assist in the bombardment, but, Major Anderson capitulated before they were ordered out.

After South Carolina seceded she was not long alone, Georgia soon followed, then Florida and on, until thirteen States determined to form a Confederacy, have their own president, and make their own laws. The day S.D. seceded, Georgia stretched a huge rope across the Savannah River in the middle of the rope, were two great iron hands, clasped, showing that she was heart and soul in the movement.

Jefferson Davis was elected President of the Confederacy, he was a graduate of West Point, a man beloved by the South, and a great scholar, he was from Mississippi. Alexander Stephens also beloved, a man small in statue, and almost an invalid, but of gigantic intellect, was Vice President - he was from Georgia. Montgomery in Ala. was the capitol, Congress met there, until it was moved to Richmond Virginia, later on in the war, the White House in Montgomery is still intact, and the U.D.C. hold their meetings in it.

In our town, Chester, we sent to the war, two companies of Infantry and one of Cavalry, Gen. Alec Walker was in command of the cavalry; the Sixth Regiment, S.C.V. was composed almost entirely of Chester men, the Catawba Guards and other companies were from the District;- In town the Calhoun Guards ... and the Chester Blues

under Capt. E. McClure were Infantry. My brother William belonged
to the Calhoun Guard, Dr. Babcock and Fred to the Chester Blues. My
cousin Alan Kennedy to the Cavalry Co.

I shall never forget the morning in April 1861, when our boys
marched away; they had been ordered to the coast to assist in the
bombardment of Fort Sumter. The companies formed on the Public
Square. Mr. Richard Nail played the fife, and Tom Wright the drum.
Tom was a negro who had always been free, he was a giant in size
and with a heart so full of love for the South, that he begged to
go along with the boys and did so, and stood by them until the surrender, and came home in his tattered grey suit, proud of doing his
duty. Oh how handsome and patriotic our boys looked, on that morning in their new suits, - banners were floating. Mr. Nail marched
in front, playing "the girl I left behind me", and Tom marching
along, in his uniform, with a rub-a-dub-dub- that nearly broke my
heart, for I well knew, that some brave fellow would never come
back again.

We went to the depot to see the troops off, the Reg. from Yorkville, Col. Micah Jenkins in charge and the companies from the
surrounding country met here, what a mass of humanity, and, all in
grey. Oh how many sad adieu' s, mothers, daughters, wives, sweethearts, all come to say farewell and many with faces as white as
death. One wife nearly fainted when she told her husband good bye,
poor child wife, she did not live to see him come home, but died,
after the birth of a little girl, and died of a broken heart. My
mother did not go to the depot, she told my brother good-bye at
home, he was her idol; I almost ran from the house with grief when
I saw the parting between the two, my mother did not cry, but the
look in her large eyes, haunted me for days.

I remember too, that when the last soldier boarded the train,
and I stood on the platform and saw the train turn the curve, and
pass out of sight, I thought the war would soon be over, for who
could resist such an array!- The companies went to Charleston,
where Gen. Beauregard was in command of all of the military. They
reached there the night before Ft. Sumter was attacked. Mr. Ruffin
an old gentleman from Virginia was allowed to fire the first shot
at Sumter; he had joined the Palmetto Guards, and wore his long
white hair hanging over his shoulders. Our troops remained near
Charleston on Morris', Cole's and other islands, until they were
ordered to Virginia in July, 1862. Willie Martin from Columbia was
our first martyr. He wrote under the name of Ruby and died on the
Island.

CHAPTER TWO

We arrive in Charleston at midnight. The city is humming as if it were midday. Everywhere, excited people are scurrying and chattering. There are soldiers everywhere, many of them drunk and most of those who aren't drunk trying to bring those who are to heel. Every uniform imaginable is in evidence. Carts and wagons rumble everywhere over cobblestones, the horses and mules adding their braying to the excitement. All is lit by the gaslights of the town and by torches, thousands of them, carried by men, stuck in the ground, mounted on posts.

We have marched by torchlight, in stumbling steps, into the heart of Charleston from outside the city. So many troops are being rushed into the seaport that our train – two days of clanking, shuffling, wheezing travel that was more halt than movement from Chester to Charleston – could not get closer than three miles to the station. Our baggage is somewhere along the track, at one of the dozens of plantations where the darkies are nursemaiding the first tender shoots of Southern wealth in this year's crop of cotton. It was interesting to note as we traveled south how the stage of production changed. At home the farmers are still preparing the soil for planting; here near Charleston the crop is under way and above the ground, although barely. Surely they will harvest first, and get the best prices. That is something to remember — our farmers are at a small time disadvantage, it may affect the prices they get, and it is definitely a factor in loaning the bank's money to farmers.

The Calhoun Guards are now part of the Sixth Regiment of South Carolina Volunteer Infantry, numbered sixth because it is the sixth regiment formed since the call for 10 regiments went out in December. We are 10 companies strong, all formed from various militia units. We have the Fairfield Fencibles, under Capt. John Bratton; the Boyce Guards, under Capt. J.N. Shedd; the Cedar Creek Rifles, under Capt. Jno. R. Harrison; the Buckhead Guards, Capt. Edward Means; the Little River Guards, Capt. J.M. Brice; the Chester Guards, Capt. Obadiah Hardin; the Chester Blues, Capt. E.C. McClure; the Catawba Guards, Capt. G.L. Straight; the Pickens Guards, Capt. J.M. Moore, and our own Calhoun Guards, under Capt. Lucius Gaston. There's an astonishing assortment of men, from rich planters deigning to serve as gentlemen privates — albeit with their own personal servants — to rough farmers and colliers and railroad men, carpenters, teamsters, and even a bank clerk or two.

Our spiritual needs are attended by a Yorkville Presbyterian minister, Ichabod Barak McCausland, a man from parents who were clearly in the grip of a Biblical frenzy when it came to naming the children. His siblings include Hepzibah, Ismael, Japheth, Esther and Neriah. He is a portly and pompous man of the cloth — broadcloth, the men snicker — who is full of Biblical quotations having to do with girding ones loins and smiting the enemy mighty blows. It appears that he does his best girding and smiting at the dinner table, and no one takes his prattle seriously as he lumbers about, seeking to engage busy and impatient officers in conversations seemingly aimed at reminding them he is there. He will announce his presence with a Bible verse, as he did when happening upon a company officer struggling to put on his sword.

"'Gird your sword upon your side, O mighty one, clothe yourself with splendor and majesty,'" McCausland beamingly bestowed upon the man. "Psalm 45, verse 3."

"Yes, well — yes," the red-faced captain responded.

James H. Rion, who had recruited the Fairfield Fencibles, has been elected colonel of the regiment. A.J., to my astonishment, has been elected lieutenant colonel. Jonathan Harrison will become major as soon as the Cedar Creek Rifles figure out how to replace him. Lucius Gaston replaced A.J. Mantour as captain of the Calhoun Guards, and a quiet, dark man named John Bratton, a doctor from Winnsboro, took command of the Fairfield Fencibles. There is great jockeying for position, as everyone wants a military title to take home when this nonsense is finished.

A.J. is still strutting, although the strain of keeping all of us together and fed has worn him down. To tell the truth, he is not without leadership ability, although having worked with him at the bank I am amazed to see it. A few days away from his father have worked a transformation.

I have been in the Calhoun Guards for a week and the change from bank clerk to soldier is taking place, no matter how much I resist. My mess includes Willie McClure, a wiry little farmer from just outside Chester with the blue-black hair my mother always said was the sign of the "black Irish." There are six others, we pool our food and share cooking chores, but McClure has all my attention right now because he knows a hundred tricks for making himself comfortable in the impossible conditions we face. He actually managed to sleep during the train ride, waking up refreshed and excitedly pointing out each item of interest on the trip. He obviously has never been outside Chester district. Well, neither have I, but I hope it isn't so obvious. I am already an object of some suspicion because I can read, write and do mathematics. Almost the only others who can do so are officers. I suspect it will take some time before I fit in. Perhaps it will be over before that happens. It is so disconcerting: In uniforms, we have new distinctions based on insignia. Distinctions from civilian life don't matter. A farmer can give orders to a lawyers or a pastor — to a bank clerk, yes — if he has what A. J. calls "officer straps" on his shoulders, the gold epaulets that signify rank. The wrongness of this grates on my nerves. Who would subject themselves to this voluntarily? Yet I am surrounded by men who are as happy as if on a church picnic.

The company has been marched down a narrow street and it appears we are to be issued weapons to replace the ancient Brown Bess muskets many of our militia companies had used for drill. We go into a huge building, the federal armory. The former federal armory; it is a state armory now, has been since December. It was one of the first buildings seized when the secession ordinance passed. We are marched in a company at a time. We walk in lantern light to the sound of wood being smashed and nails being wrenched loose; empty boxes are everywhere. An officer in a deep blue uniform gleaming with gold braid meets us as we move deeper into the building. We are stumbling now in semi-darkness and not even trying to keep in step, although we are marching four abreast; one feels oafish.

"Who's in command here?" the officer sneers, pulling off his white gloves and looking down from the box he jumped upon.

A.J. moves up from the rear of the company where he has been trying to find out who has the company roster so he can call roll and find out if we lost anyone in the march along the railroad. He salutes the officer.

"Lieutenant Colonel A.J. Mantour, sir, at your service, with the Sixth Regiment."

The officer curls his lip. He is a major; he should be saluting A.J., but A.J., eager as a puppy and trying to be friendly, saluted him first instead. The arrogant major pulls papers from inside his jacket and consults them, without returning A.J.'s salute. After a minute he speaks.

"I am Major Brett of General Beauregard's staff," he tells A.J., speaking slowly as if to a child "It appears this rabble is to be armed, though God knows they don't look bright enough to keep from hurting themselves."

A ripple of murmuring surges through the company, a mixture of whispered curses at the major's condescension. There are apparently limits to my companions' willingness to be abused by "rank." There is also excited speculation on what weapons we'll receive. It is known that Southerners in President James Buchanan's cabinet arranged for the shipment of thousands of the best rifles in the U.S. arsenals in the north to depots and warehouses in the South prior to the transfer of government to the Lincoln administration. And we, like a lot of the upstate companies, have men who are crack shots with rifles. Designation as a rifle company or a sharpshooter company would surprise none of us. Anticipation of such weapons led our officers to direct us to stack our old militia arms by the side of the train, and leave them for the quartermaster.

A.J. orders us to be quiet, then the officer and A.J. move to the rear of one pile of boxes. The sergeant in charge of one of the companies that has already gotten muskets orders his men to stack arms; they try several ways to get the bayonets on their muskets to interlock, but can't get it right. The sergeant, a bearded giant, grabs the two closest men by the neck, knocks their heads together and roars at them. All this accomplishes is to make the men keep one eye nervously on the sergeant while trying to get their muskets to lean together in the appropriate fashion, and the job slows down even more. The major ignores it all. Finally the muskets are in more-or-less orderly pyramids, and the sergeant orders his dozen men to split into two groups and start unpiling the big boxes. Their first attempt produces a thunderous crash as the 300-pound load gets away from the men and crashes to the floor. The sergeant curses and more heads are knocked together. The men knock the lids off some of the crates with hatchets, then start to laugh.

The other company had drawn Mississippi rifles, the kind used by some troops in the Mexican War. They are fine weapons. We are not so lucky.

We are counted off in twos, then marched forward in groups of four to get our weapon. We quickly find out why the first group laughed. There are noises of dismay as the first groups put their hands on the weapons.

"Never seed anythin' like this," a lanky farmer from Great Falls says in dubious wonder as he walks back into the ranks with a heavy, clumsy gun. Whatever it is, it is a flintlock, not the modern percussion cap. Closer inspection reveals the muskets to be 1816 Springfields. Most are rusty, some are broken. There are no bayonets, no ball, no flints, and, we discover shortly, no powder.

All the guns are in crates bearing the mark of Watervliet Arsenal in Troy, New York state. There are 20 guns in a crate and crates are stacked in every direction. Obviously some crates have better guns than others, but who is issuing what to whom, and why, is a complete mystery. We look at the heavy, ugly guns.

"We're ready now!" some wit pipes up sarcastically when the situation in all its foolishness is finally clear. There is a ripple of laughter.

This is not what we expected. Our adventure into soldiering is deteriorating rapidly from the promise of glory that seemed within reach in Chester only two days ago.

Then, the entire town turned out as all five Chester infantry companies assembled at the top of the hill. There were speeches and cheers and ladies gave the boys food and stuffed more in their knapsacks. Everyone waved Palmetto flags and wore bright cockades; A.J.'s fiancé presented us with a company flag sewn by the ladies of Chester, a pale blue square of silk with a Palmetto tree in white on one side and a big white star on the other. The officers thanked the ladies, the ladies simpered and giggled and waved their hankies, so the street looked like it was lined with fluttering butterflies. Huge, black Tom Wright started beating the drum and tiny, blond Richard "Tack" Nails played "The Girl I Left Behind Me" on the fife beside him and we all marched off to the train station at the bottom of the hill, with the whole town lining the streets and cheering at the top of their lungs.

Well, I didn't exactly march. I'd just joined, and I didn't know how to march. I did have a uniform. A.J. produced one for me, surprise, surprise, that fit like a glove. But no hat. I wear my civilian hat. But I didn't join the ranks, I strolled behind the Calhoun Guards, carrying a satchel that A.J. gave me to hold the company paperwork. The rest of the men carried their old Brown Bess muskets, relics of the Revolutionary War; they'd shined the barrels and oiled the stocks and the guns looked good, but in fact quite a few of them were missing parts and couldn't be fired. Still, they, in blue militia uniforms with feathered shakos and shining weapons, presented a far more warlike appearance than I did. Some of the men look at me with hostility, and I heard one ask another why "A.J.'s pet clerk" was tagging along. I didn't hear the response, but both men laughed. Louts.

A word about Tom. Some of the men say it isn't right, bringing along a darky. But A.J. pointed out he was a freeman, he volunteered to serve with the militia company just like all the others did, and, besides, nobody else had the slightest idea how to play the drum properly. He said other regiments had darkies, mostly as body servants to the slave-owning members, so Tom wouldn't stand out that much. There is still some grumbling, but it must be admitted Tom knows how to make the drum shout. They march in step when he beats the cadence.

And so we marched down to the depot, led by a giant black man and a diminutive white man with blond hair and trailed by a bank clerk in a civilian hat, the ladies of the town lined along the streets, crying and laughing and frantically waving handkerchiefs at us all.

That is all in our past. Our less than glorious future appears to center around antique weapons fit for a museum, not for actual use.

We are ordered out of the armory, to make room for the next group coming in. A.J. is winding himself up to argue with the major when the boom of a cannon rolls up from the harbor. We fall silent; it seems the entire town falls silent. Far out over the water, where Sumter hulks like a black stain on the horizon, there is a burst of light in the sky, and a few seconds later we hear a loud pop. Then all hell breaks loose, with guns opening up from all around the harbor. A huge cheer rolls across the town, and we see men and women opening their doors to run out in the streets, and climbing out roof hatches to get a better look. The concussion of the guns is palpable, you can feel it across your chest.

A.J. and the snotty major confer, then A.J. orders Tom to beat assembly. Nobody recognizes the drum call, though, so A.J. has to shriek orders over the deafening thunder of the guns. We are finally in the formation A.J. wants, whatever it is, and we march down to the Battery, where a dozen guns are blazing away at Sumter, clearly visible across the harbor. All of us are convinced we are going to assault Sumter, and everyone but me seems mad for the chance. Hours go by; the sun rises, and other companies from our regiment are brought to our location, then other regiments. Thousands of men are assembled on the Charleston waterfront. We have the best view in town for the start of hostilities. Because we are right in town, we are the object of the lavish affections of the Charlestonians, who smother us with food all day long. Some of the men manage to get drowned in drink, as well, and provost guards are busy everywhere. Nobody from our company behaves disgracefully, I'm glad to say.

Finally, even the bombardment becomes commonplace. Some effort is made at figuring out how to stack our weapons. We are instructed by none other than Farmer Michael Moore, to my chagrin and deep apprehension. It turns out his best suit of clothing, by far, is his militia uniform, which bears those insignia denoting him as a lieutenant. Moore, an older man, served with Jeff Davis and the Mississippi volunteers in the Mexican War. He shows the noncommissioned officers how to pull the ramrods a few inches out, then weave barrels and ramrods together until three muskets are locked in a tripod, with a fourth leaning against the stack. The noncommissioned officers then spread out among the hundred men in our company and try to show us how to do it. All this is done at a shout, to be heard over the boom of the cannon a few dozen yards away. It takes a long time, and we all must wait while everyone "stacks arms," but our weapons are finally in stacks, the stacks are in neat alignment, and our state flag and company flag are furled and laid across two stacks. We are released from formation and told to stay in the area; that is not a problem, as most of us are exhausted. Quite a few of the men drop where they are standing and fall asleep in the warm April sunlight.

Some of us are in urgent need of a privy. It is something we hadn't really considered, this problem of a hundred men or 800 men needing to answer the call of nature, but it is indisputably a part of soldiering. While we were in Chester we were never assembled for more than a few hours, so the problem simply didn't come up. On the train ride down there were so many halts in the wilderness that men could clamber down off the tops of the cars or climb out the windows, and leave the train briefly. But now we are in the middle of the third largest city of the South. Even worse, we are in the Battery, which, regardless of its current military use, is still a large park fronted by the homes of some of the wealthiest people of our new nation. Half of them are women, and most of them are on the roofs of houses.

Clearly, though, the artillerists now manfully sweating at their guns have been based here for some time; their tents, huge cone-shaped affairs, are pitched at the north end of the battery. A few of us walk over to see what solution they found to the problem we now urgently confront. We find a new dock into the harbor, with a pavilion at the end, surrounded by canvas screening. Inside the screening are the familiar benches. It is extremely inelegant; it is also a nerve-wracking kind of place, because it is in front of some of our batteries and between our batteries and Sumter. So far the Yankees have not fired toward the batteries actually in Charleston, but if they do and the shells fall a little short, the privy is a bad place to be. There is no dignity here, with the canvas screening shuddering every time a cannon blasts. Becoming a soldier is every bit as nasty as I thought it would be.

Lt. Moore seems determined to break me. I do not know the usual procedure for training a new man to become a soldier, but Lt. Moore has made me the object of his special attention, complaining loudly to all within earshot of his booming voice about my woeful deportment, ignorance of all things military, and clumsiness in executing drill. I have been given every dirty job there is, twice as much as any other man in the company, and every demeaning job. The source of his animosity becomes clear, finally, when I hear him tell an officer from another regiment that Fate has turned over to his tender mercies the "impertinent pup" from the Chester bank. My first thought is to confront him, but I am stopped by the thought that after all, this will only be for a few days. My second thought is to protest the injustice and indignity to A.J., but I am stopped by the realization that invoking A.J., while it might put a halt to Moore's provocations, would hardly improve my standing in the company — and that, for reasons I am still not sure about, has become important to me. These men think me a mere clerk, a shuffler of papers — Mantour's pet clerk — and I am determined to show them I can master their pathetic drills as well as they. I resolve to wait it out — to endure the siege, as it were — and see if the same Fate that delivered me to the merciless Mr. Moore will undeliver me.

But I will not give him the satisfaction of showing the white feather, no matter how many bags of rice he forces me to carry or how many officers' trunks I must fetch.

Chester, S.C.
May 5, 1861

Dearest William,

I take pen in hand to tell you — oh, I cannot do this! Is it not glorious? We have sent the Yankee thieves fleeing for their lives. Surely God has blessed the South! Chester has gone wild with the news of Fort Sumter and everyone is sure the war will be over in weeks. We have parades and speeches every Sunday afternoon.

I trust my package to you has made it safely with Gus. He was going to Charleston to visit his brother Cato, who is servant to Capt. Lemuel Hart of Lancaster, and is sick with swamp fever. I hope you will think of me when you wear the vest, although I know my poor skill with a needle is nothing you can show to your friends.

I will write more later. Mrs. Horace Dorcutt has organized a large group of ladies to meet in the hotel lobby tonight to knit socks for the soldiers. Remember when decent women could not go to the hotel unescorted? How the war has changed things!

Lovingly,

Elizabeth

CHAPTER THREE

Sumter fell, but nobody believed the new President would leave it fallen for long. The military authorities in Charleston — that is, General G.T. Beauregard — funneled men and arms into all the approaches to Charleston. The Sixth Regiment was flung far and wide around the town, an arrangement that might have suited a veteran United States regiment of Regulars with an established command structure and supply system, but which suited the volunteers not at all.

Col. James Rion had been elected colonel of the Sixth. He knew what had to be done, but was powerless to do it. He was powerless to stop the dispersal of the regiment and powerless to meet its needs once it was scattered across James Island, Morris Island, the Battery, Fort Moultrie — it seemed the 10 companies were sent to a dozen different locations.

Supply became difficult. The troops quickly became acquainted with the most eager volunteer in all the armies, the grey louse, who was relieved from duty only by the sand flea, the wood tick, the mosquito and the huge blue-black flies that seemed to gather out of the sky whenever fresh — that is, raw — meat was issued.

Everything that went wrong flew home to roost on Rion's perch. If a company didn't get meat for a week, Rion was at fault. No flints for the guns? Rion was to blame. The eager volunteers spent April and May and part of June learning that soldiering has more to do with effective supply lines and dealing with boredom than it does with battles and glory.

It had this benefit: One had to have some faith in the goal of the exercise in order to overlook the human frailties that inevitably accompany an army in the field. Fervor and faith seem to go hand in hand in these days of hope; some bad meat, a poor choice for a camp site, not enough shoes — are these not a small price to pay for creating a new nation? Those who think we are doing no more than our grandfathers had done in 1776 are willing to overlook some hardship. I admit I am as susceptible as anyone to the patriotic fervor that seizes us all after the heady experience of firing on a federal fortification and seeing it surrender. Some say it will be over in weeks, that Lincoln's refusal to come to the aid of Sumter shows the Yankee lack of resolve. Most think Lincoln will respond, in his own good time.

The Calhoun Guards were sent to Sullivan's Island, with the Catawba Guards. Lt. Col. A.J. Mantour and Maj. Thomas Woodward went to Morris Island with the Cedar Creek Rifles, the Pickens Guards, the Chester Blues, the Chester Guards and the Little River Guards. Then they moved the Chester Guards to the pesthole of Fort Johnson, and Maj. Woodward went to Cole's Island with the Blues. There we joined them, along with the Catawba Guards, and finally A.J. arrived and actually found himself in command of all of Cole's Island. Col. Rion, meanwhile, was at Battery Island with the Pickens Guards, the Cedar Creek Rifles and the Little River Guards. Why, no one knows.

We labored and we persevered, we set up camps and tore down camps, we dug fortifications and then we walked away from them; and our Chester companies grew strong. That was not the case with other companies. At about the time everyone realized the war would be in Virginia, not Charleston, our first crisis arose. We were to be accepted for Confederate service, rather than strictly South

Carolina service, and some of the loudest voices of April were hushed in June, after a few weeks of military reality had adjusted notions of what war was all about. To put it bluntly, a lot of men wanted to go home. Charleston was an adventure, but there was not the same attitude toward service in Virginia.

The regiment was removed from the islands and assembled at Goose Creek outside Charleston, and the proposition was put to the men: Would they enlist for a year in Confederate service, or go home?

One company, Rion's own Fairfield Fencibles, arrived at Goose Creek after all the rest, somewhat the worse for wear from all the mint juleps and sherry cobblers forced on them during their march through Charleston. They were a mob, and when they found their tents had not arrived, they created such an uproar that Rion turned them loose into the villages around Goose Creek to find what quarters they could. That was almost the last we saw of them, until their captain, Bratton, went after them and started bringing them back one at a time.

Rion was very down at the mouth about all the complaining going on, and in a fit of pique made a melodramatic gesture that turned upon itself and bit him. He asked the men to conduct two votes, the first being whether or not he would continue as colonel if they did later vote to stay together and go to Virginia. He apparently expected a vote of confidence out of this, but he didn't get it. The men quickly and with no emotion other than polite eagerness voted him out.

Immediately his supporters in the regiment were furious and wildly indignant. The Fairfield Fencibles, the Little River Guards and the Cedar Creek Rifles pretty much disbanded on the spot and voted with their feet to stay in South Carolina. Only three men from those three companies put the new nation ahead of their personal feelings and stayed behind.

A.J. was in a fix. As lieutenant colonel, he would take command if Rion were disabled on the battlefield. But he wasn't disabled and there was no battlefield and there was, if the truth be stated bluntly, no regiment until further voting took place.

Rion left in a huff for Columbia, to see what else he could scrape up in the way of a command. We were left to sort ourselves out.

General Beauregard sent word through Major Brett, his arrogant, dandified aide-de-camp, that if we could muster seven companies, each of 65 enlisted men, we could keep our status as the Sixth Regiment and we would be given time to make up the other three companies before being shipped to Virginia. If we failed, the unit would be broken up, with companies willing to enlist in Confederate service reassigned to other regiments.

Brett — his first name was Quincy and he was reportedly some sort of secular minor factotum within the Catholic Church hierarchy in Louisiana, perhaps accounting for the aura of sanctimonious judgement that seemed to ooze from him — clearly found his mission distasteful. Just as clearly, he hoped we would fail to muster the necessary men so he could get back to the seat of power in Charleston. We, however, did not take things lightly, and scoured the camp for recruits and sent urgent telegrams home to drum up all who might join us.

Within days the recruits summoned by telegraph began arriving in our Goose Creek camp, where they were drilled in the fields surrounding that quiet village, to the delight of the community's youngsters. The Carolina Mountaineers arrived from Greenville, each with a huge bowie knife strapped to his boot, and the Limestone Guards marched in from Spartanburg, the company flag waving from a hickory pole cut from the Revolutionary War battlefield of Cowpens. And John White arrived with the York Guards, from York County.

The ever-impatient Brett was joined by the recruiting officer, John Dunovant, after three days, and we were informed it was now or never.

The Chester companies each mustered their 65 men with no trouble, as did the Buckhead Guards. Then the Boyce Guards found to their horror that they had miscalculated and were one man short of the 65 enlisted men required by Beauregard.

We were all drawn up in a hollow square facing inward, several hundred men eager to keep an organization together. The regiment consisted of the following seven companies: Boyce Guards/ Buckhead Guards; Chester Guards/ Chester Blues; Catawba Guards/ Calhoun Guards; Pickens Guards; York Guards; William Camp's company from Spartanburg; and Spartan D. Goodlett's company from Greenville.

We looked at each other. Brett walked over to A.J. and brushed imaginary dust off his immaculate uniform.

"I say, it looks like no go," he told A.J. He smiled. Or sneered. Hard to tell the difference.

A dark-haired man wearing captain's bars broke through the formation and walked over to Brett.

"I guess there's enough officers," he said. He took off his militia jacket and ripped the captain's insignia off the collar. Dunovant handed over a muster book, and John Bratton of Winnsboro signed on for a one-year hitch as a private with the Boyce Guards. He joined the rank and file of the company he had just commanded in the most complete silence imaginable.

"Gentlemen," Dunovant said. "The Sixth Regiment is formed. It will leave for Virginia as soon as three more companies are mustered."

A cheer broke out, the formation joyously shattered and Bratton found himself in pain for several days from all the thumps of congratulation his back received.

I myself was in quite a bit of anguish. None of the movement and confusion and politicking had done a single thing to relieve me of the bane of my life, Lt. Michael Moore. Our captain, Lucius Gaston, is a fair man. So is Lt. Moore, in all respects save one. He has an unyielding hatred of me and takes every opportunity to direct the sergeants to give me extra duty, extra drill and always at the most inconvenient times. I have dug more sinks than any man in the army, and performed the manual of arms more often than U.S. Regulars who have had ten years of service. I do not know what to do; to object would truly be gratifying, especially since the dull creature could not stand up to me if I really elocuted on his injustices and shortcomings. But so far I have stood it, and I am taking delight in the fact that "the pale clerk," as he called me one time when he thought I couldn't hear him, has carried out every duty without flinching, no matter how odious. And sooner or later he will appear before me again as a farmer seeking a bank loan. I carry that image in my head constantly, while wielding a shovel.

We were ready for Virginia, except for the colonelcy. And here A.J. did something that changed my opinion of him forever for the better. He had truly changed.

A.J. called a meeting of the company commanders. Naturally, the wind was up and most of the regiment crowded nearby, curious to see what the officers would decide. The military regulations of the United States, which had been pretty much kept in operation by all the officers who left to enter the service of their states in the Confederacy, said that if the colonel wasn't available, the lieutenant colonel took over. But that was a regulation everyone felt applied to a battlefield vacancy, not a vote of no confidence from troops. Indeed, a vote of no confidence from the troops would appear to be a contingency not remotely contemplated by the Regular army. Still, if A.J. wanted, he could have seized the moment. The high brass would have probably backed him up, simply because it was a simple answer.

He gave the opportunity back to the regiment.

"My opinion," he told the captains, Major Thomas Woodward, Surgeon John Douglass and Adjutant Julius Mills, "We need a Regular."

"I can understand what needs to be done in camp, and on the march," A.J. said, "and I can carry out a plan. But I am going to admit that being a militia captain is not enough qualification to lead this regiment into its first battle."

The men were split on whether A.J. had done right or not. Some thought he was being sensible. Others said it showed he'd never be a real leader; he had the colonelcy in his hands and he threw it away.

The officers decided Woodward and Capt. E.C. McClure of the Chester Blues should be detailed to find us a colonel, and they left the next day. Meanwhile, the rest of us kept on with preparations for traveling to Virginia. For A.J., it was a time to use the authority he had as acting battalion commander. He weeded out men who were plainly not up to the job. Our incompetent surgeons were dismissed — they'd only killed a few of us, but they clearly were not familiar with modern medical practices — and he somehow brought in Dr. A.F. Anderson of Columbia as surgeon and Dr. S.E. Babcock of Chester as assistant surgeon. All the Chester men knew Babcock and had confidence in him; both he and his father are good doctors. It gave a significant lift to our morale, and my respect for A.J.'s hidden, unsuspected talents as an organizer grew.

As for me, Bill McClure and I started the Aaron Burr Mess. Burr had passed through Chester in 1807 after being captured and charged with treason, back in the turmoil that surrounded his apparent scheme to create a new nation out of the southwestern territories. We picked the name with nothing more in our minds than a certain wryness. It merely reminded us of home and added a little class to what was a very makeshift arrangement. The mess — all from the Chester district, and all boys I'd known before we'd become soldiers — included sturdy Tom Farrar, a farrier; Fred Babcock — younger brother of our surgeon; Rudy Brandt, whose people were originally from Pennsylvania; J. Major Hall, who took great delight in telling everyone he really was a major; Andy Lindsey, quickly known as Lindsey-Woolsey; A.D. Lael; Bill Lucas, who can play the cornet; Henry McElduff, a dour young farmer rapidly named "Gruff" by the regiment; Sean McWalters; and J.R. "Green" Peay. I am, at 29, the second oldest man in the mess. Only McWalters, who is 43, is older than me. They are all good boys and some of them have gone out of their way to help me catch up on the soldier knowledge we all must learn.

McClure and I also started the Goose Creek Frying Pan Company, Ltd., as a subsidiary venture of the Aaron Burr Mess. I spent $5 of the money I'd brought from home and bought a big steel frying pan from a Charleston dry goods store. McClure agreed to do the cooking; we sold shares in the frying pan to 10 other men for $1 a share, giving me a profit of $5, of which I invested in $2 worth of relish, which it seemed to me would help along just about any of the bland fare we found issued to us daily by a commissary that seemed unable to realize it was being robbed by vendors. We got moldy flour, sugar that was half sand, and fly-blown pork. Hunger was a good sauce, and we had already reached the point where plain pig was no longer a meal we would disdain as too plebian for our refined tastes, but we could not eat some of the rations we were being issued.

I offered $2.50 to McClure as his share of the profit for his cooking chores, but he told me to keep it and invest as I saw fit, saying it looked to him like each partner should stick to what he knew best. He knew johnny cakes and how to start a fire in any weather; I knew sums and values and what would likely go up in value. A deal was struck, and a better deal I never made.

We couldn't put up with the commissary, and the good people of Goose Creek could help just so much before a regiment of nearly 800 men cleaned out their larders. Still, we had to eat. The solution came when one of the Winnsboro men who formerly had lived near Charleston pointed out that the streams and the ocean itself were filled to overflowing with good things to eat, if only we could figure out how to tap the rich resource. The nigras had already been down this road, and we convinced an old uncle to help us out.

He had about two teeth in his head and spoke with a Low Country accent most of us could just about understand, but he did know how to find food. In a short time our mess had built a couple of fish weirs, funnel-shaped baskets with inverted baskets inside, so a fish swimming into one would be forced into a narrow hole where the end of the funnel almost closed on itself. Once inside, the fish could look around and never find the door, because from the inside it all looked like woven reeds, with no hole. These fish traps would be dropped in the tidal streams, usually without bait, and checked on every low tide. They invariably yielded 10 or 15 pounds of fish, everything ranging from perch to sea trout and striped bass, along with some blue crabs.

The Aaron Burr mess ate like kings for a day, attracting the envy of those still picking out the maggots in the commissary meat. We soon found ourselves quietly followed in our twice-daily trips to the tidal stream near Goose Creek, and soon fish trap manufacture became the boom business of the Sixth Regiment. We worried some that over-investment would upset the market, that is, clean out the fish, but it didn't happen.

We had fried fish, fish broiled over an open fire on a split green sapling, poached fish boiled in a pot, fish chowder, and fish baked in green leaves buried beneath hot coals. We had fish and crabs three times a day, and after three weeks we were ready to go to Virginia just to get away from the fish. Still, it was better than moldering pork, it kept us alive and healthy, and we forced ourselves to dry some split fish on sapling racks in the hot July sun, creating a leathery item that could be chewed like jerky or restored to something that resembled fish by boiling it in water. It would keep quite a while without spoiling, we found, and we kept a few pounds in the reserve supplies of the Aaron Burr Mess.

It was a good time. I had never cooked, and learning how to do it under these conditions I somehow found very satisfactory — the ability to cook was something that was now mine, and it occurred to me that in the future this would be a great tale of hardship overcome. My ability to endure Lt. Moore's depredations had improved my standing in the company, especially when McClure, in whom I had confided, let it be known I was the victim of retaliation based on nothing but class distinctions. I denied anyone permission to take the issue up with Moore, telling them I'd take care of it myself.

Finally, in July, our good time ended and our new adventure began. We marched from Goose Creek to the railroad; a train arrived and we all boarded, filling up passenger cars, boxcars, flatcars, even the caboose was crammed with soldiers inside and on top. We jammed our baggage on as best we could, and the field officers' horses got their own boxcar. Then we were off for Virginia, a horrible three-day trip with half the men sick from the heat and the motion of the cars and the other half complaining about the lack of water. There was no lack of food; at every stop, and there were many, people in the towns brought boxes and baskets and even wagons of food, pitchers of milk, all served by pretty girls in bonnets and hoop skirts who ventured as far as the loading docks at each depot but would under no circumstances board the troop train. If they had, even for an instant, their reputations would have been ruined, and they knew it.

We jolted and bounced north through the sandy pine hills of eastern South Carolina and hit the North Carolina salt marshes where they merged into dry ground and fresh water, then we were in Virginia. We could have more easily gone through Chester, but somebody let it slip that the generals were afraid that if we made a stop in our home town, we'd desert in droves. Opinions contrary to the good names of the generals were aired, and great indignation was expressed by many at their lack of faith in our patriotism, but a few men did look suspiciously thoughtful.

We rattled on uneventfully until we hit Petersburg, where a man named Wrenn from one of the other companies fell asleep atop one of the boxcars and was jolted off between the cars when the engineer hit the brakes. I did not see what happened to Wren, but I saw the faces of the men who did see him and who helped get his body out, and that was plenty for me. A lot of men strapped themselves to the roof hardware with rope or belts after that.

It was a tired and dispirited group of men who gathered at the new Sixth Regiment headquarters outside Richmond. There, at least, we found the efforts of Maj. Woodward and Capt. McClure had produced results, although we were later to be of several minds about those results.

It seems they'd met with Jefferson Davis himself about the matter of the Sixth Regiment's colonelcy. He told them, they said, that the officers of the Sixth had, by refusing promotion, set a precedent of humility that he found "a wonderful occurrence," humility then being in very short supply among the officer corps.

"You have shown your patriotism and good sense," Davis told Woodward and McClure. "You shall have one of the best men at my disposal, and a Carolinian if possible."

They had already approached Maxcy Gregg, colonel of the First South Carolina Volunteer Infantry, whose enlistments had run out. But Gregg had promised his staff officers that he'd try to get them a unified command, and regretfully turned down the colonelcy of the Sixth.

Davis had a name for them, and it later became a source of wonder and mystery as to whether Woodward and McClure had tracked down the right man of that name. The name was Thomas Jackson; they found a former Regular of that name in Richmond, but, upon inquiry among his acquaintances, were horrified to find out that the man drank and frolicked and was known in the old Army as "Hell Roaring Jackson."

"'Be careful, or your hearts will be weighed down with dissipation, drunkenness and the anxieties of life, and that day will close on you unexpectedly like a trap," Chaplain McCausland intoned. "Luke 21, verse 34." No one was sure what he meant, but everyone was sure no one named "Hell Roaring Jackson" should ever lead our regiment.

Woodward, McClure, and this time McCausland, went back to Davis, who, with infinite patience, heard their laments and then gave them the name of the man who would be the making of the Sixth, Charles Winder of Maryland.

He was the youngest captain in the old Army, a 10-year veteran and a graduate of West Point. He hated, through some unknown source of vexation, all Yankees. He was the strictest disciplinarian we had yet come up against, and wasted no time making our lives miserable. Everyone now joined me in the same level of hell that Lt. Moore kept me in.

We only thought we'd drilled, up to that point. Winder showed us drill. A.J. lost weight putting us through our paces in the hot middle weeks of July, and it is no lie to say we drilled from dawn to sunset for more than a week straight, breaking only for meals, which were considerably better than we'd been getting from the commissary at Goose Creek.

We went through the manual of arms with our old muskets thirty times a day, under Winder's stern gaze. He never missed a thing; out of nearly a thousand men, if one private had his musket out of proper alignment at right shoulder shift, Winder would spot the musket at the wrong angle from a hundred yards away and pounce. The private would get a dressing down, the nearest corporal would get a dressing down; the first sergeant would be told it was his job to see that such things didn't happen; the second lieutenant, the first lieutenant and the captain would all be brought over to inspect the miserable private, whose only wish now was to become invisible. They were told the shortcomings of the first sergeant, the corporal and the private were all upon their gold-barred necks; if they wished to keep the gold bars, this had better not happen again, etc.

The end result was that the corporals, sergeants, lieutenants and captains tackled Hardee's "School of the Soldier" and "School of the Company" as if their lives depended on memorizing the contents, which, in Winder's mind, was exactly the case.

After a day at the manual of arms and turning from a battle line two men deep to a column of men four abreast marching "by the flank," both by the right flank and by the left flank, we moved into company maneuvers, splitting into platoons, forming a battle line to the left, to the right, and to the front from a column marching by the flank and then from a column of companies. Our knees ached and our necks throbbed from the weight of the clumsy muskets. We tackled marching by the left oblique and by the right oblique, we kept our guide to the left when marching by the right flank and our guide to the right when marching by the left flank, and kept it all straight when, after two days of this, we moved into battalion drill, with all 10 companies on the field.

We marched with flags centered and guides posted at each flank, and got it wrong until we got it right. We kept at it until the slowest private in the Sixth Regiment understood what was expected from each of the dozens of commands an officer might choose to hurl at a group of marching men. We quickly figured out that when our company marched at the head of the battalion, it paid to have a mighty sharp man with very good hearing at the head of the column next to the first sergeant. The ability to hear the general tell the colonel what he wanted before commands came down through the company captains meant he had time to think about what he was going to do, and so could do it right; and if the first private at the head of the Sixth Regiment did the right thing, all the others would follow and so we would all do the right thing and escape the wrath of Winder, which was a wonderful thing to behold but a terrible thing to incur.

After several days of battalion drills and long marches, we moved into skirmish drill. Instead of behaving like mindless animals answering to a rein, we were now expected to exercise some initiative and work in largely independent four-man teams, stinging the enemy with fire from a dispersed battle line and trying to goad him into deploying his main force so it could be assessed and dealt with.

All through this we fired not one round. The officers acted like target practice was out of the question, due to the scarcity of powder. Actually, there was plenty of powder, and after overhearing a conversation I grasped their dilemma. They knew our muskets would be accurate out to only

50 or 60 yards. There was no sense practicing; it would have done no good and would, at that point, only have made us doubt the effectiveness of the weapons we'd been given. We knew the range of the guns, of course, but we didn't really know it in the sense of understanding the implications. We found out soon enough, in a meaningful way, about the limitations of our clumsy old guns.

We did practice loading and firing, hours of it, without powder and lead. Like little children, we yelled "Boojow!" to simulate the noise the gun would have made had it gone off. It was, one of the officers joked, the French word for "Bang!" In an army that still studied the campaigns of Napoleon and thought the French army was the best in the world, this was a logical development and a fine joke.

We became a viable military unit so quickly it stunned us.

We were even more stunned when we found ourselves one scorching hot July night being urged aboard a train that had just come empty from northern Virginia. It was immediately given a new crew and turned around to head back with the Sixth Regiment. The Yankees, it seemed, had decided to open the ball and were marching south.

CHAPTER FOUR

The trip took all the rest of that night and most of the next day, but we had no opportunity to speculate among ourselves on what we might find. The railway was in pretty good shape and the engineer ignored speed limits; we flew up the tracks. It was too noisy for much talk. We watched the moonlit Virginia countryside streak past in a shower of cinders and sparks and dirty white smoke that sometimes eddied and blew into open doors of the boxcars where we swayed and hung on to each other to keep from falling down. Then it was daylight and we were jumping out of the cars, forming up into companies beside the tracks.

Our train pulled away and another roared into its place, shuddering to a squealing halt and belching steam like a panting wild animal that had been racing for its life. Jefferson Davis jumped out of the train, flanked by a group of staff officers and civilians. He ignored them, jumped on the platform of the railway station and crossed it in three quick strides, then sprang to the back of a horse that had been kept waiting there for his arrival. And he was gone, heading for what we now realized was not thunder, but the distant thump of cannon. And we were formed into a column, right in front, and marched that same direction ourselves, in a matter of moments, Tom Wright and the other drummers beating the step with sure hands.

Now we found out something about war.

The afternoon of July 21, 1861, saw the first major test of arms between the Yankees and our army, at Manassas. We won, as all now know as I write this three days after the battle, but we never would have believed it from what we saw when we marched up to the battlefield.

Everywhere there were men in uniform, drifting back south along our line of march. Some had wounds; most did not. All who would speak had tales of disaster and strife, and counseled us to flee. Winder, furious, posted the lead company in a battle line, with orders to move ahead and stop all stragglers moving to the rear. The stream of dispirited soldiers merely moved off the road and into the woods and fields beyond the flanks of the lead company and kept on trudging to the rear.

It was here, still three miles from the battlefield, that we started to change our opinion of Winder. He had been feared and despised for his meticulous adherence to drill and regulations. Now we found that, despite the haste with which we had been put aboard a train, he had nevertheless arranged for us to be met by our own supports, with food and ammunition, when we arrived. We dispensed with the usual tedious issuing of rations with paperwork and ceremony; we swept through the commissary staff like an especially efficient swarm of locusts, scarcely slowing down, and when we came out the other side we had both food to eat and ammunition to shoot. "Food for the stomach and food for the soul," one man quipped. We ate on the march, rolling relentlessly toward the battlefield, where we could still hear the booming thud of cannon and the peculiar rippling "Crack!" that a regiment makes when a thousand muskets go off almost at once.

We saw more men coming our way, and now there were wagons full of wounded men, and individuals carrying their wounded friends; some men escorted Yankee prisoners, big, stunned-looking fellows who stared about them as if in wonder at their surroundings and fate. All announced the day lost and our troops surrounded, with one exception: Col. Wade Hampton. We found our brother South Carolinian near the field with a minor head wound; he saluted us and told us that so far as he could see, the day had gone well for our side.

We finally got to the battlefield at 6 p.m., too late to be of any use but not too late to smell the coppery wrongness of blood and the sulfur stench of black powder and hear the groans and screams of wounded men and horses. It was a nervous time; my bowels felt shaky, and for once it wasn't from the food.

We fully expected that we would be used to start pursuit of the broken enemy hosts, but we reckoned without the ability of generals to misunderstand a situation. Indeed, until that moment, we hadn't realized such a thing existed.

Hampton had the right of it; he cut through the smoke and screams and blood and perceived that the enemy was routed and that, with a little more grit, we soon could be in Washington asking Abraham Lincoln in person if he felt this conflict was a good idea. But Beauregard and Joe Johnston and Jeff Davis himself appeared as stunned as most of the stragglers we'd seen earlier. We could see them huddled near the wreck of a house, standing in a cluster and gabbling amongst themselves, as the rain began to fall. That appeared to be the clinching argument in their minds, for we soon realized, with no actual information passing our way and no orders given, that there would be no pursuit. Our army — except for the Sixth Regiment and a couple of others that arrived after the battle — was almost as shattered by victory as the Yankee army had been by defeat. We merely retained possession of the battlefield.

That was no mean accomplishment, for it yielded thousands of weapons and tons of equipment, all discarded by the frightened Yankees in their haste to lighten their load and get back to Washington. Unfortunately for us, those wonderful new Springfield rifles and modern accoutrements went to regiments that had actually fought on the field.

We stayed on the battlefield for 24 hours, in pouring rain, without further provisions and without shelter. There were 983 of the most miserable soldiers in history by sunset on July 22, and part of our misery was the feeling that we'd walked up to a question we each had about ourselves and not been given a chance to answer it.

Would we run? Would I, William Coleman of Chester, respectable citizen and dependable bank official, disgrace myself and make it impossible to ever return home by giving in to the fear that had nearly crippled me in the last mile up to the battlefield? My mind said no, but my bowels had given me another message. I thought I was alone in my fear, until McClure came up to me in the dark with a made-up excuse about double-checking on the relish supply of the Aaron Burr Mess.

"I doan know if I'm happy or sad," McClure said. "Seems kind of a shame — got all riled up to go into a fight and now all we do is stand here in the rain and wonder what it would have been like."

It was like setting fire to a trail of black powder in dry grass; in moments, everyone was echoing his comments, with some men candidly admitting they'd been scared so bad they were shaking as they came up to the hill at the wrecked house and saw the dead lying in bloody rows.

Still, other men like us had been there and stayed there, and the name Stonewall Jackson was heard. His men refused to give an inch, we were told, and the Federal attack broke on the unyielding ranks of his Virginians. We were told this was Thomas Jackson's regiment, and immediately we assumed it was the Thomas Jackson our officers had rejected as colonel; we thought "That could have been us out there," and we looked at the bodies and heard the admiration in the voices of everyone who'd witnessed their stand, and we didn't know whether to be glad or not. We'd missed out on a singular honor, but death was pretty singular as well, and giving that a miss seemed like a good bargain. Some of the men said those who died achieved immortality in that kind of a desperate stand, but these were the same childish fellows who thought the Yankees wouldn't fight at all. An older man in the Chester Blues, a man whose son served in the ranks with him, grabbed one of these romanticists, shoved his nose toward the bloody, exposed rib cage of a dead Virginia youth who'd got in the way of a shell burst, and told him to take a good, long look at immortality and then shut up.

Chaplain McCausland led us in prayers, but he apparently prayed with the dead as well, giving them bits of Calvinism as they lay grotesquely on the ground.

"'You did not choose me, but I chose you,'" he intoned to one corpse. "John 15, verse 16."

A.J. came by about midnight and told us it wasn't the same Jackson, that this Jackson was a rock-ribbed Presbyterian, not a hell-raiser, but all that did was make us wonder if Woodward and McClure had got hold of the wrong Jackson in the first place, and this one was the one Davis had in mind for us all along.

The rain stopped and we listened as mockingbirds opened up with song in the warm darkness.

Two days after the battle, with the stench of putrefying bodies heavy in the air despite the efforts of negro work squads to get them buried, we finally moved off the Manassas battlefield. We marched a few miles north along the railroad, to Centreville, and then to Camp Pettus, a site already occupied by a Mississippi regiment. It proved our undoing; the Mississippi troops had measles and it followed us from Camp Pettus to Germantown, only 14 miles from Alexandria and the Yankees. Here we had the worst campsite yet, a hollow that flooded after every fog or heavy dew. We christened it "Camp Misery," and it proved to be the final resting place of quite a few brave fellows. The measles, a disease that is nothing when a child gets it, proved deadly. The Sixth Regiment lost 34 men to measles, and had another 64 laid so low they had to be sent home to recover. And every day we heard the big Yankee guns booming from across the Potomac, not shooting to do any real damage, just letting us know they were still there and still willing if not quite so eager.

Our leaders seemed to think one victory would be the war; they sat back and waited for Abraham Lincoln to announce that the secession of 11 states was an accomplished fact. They reckoned, not for the first time, without understanding the peculiar mulish nature of the Yankee mind.

We had plenty of time, while we were watching each other sicken and die in bad camps, to do our own reckoning. Our understanding of the politics — which we considered crucial to understanding why we were camped and dying in a mudhole in Virginia — centered on Fort Sumter.

Those who had paid attention while the crisis developed wondered why Beauregard had attacked Sumter when he'd been told by Maj. Robert Anderson, Sumter's Yankee commander, that without resupply the fort would surrender within days. Within hours of getting that message, we bombarded the fort.

There were a lot of explanations. Some said Beauregard just plain didn't believe Anderson, and expected some sort of attack from the Yankee fleet everyone knew was just off Charleston. Others said it was a matter of honor, that starving out a garrison lacked the dignity of forcing a military surrender by battle. The devious minds in our ranks — and there were some — said we did it to force Virginia to join the Confederacy. Others protested, asking how firing on Sumter could have forced

Virginia to join. The devious ones pointed out that in fact, our firing on Sumter forced Lincoln out of a stupor and prompted him to issue a call for troops from all the states to suppress the "rebellion" in the seven Confederate states that then existed. Lincoln sent telegrams to North Carolina and Virginia asking for troops; that enraged people in Virginia and North Carolina, and those states cast aside their doubts and threw themselves completely into the Southern cause. And that, the devious ones said, was exactly what Beauregard and the politicians wanted. They probably didn't want to arouse the North to the extent the North got worked up, they admitted, but it was absolutely necessary to force the issue, and Sumter was handy.

A Confederacy without Virginia's long tradition of leadership and North Carolina's factories, the devious ones said, stood little chance of standing up to the North, whether the issue was joined now or in 20 years.

"A gamble," was the opinion offered by a Winnsboro dry goods clerk.

"No choice," was the rejoinder from the devious ones.

John Bratton, the captain-turned-private from Winnsboro, was among the devious ones. It turned out he was only trained as a doctor, he'd not practiced. He had unusual ideas about medicine that made him a pariah among his medical colleagues, including collecting and writing down folk remedies from the negroes and the wise women in the backwards areas of our state. He walked among the sick at Camp Misery, helping those stricken with measles and with the bloody flux, and talking politics the whole time.

Bratton felt the gamble had to be taken, that the South had no chance without all the states that had anything at all in common bonding together. He — and McClure and many others — felt that the basic difference between North and South wasn't slavery or the tariff or states' rights, but love of the land. Land was the mark of success in the South, while money was the mark of success in the North. Whether it was an Irish tenant farmer forced out so the English absentee landlords could turn his ground over to sheep, or the dispossessed Huguenots in South Carolina who'd lost their land in France because of opposition to the Catholic Church, or the younger sons of English nobility sent to the New World because there was no more land for them in the old country, the South seems to have a lot of people who feel land is security and the measure of success. That, said Bratton and others, is not the case in the North, where factories and cities are rapidly severing the connections between people and the land that, ultimately, supports them.

"You can't even talk to some of those people. They don't understand what we think is important," Bratton said.

He felt the gamble was necessary. But he didn't think our lives should be wasted because generals couldn't figure out that low ground harbored disease.

Others pointed out that it really didn't matter what had gone before: The issue at hand was force of arms, and it is necessary to defend our homes regardless of politics. To them, our first duty is as clear as if it had been engraved on tablets of stone.

We get to see quite a bit of Northern Virginia, marching out on excursions to Falls Church and Munson's Hill and Upton's Hill and Point of Rocks. At times we were close enough to Washington to see the still half-built Capitol dome.

And on one of these excursions we draw blood, at Hall's Hill. It is just a skirmish, but it looms large, especially since many thought the lack of action out of Washington and Richmond means peace talks will soon send us back to our farms and jobs.

We are teamed with some companies from a Maryland regiment — orphans, we call them, since they are cut off from state support by the entire Yankee government in Washington. We also have with us the Washington Artillery of New Orleans, under Capt. Thomas Rosser, a West Pointer. We march through a hot fall day — shots ring out from a wood line to our left. They are firing from more than 400 yards. They do no damage and we could easily pass by. But peevish Winder gets a burr under his saddle, and the next thing we know we are deployed across that field, the artillery in the middle of the line and the Maryland companies on our left flank. It was "Charge bayonet! Forward, march!" and across a field of clover and into the woods, to find the enemy gone. Or almost gone.

We are congratulating ourselves on our courage when uproar breaks out at the farmhouse down the wood line. The farm, it turns out, is owned by Quakers, who show themselves to be true to their faith and not interested in the mortal combat taking place on their quiet acres. They own a bulldog, however, that apparently does not subscribe to their peaceful religion; he attacks Bill Jamison of the Boyce Guards, who has quite a time with the beast before finally resorting to the bayonet and putting an end to the dispute. The dog flees, spewing blood and howling. Other soldiers, coming up some moments after the incident and not realizing what had transpired, attribute the blood to wounded Yankees. They proceeded to tear apart the farm, whereupon Corporal Dunlevy of the Chester Blues indeed discovers three Yankees, including a Lt. Kittrell from a Maine regiment, hiding in a bank of potatoes in a cellar under the farmhouse.

"I see you in thar, come out from them potatoes!" we hear him shout. Laughter sweeps through everyone who hears his muffled roars coming from under the house, and shortly Dunlevy emerges, with three Yankees in front of him, picking small spuds out of their traps and looking sheepish. He is proud of himself. Capt. Walker orders Dunlevy to bring the prisoner over to the Calhoun Guard, which is reforming in front of the house. He should take them back to his own company, but back in Chester Dunlevy worked for Walker's father, at Walker's Mill.

This is quite an event. Three Yankees, potatoes and goodness knows what else in that Quaker basement. Walker puts us at rest — we can move about — while he talks with the Yankee lieutenant. McClure is with me — by mutual agreement, he is now "Willie" and I am "Bill," to reduce the confusion — and we quickly go to work. I would have been ashamed of myself six months earlier. The sight of all those Quaker men not in uniform, rosy cheeked, enjoying the fruits of the land and of life while we wear worn-out uniforms and pick lice off ourselves in their defense, has triggered something in me: Some old-fashioned resentment.

The old Quaker patriarch is wringing his hands and asking what will happen to the prisoners. I look around: There are no officers nearby.

"They won't be shot," I say. "They are in uniform and were acting as honorable soldiers. You should look to your own soul, sir."

His hand wringing gets more agitated. McClure looks at me in wonder.

"What do you mean? Speak plainly, young man," the old Quaker says.

"They were hiding in your cellar," I say. "You are part of a sect that has not embraced the Confederate cause. Some might say you gave sanctuary to our nation's enemy." Willie, figuring out where I'm heading, has lined up several members of the Aaron Burr mess and put them at attention in the old man's front yard. The Quaker family looks on; there are several healthy young men, who would have graced any military force, and yet they were sitting out the war on a farm bursting with plenty while we are issued wormy pork. Really, anyone could tell the Yankees had just ducked into the first hole they found, but here was a situation where soldiers could take revenge on noncombatants. And revenge is sweet: Already we had seen ourselves transformed from being heroes defending the nation to "Filthy soldiers, stay clear of them, Amelia," whenever we went through a town. The Aaron Burr mess looks grim but eager.

"Fix bayonets," Willie orders. The men don't even blink at his assumption of noncommissioned officer rank. They just fix bayonets, by the book. They are willing to implement the fib, especially with me in the lead — I think seeing me riled up is the main draw for them. I've always laid low before, and they are intrigued by the novelty of me stepping out in front.

The old Quaker has sweat beading his forehead. He stops twisting his hands long enough to wipe his head.

"I couldn't stop them," he tells me. "They ran into the cellar, we didn't know they were there until you fellas found them."

"Show me this cellar," I say. He takes us down a set of stone steps to the foundations of the house, and into a coolness that reeks of food. I smell apples, ham — butter ? — and spices, cinnamon and cloves. My mouth waters.

"Old man," I say. "The Calhoun Guard now has your Yankees and nobody but the Calhoun Guard ever needs to know exactly where they were found. We are willing to do you a favor, because we are true Christians. We are willing to turn the other cheek." And I turn to present him with a cheek, and look unblinkingly right at a huge ham hanging from a beam.

He isn't slow. He may be a Quaker, but he's also, apparently, a businessman.

"I am a Christian also, and Christian charity should be shared," he says, following my gaze.

"You will be rewarded in heaven, sir, and will be given every opportunity to share," I say. Then I call for Willie. He brings down the Aaron Burr Mess, and we leave heavier than we came in. Indeed, the Calhoun Guard eats well for the next couple of days.

The day before this, we killed our first Yankee. I guess I have put off telling of it as long as I can. I am left with an uneasy feeling, but it must be told. It is what happened, and I'm resolved not to flinch from recording everything. We — the Calhoun Guard — "tallied the first score for the regiment." I guess we should be proud.

Three members of the Calhoun Guards had been on picket duty in a field overgrown with weeds. To their left was another picket post, at a large pine, behind which the pickets were sheltered — except that there was a hill a couple of hundred yards away that looked down on the spot. A Federal sharpshooter, who had been murdering pickets along the line, came up to the area, saw our soldiers behind the pine and managed to creep up into position to shoot — his target appeared to be Lt. J.L. Agurs, who was Officer of the Guard and visiting the picket post to make sure things were as they should be. But Sgt. S.C. Morrison, "Tack" Nail and Jacob Baker of the Calhoun Guards were on a defensive patrol, and spotted the Yankee sneaking across the hillside above them, only about 50 yards from where they'd halted to take a rest and look around. They watched him, to see what he was up to before capturing him. When he smiled and raised his rifle, they shot him and sent him to his Maker. One bullet hit the brass plate on his belt, on edge, and tore a furrow across his belly. Another hit the lock of his gun and smashed it. The third went through his cartridge box, on his left hip. That one went through his body, angling up and breaking his wrist when it came out. Morrison, Nail and Baker called for the corporal of the guard and brought the Yankee back into our camp. Nail stayed with the Yankee for the several hours it took for him to die. He wasn't overjoyed.

"His gun was dirty, his cartridge box was almost empty; he'd been sniping all day," Tack told his cousin, Richard, when the man's ordeal was ended. "He'd been gunning for us all day and he was taking an un-Christian delight in his work. But God! It is hard to see anyone die gutshot! He'd ask for water, and at first we gave it to him, but he'd cramp up and scream after he drank it, so we stopped givin' it to him."

Surgeon Babcock attended to the man in his last hours, but told him and us there was nothing he could do, the man's guts were all twisted up and cut by the .69 caliber musket ball. The Yankee's name was Archibald; he was from Marblehead, Massachusetts, and he had blue eyes and blond hair and looked to be about 25 or 26 years old. We got a lot of praise for killing him, and it was undoubtedly our duty to do so, but the men who shot him agreed later that we got more satisfaction out of the Quaker ham.

A.J. took Archibald's wallet and sent it through the lines later, under a flag of truce, with a note explaining the circumstances of his death. His note regretted the necessity for killing the man, but warned that other "murderers" of pickets would face similar fates.

It was still that kind of war.

In December, it changed.

My Dearest Brother,

I hope this letter finds you and all the Chester boys healthy and doing your duty. Oh! I wish I was a boy! Then I could join you and fight the cowardly Yankees instead of staying here and making socks!

The trains run all the time now. There is hardly an hour of the day or night when we don't hear a whistle coming or a whistle going. It seems all the South is sending soldiers and wagons and guns and horses to Virginia. I never knew there were so many people in our Nation! Some of the boys are not much older than me and very handsome, although Mamma says I am to take no notice because I am too young for such things. It is not fair! I am not old enough to take a woman's part, I am not a boy — God has singled me out for this special affliction, to have nothing to do that is worth doing while great things are being done.

I have knitted you a cap, since your last letter said some of the men were having great sport with hats to wear in camp. I am sorry about the missed stitches, but perhaps if you only wear it at night no one will notice. It will surely keep you warm, and if you wear it I will feel that not everything I have done since you left was some worthless act done by a silly little girl.

When will you come home? Others have come home for a week or more, but you and your company have not. Have you no officers who look out for you? Surely they must know how much you all would like to see home.

I will write again, soon.

Hanna

CHAPTER FIVE

In late December five companies of the Sixth Regiment S.C.V.I. were detailed to join a makeshift force under the command of up-and-coming Brigadier General J.E.B. Stuart and guard a wagon train sent to collect forage for the army. We were accompanied by the 11th Virginia, the 10th Alabama, the 1st Kentucky and Cutt's Georgia Battery.

We marched 16 miles on the 20th of December, with A.J. in command of the regiment simply because Winder had been assigned to a court martial. We came up to the little town of Dranesville. A cavalryman galloped up and, as bullets whickered past him and kicked up dirt near us, gave us an intimation that the enemy was at hand and bloody work was imminent. We rapidly got orders to halt and load, and we moved up the road and marched by the left flank into the woods bordering the road. Cutt's Battery stayed in the road, and the 10th Alabama and 11th Virginia went to the right. The 1st Kentucky moved off the road with us, slightly to our rear.

We filed into the woods and prepared to meet the enemy, whose noise was plain in our front, somewhere beyond a dense thicket. My knees commenced to shake and the shaking spread up to my shoulders, so that my musket shook. McClure was ahead of me; I couldn't see his face, but his musket wasn't shaking. Fine. Willie has about as much common sense as anyone I've ever met. If he sticks it, I'll stick it. But when I see him go, I'm going, those were my thoughts at that moment.

The 1st Kentucky lined up about 60 yards behind us. We thought nothing of it; we'd been with them for 16 miles and our pale battle flag was clearly visible, held aloft by William McAlily. The thick woods didn't begin for 10 yards to our front, and it was all clear woodland between us and the 1st Kentucky.

Suddenly we heard clear, ringing commands to "Ready, aim!" and when I turned to see if the 1st Kentucky was being flanked, I found every gun in the Kentucky regiment aimed our way. "Fire!" came the command, almost drowned out by a crashing volley. The man next to me went down, blood gushing out of his mouth, and I admit that for a minute or more I was useless. I stood there and shook. One moment he was next to me and talking, and the next he was nothing, something to step over. Five other boys fell dead up and down the line, and more than two dozen were wounded. A scream of rage and sorrow went up, and the Kentucky boys immediately knew they'd made a mortal mistake, but there was no time to think about it because suddenly our front was filled with blue. Now, even while I was pretty much useless as a soldier, my mind refused to stop and it said "Blue? Blue? Goddam it, we're shooting at blue and we're still wearing blue, too! No wonder they shot us." Some of us, especially in the Chester Blues and the Calhoun Guards, still had our blue swallow-tail militia coats, just about worn out but better than going without any coats at all, and it has to be admitted that in the gloom of the forest, there was not a lot of difference between South Carolina militia blue and Yankee blue. And the 1st Kentucky? Blue coats, blue pants. All the ingredients for disaster.

The 1st Kentucky marched farther out to our left, to keep the Yankees from flanking us. Our officers noticed that Cutt's Battery was aiming at us, apparently taking their cue from the 1st Kentucky's volley. A.J. screamed at them, and they redirected their guns before they fired at us, but it was a near thing. I saw Stuart grab Maj. Woodward and point toward the enemy, then Woodward grabbed A.J. and the order came down through the captains to "Advance! Advance!" and so, with Winder's good training coming to our aid in the midst of horror and rage and frustration, we advanced. "Battalion! Forward! Guide, center! March!" and into the thicket we moved, our line curving and breaking in the underbrush, but moving, moving, leaving our dead and wounded behind. The relentless push gave its own life to our movement, bringing those like me along like dull animals, capable of little but following the herd; and our luck changed, because no one was in the thicket to greet us with deadly fire and gleaming bayonets. We came out the other side, reformed in good order, and pushed ahead. I was shaking so bad I thought I might drop my gun.

And there they were.

A long, thick line of blue tipped with glittering bayonets was moving at us across one of the fields behind the collection of houses that formed Dranesville. To the left and right, as far as we could see through hedgerows and fields, there was a line of blue. And behind the first line, a second, perhaps a hundred yards back.

Cutt's Battery moved up the road to join us; huge, crashing volleys broke out on our right, across the road, and we could hear screams and cheers and the wild noise horses make when they are in mortal pain. Then a Yankee battery opened up from somewhere in Dranesville, and Cutt's Battery began taking hits.

The blue line in front of us advanced to within a hundred yards before A.J. gave the order to fire; 315 muskets boomed, and the Yankee line melted. Men fell; others stopped, while even more decided they'd had enough and began moving away from us. We wanted to give them another volley, but A.J. wouldn't let us.

"Too far," he said.

Somebody on the other side figured out what our problem was: Muskets, effective range 100 yards or less. The first Yankee regiment melted into the second and went to the rear, disappearing in the distance. The second regiment advanced to about 150 yards and opened up on us. Men started dropping immediately, five or six with every volley, and there was a kind of movement up and down our line, a ripple; men didn't leave, but they fidgeted. I checked: Willie was standing fast, so I stood fast.

The Yankees only got off two volleys before A.J. had us moving back into the woods, not in a battle line but with every company forming a column at right angles to our line of battle and marching directly away from the fight, a move we'd drilled for countless hours without ever appreciating the practical uses it might have. We disappeared into the thickets, and we could hear the Yankee "Hurray," and their officers pushing the men to move after us. A.J. halted us about 75 yards into the woods, and we quickly moved by files left, then fronted; it wasn't that simple, because the woods and thickets made it difficult to align. But we knew what A.J. wanted: He wanted us facing the enemy and ready to fight in an area where the greater range of the Yankee rifles meant nothing, because of the woods. So we formed two ranks and made sure we were loaded.

Sweat was rolling off us, even though the sun was low on the horizon and the temperature was dropping. Our breath was steaming in the cold air, and a cloud of vapor went straight up from the Calhoun Guards. I'd stopped shaking; too busy trying to make sense of the complicated commands to worry any more. And it felt good, holding formation and fighting with others close by.

The Yankees came running into the woods and thickets, and when they were good and caught, each company ripped it into them. A.J. had turned the firing commands over to the companies, because there was no visibility for a battalion front. Sometimes the blue uniforms got within 30 yards before a captain would let his 70 or 80 muskets fire; sometimes the woods were more open, and the firing would begin when the enemy was still 70 yards away but trying to form a company front. They were all broken up by the woods, because they hit it the way we did the first time, in a battalion front, and some of them moved fast while others got hung up in briars.

We tore them apart. Our big, old muskets had no range, but they could be loaded swiftly. After each company's first volley, we were given the command to "Fire at will!" and as targets presented themselves in the gloom and smoke, we fired, sometimes one at a time and sometimes in a clump of three or four muskets. No Yankee got closer than 10 yards, but it has to be admitted they kept on coming. They had bucktails pinned to their hats.

Cutt's Battery had stopped firing, but the Yankee guns kept booming. We heard nothing on our left; to the right, the shooting and yelling kept up, but seemed to be moving to our rear. We held our ground.

Suddenly we began taking fire from our left. Nothing dramatic happened, just the companies to our left began bending as the captains tried to bring their lines to bear on the fire coming through the woods from the left. Where was Kentucky? Gone, as it turned out. They ran into the Yankees before getting out of the woods and, unnerved by what happened the first time they fired, waited too long this time for fear of making another mistake. The Yankees were on them before they truly got ready, and the Kentucky regiment was drifting to our rear out of the fight. They had lost momentum and never got it back.

It now looked like we were in a fair way of being surrounded. The firing on our right was clearly moving to the rear, and our left companies were bending, bending, trying to keep the Yankees from sinking steel teeth in our flank. We began taking shell fire from the Yankee guns, which were firing blind into the woods and killing as many of their own men as ours. The captains wanted A.J. to order a charge, but he refused, saying he knew too little of what was in front of us to do such a thing. On the other hand, no one had told A.J. to retreat, so we hung in like bulldogs.

About this time Major Woodward went down right behind us, and A.J. was at his side in an instant. His horse was down with a mortal wound and Woodward had no more than jumped clear when he caught a minie ball through the meaty part of his thigh, spinning him around like a top and dumping him on the ground. He had a silly look on his face and he kept saying "What? What?" A.J. grabbed me out of the line and got George Ladd of the Boyce Guards, who had been detailed as a courier, to pick up Woodward and get him out.

We stumbled to the rear, with Woodward slung between us and hopping on one leg through the open woods and letting us pull him through the briars, which were not as bad on the way out as they had been on the way in, because they'd been torn up by shot and ball and tramped into the dirt by the regiments passing through. We passed the Kentucky regiment, which was being reformed by their major. He gave us his dead colonel's horse, and we put Woodward in the saddle and moved off, with me leading the horse and Ladd keeping him propped up; he was groggy and talking nonsense.

We moved to an ambulance, and waited to make sure they took care of Woodward. Stuart was trying to enlist stragglers to help Cutt's remnant pull out the guns by hand; almost all the horses were dead. Quite a throng was moving to the rear.

"Jest listen to those South Carolina fellers taking on that whole Federal division! Damn fools!"

one man said as he scuttled to the rear. The hair on the back of my neck stood up.

Stuart finally sent couriers into the woods to tell A.J. to move back, and soon we saw the Sixth Regiment's pale flag coming through the woods, with a battle line moving backward on each side. That flag — one of the new battle flags ordered by Beauregard after Manassas — had been a source of some discontent among the troops because it was a very pale tan, rather than the rich red adorning some of the other new battle flags. But this day it proved its worth; it stood out boldly in the gloomy woods and was clearly visible to the rank and file, who aligned on it — unevenly, it's true, but straight enough to mass the regiment's fire — with no problem despite the underbrush and growing darkness.

The regiment was preceded by the Rev. Ichabod Barak McCausland. The preacher, having no worldly functions as chaplain during the actual fighting, had taken it upon himself to minister to the injured, becoming a physical healer rather than a spiritual one. The move out of the woods caught him somewhat by surprise, while trying to bind a young fellow's shattered leg to stop the bleeding. Uncertain whether to leave the boy in the woods or to stay with him, McCausland resolved his indecision by picking him up bodily and carrying him out — only to find out upon emerging into the road where the Sixth was reforming that the youngster had died.

"And our hope of you is steadfast, knowing, that as ye are partakers of the sufferings, so shall ye be also of the consolation," he intoned, with a quaver in his voice. "We were pressed out of measure, above strength, insomuch that we despaired even of life: But we had the sentence of death in ourselves, that we should not trust in ourselves, but in God which raiseth the dead."

"Corinthians," McCausland said to me, "but I know not which." He appeared somewhat dazed — but he was there, and my respect for him grew.

There we stood, the Sixth Regiment backed by an uncertain group of Kentuckians, while the rest of the expedition drifted to the rear. Stuart had orders to protect the wagon train, which was nothing more or less than every wagon the army in northern Virginia could assemble for the purpose of harvesting fodder for the army's livestock. We all had felt the hugeness of the enemy force opposing us, and waited grimly for the first blue uniforms to poke through the underbrush and push us out of the way.

Minutes passed, and finally we realized they weren't coming. At least, they weren't coming in our front. There was time to reflect. It had been my first battle, and while I had been scared, I hadn't run. After the Kentucky troops fired on us, there really hadn't been time to be scared. Winder's training paid off; I concentrated on hearing and obeying the orders, and that was enough. Almost none of the Sixth had broken to the rear, and those who had were showing up now, with shamefaced looks and weak tales about getting separated. But I was tired, weary to the bone.

On the other hand, some of the men absolutely glowed. Combat transformed them; they were almost breathing fire, and had to be addressed sharply before they would respond. I saw the lieutenant strike one man, knocking him down; the soldier simply got up and kept on looking into the woods, ignoring the lump that grew on his forehead. He was in the grip of strong emotion; I didn't understand. It bothered me. Getting past the fear was enough for me, it was the goal I'd set for myself. The possibility that this fighting could be enjoyable horrified me.

One of the fire-eaters had a Yankee kepi he'd managed to snatch from one of the dead. It had a bucktail pinned to the left side, with the base of the tail touching the front of the cap and the tail sweeping sideways, with the tip of the tail pinned to the rear. He was wearing it and doing a dance.

"I got me a trophy, hyars war I send sumpin' home so Martha kin see weuz in a faht," he chortled.

"Brownley, you lift up a buck's tail, what's usually under it?" a wit called out.

Brownley got mad.

"I'll smash yer smart tongue down yer stinkin' throat," he roared, throwing down his gun, knocking the cap off his head and lunging toward the wit. Most everybody else was too busy laughing to realize he was deadly serious, but McClure, quick as ever, stuck out a foot as Brownley lunged by and sent him sprawling into the dirt. Five of the boys sat on him; it took that many before he cried "Uncle!" and said he'd leave off.

I picked up the cap and looked inside. There was a piece of paper pinned to the lining, with a carefully written message.

"If I fall, please write to the widow Sarah Potter, 114 Morris Avenue, Germantown, Penn., and inform her that her son, Thomas, died with his face to the enemy."

"Brownley," I said, taking him the cap and showing him the writing, " it looks like you've taken on more than just a cap."

Brownley scowled.

"Cain't read," he muttered.

I told him what it said.

"Shit," he replied. "I cain't write, neither."

He spit tobacco juice, turned and walked away, leaving me holding the cap with its bucktail and message.

Stuart got word the wagon train was moving away, and at last ordered us to leave the field of battle.

Thus ended the battle of Dranesville, which sealed A.J.'s doom.

We lost Obadiah Hardin, captain of the Chester Guards. His had been the color company, and with three flagbearers shot down, Hardin picked up the colors himself rather than send another man; he was shot down and killed on the spot. The pale flag was very visible to the Yankees, too. Fred Moore, a lieutenant with the York company — another Moore, there were a lot of them — was also killed, along with 43 others from the Sixth Regiment. We had more than 100 wounded. All that blood spilled just to protect a bunch of wagons. Those of us who fought there knew we'd been well handled by A.J., but not all the regiment was present. And even those who were there tended to blame A.J. for the incident with the Kentucky regiment. A lot of men lost friends at Dranesville, and Stuart made it worse by singling out the Sixth Regiment for its courageous stand; the mood was such that everyone perversely took it the wrong way and interpreted it as a sarcastic slight for standing fast rather than not making a charge that could have turned the battle our way.

It is absurd, but leadership, it turns out, depends on perception as much as it does on reality, and the men perceived that A.J. had been at the head of the regiment when bad, discouraging, awful things had happened.

We spent four months in a gloomy winter camp, eating bad food, getting sick and dying, and thinking again and again about the disaster at Dranesville. Winder, whose zeal for discipline and drill was surpassed only by his ambition, left us; I think he believed we would not re-enlist after our one-year term of Confederate service ended. I think his ambition moved him away from a regiment that did not seem to be creating a good name for itself. When the regiment was re-organized in April, with companies added from the broken-up 9th Regiment to take the place of those who had fallen or died of sickness, A.J. was not elected to any field officer post. Instead, the men remembered things that needed to be remembered. John Bratton became the colonel of the Sixth Regiment.

A.J. went home much, much older than when he'd left a year before.

My recollection
of the War of Secession
or the War Between the States

By Miss Hanna H. Coleman

On the Wilderness, or Seven Pines battle field my brother William picked up a Bible, that had belonged to a soldier from Maine,
it had a bullet hole through it, he sent it home also, a large
black new foundland dog, the boys named him Rover, he was found on
the battle field, lying by his dead master, who was a Northern soldier, he was taken away by main force; my mother had Rover sheared,
and, had his hair spun and woven and made my brother a beautiful
vest out of it.

CHAPTER SIX

The Sixth Regiment shook itself together under John Bratton, who had anticipated events and tried to get the entire regiment to re-enlist. The war, he said, would not be over any time soon. The Confederate government would have to take bitter measures to keep an army in the field; he believed we would be ordered to stay in the field until hostilities ended. He felt any regiment that first volunteered to serve until the fighting ended, without waiting to be ordered, would be in a strong position later to demand honorable service and treatment.

A lot of men just wanted to go home. And most of the winter was spent believing that when spring came, the Yankees would recognize the Confederate government, and that would be that.

It was with a great deal of consternation, then, that the government realized in April that the Yankees weren't quitting and were instead building and training a huge army. The Confederate government had not planned for this; one-year volunteers were nearing the end of their enlistment, while the Yankees were training and drilling and piling up mountains of supplies.

So when April inevitably rolled up and the muddy roads dried, the Confederacy was faced with invasion and had an army that was about to evaporate. It did what John Bratton said it would do. We were told we were in for the duration. We were conscripted.

Even so, we were gutted. A lot of men had been invalided out. Others had been killed or wounded at Dranesville. We were down to around 400 men in the Sixth when the order came to re-organize the entire brigade. The 9th Regiment was disbanded, with some of the men coming to the Sixth and others to the 5th. The 5th had been gutted by Micah Jenkins to form a new regiment, the Palmetto Sharpshooters, an elite unit armed with the scarce Enfield rifles, a unit Jenkins hoped would win a name for itself and, not so incidentally, for him. The 2nd Regiment Rifles had also been torn apart to provide men for the Sharpshooters. The 5th was replenished by men from the 9th and other disbanded units. It was a mess, but when it was over — when the politicians' sons pulled in all their favors and got sent home, when those with weakening resolve were bucked up, when those with nothing going at home realized they actually enjoyed life in the army if it weren't for the fighting — we mustered just about 700 boys under John Bratton's leadership, all veterans. We quickly began learning what our new colonel expected of us.

The new Sixth Regiment consisted of: Company A, the Calhoun Guards, under Capt. John L. Agurs; Company B, the York Guards, Capt. John M. White; Co. C, Capt. Edward Cantey; Company D., Capt. J. Walker; Company E, Capt. James L. Coker; Company F, the Pickens Guards/Chester Blues, Capt. J. Lucius Gaston; Company G, the Boyce Guards under Capt. James M. Phinney; Company H, the Buckhead Guards, under Capt. Boykin Lyles; and Co. I, the Chester Guards, Capt. Crosby.

Bratton had been trained as a doctor before the war began. He remained a doctor in his heart. We also found out he'd spent his time as a private studying his colleagues in the regiment.

He summoned me to his tent one warm night in late April, after we'd been moved from north of Richmond to the east. Frogs were singing in the dark in the swamp down the hill; a gentle breeze kept the mosquitoes on the move. The smell of wood smoke from cook fires mingled with the odor of wool and leather and metal and horses; another typical army camp, this time on a hillside with good air.

"We need a regimental commissary sergeant," he said, with no small talk or pleasantries. "I want you to take the job."

I considered. Commissary sergeant — usually a brigade-level job — is not a particularly popular post in the Confederate Army for anyone with any sensitivities, especially anyone afflicted with the curse of honesty. The regimental commissary sergeant is responsible for dividing the rations received from brigade and division commissaries, and apportioning them among the regiments, or, in my case, among the companies of the Sixth Regiment. The sergeant gets full blame for bad rations and no credit for stretching limited amounts of food to a sizable assembly of voracious young men whose naturally healthy appetites are fueled by exercise and living out of doors. The commissary sergeant is also at the mercy of the commissary itself, which we suspect of "condemning" the best food and clothing and selling it privately to civilians, pocketing the money. Still, it would help insulate me from the malignant Michael Moore, who, while less overbearing than he used to be, still manifests utter coldness and disdain in his dealings with me.

"Why me?" I asked Bratton. "Whom did I offend?"

He grinned, and it was part of John Bratton's charm that his grin is a window to a soul essentially happy and optimistic.

"You offended no one. I just remembered the old Quaker," he said. "I had some of that ham. I think of it sometimes. The Aaron Burr Mess seems to eat a bit better than everybody else. I think you're the reason."

I understood; he didn't.

"Private McClure is a big part of the reason why the Aaron Burr Mess eats well, and his procurement techniques are — not regulation," I said.

"Private McClure is hereby assigned to assist you in whatever way you see fit," Bratton said, grinning again.

"Am I to understand that it is the new colonel's desire that the Sixth Regiment not be content to wait to see what the army sees fit to issue us?" I asked.

"Your understanding is correct," Bratton said. "We are of no use to the Confederacy sick from eating bad pork."

"There is one other thing," he said. "This regiment has no posts in the rear of the line of battle. Commissary sergeant or not, when we go to fight, you are fourth sergeant, Company A, and your job is fighting, not finding supplies."

I nodded. This was not dismaying news, although I knew of some men who were trying desperately to find posts that would get them out of the fighting. Like a lot of other men, I'd found at Dranesville that while the dread of anticipation is almost unbearable, it seems to fade a bit when the fighting starts. I will always be scared, but I will do my duty. I hope.

We marched southeast shortly after that, and found ourselves in dirt fortifications in Yorktown, where our ancestors had forced the British to surrender. It gave us an eerie feeling to march into the same breastworks they'd occupied, chopping brush and digging new trenches in the face of an enemy whose great-grandfathers had been our allies 80 years before.

George McClellan, the new Union commander of what is now called the Army of the Potomac, performed a miracle with the defeated rabble that fled Manassas in July of 1861. They are in our front, more than 100,000 men, equipped with modern weapons and fed by a supply line that stretched back to Washington and beyond, by wagon, train and boat. We faced one of the biggest armies the world had yet seen, and to say we were impressed is to understate the situation. We were intimidated. And yet ....

They could be fooled, these Yankees.

We fought at Williamsburg — actually Yorktown, on the north side of the peninsula. It wasn't much of a fight, a rear guard action by most of us. Two of our companies got into it when they got swept into an advance ordered by an impetuous Virginia colonel; Micah Jenkins, who had commanded the 5th South Carolina and now commanded the Palmetto Sharpshooters and was the senior colonel in our brigade at the moment, forbade Bratton to release any more companies to support the Virginians. There were no orders for an advance, he said.

But there were no orders for a retreat, either, at least not until dusk of the day that the Yankees finally made their move.

They'd been stalled for some time by the theatrics of John Magruder, the general in charge of the fighting army on the Peninsula. He was an aficionado of the theater and took a page out of the book of stage tricks to fool the Yankees, none of whom had apparently ever attended a performance of "Julius Caesar." He found a spot that was under observation by Yankee scouts, and proceeded to repeatedly run a few regiments of infantry across that spot, looping them in a circle through a ravine where they couldn't be seen. To the Yanks, it looked like thousands of men all pouring into the trenches near Yorktown, when actually it was just the Sixth Alabama and a couple of other regiments, again and again. We slept well that night — not so well as the Sixth Alabama, of course — while Yankee generals went without sleep trying to figure out where the endless supply of Confederate soldiers was coming from.

McClellan would have sat there all summer, but his subordinates were made of sterner stuff. Major General Joe Hooker, commanding a division in the Third Corps, finally got disgusted and contrived to start a fight on May 5, just to prove McClellan was an idiot, as we later heard the story told by prisoners. We had to move out of Yorktown, finally, but found ourselves again the rear guard, constantly forming a battle line to slow down eager Yankees coming up in our rear. We got to be expert at forcing them to form up, and we became even more expert at disappearing from their front at just about the time they lined up overwhelming force against us.

We backed our way west up the Peninsula for two weeks, until we could hear the church bells in Richmond. Joe Johnston had retreated us right to the ramparts of the city, and the Yankees taunted us at night from their picket line.

"Hey, Reb! When are you going to fight?" they'd call.

Tom Wright is on the regimental rolls as a musician, but he knew about Bratton's plan to have everyone on the battle line, regardless of their assignment, when a fight was imminent. He is also in the Aaron Burr Mess, which none of us think anything about since we'd all known Wright for years, even though he was a few years older than me. It was pretty useful having a musician in the mess, because his duties and a soldier's duties sometimes meant that he could take care of chores while we were busy, and the other way round. Now Wright argues that he needs to learn the infantry drill, so that when the time comes, he would be able to pick up a gun instead of a drum. There was almost a fight over this.

"You ain't gonna let a slave carry a gun," a snarling farmer from Winnsboro insisted. "It ain't natural, it ain't right; what is this all about if you let a nigger act as good as a white man?" Now, this was a bit much; slaves carried guns back home if they could shoot, and most slave owners were glad enough for some venison, regardless of who shot it. But we had all kinds of people in the regiment, even a few plantation owners' sons who were definitely in this to protect their "property," and who even brought personal servants with them. We also had some just plain ugly people like the Winnsboro farmer.

To my surprise, Willie McClure took him on.

"It ain't about Tom Wright," he said quietly to the circle of men who had gathered when the farmer interrupted Tom's conversation with us. "Tom Wright ain't a slave. Tom Wright was never a slave. Tom Wright's family was never slaves; they been in Chester district since anybody can remember and they always been free. For all I know, Tom Wright's great-grandfather was there to greet white folks and say 'howdedo' when the first white trapper come splashing up the Catawba."

"He volunteered to be here just like me and he stayed when some others called quits and left," McClure said. "I ain't got a problem with this man wantin' to fight. Any man got a problem with it needs to deal with me."

And Willie "swolled himself up" to maybe five foot six inches and stood there glaring. Tom Wright, a giant who stood well over six feet, walked out to stand alongside him. And, because nobody would challenge the pair, it came about that sometimes, when a fight was under way, Tom Wright would swing his drum around to the back, find a musket and fight. And when the Calhoun Guards went on picket, Tom Wright would sometimes go with us, carrying a musket and taking his turn as sentinel. What the field officers thought of this — the majors and colonels and whatnot — we never discovered. They never seemed to see him, even when talking to the man next to him.

He was a good shot.

These were easy times for a regimental commissary sergeant. The huge Yankee army on the Peninsula prompted every farmer in its path to turn over everything they had in their spring cellars and barns to their defenders in the Confederate army. Supplies were pouring in from across the country and out of the Shenandoah Valley; all I had to do was shunt supplies from company to company, and spend some time being pleasant with our division commander's staff. The division was commanded by James Longstreet; he was a happy man, a lot like Bratton, and left it to subordinates to take care of things like supply. I found that it was wise to diversify into quartermastering, as well, where our equipment and clothing came from, and not stick just to comestibles. If the brigade quartermaster needed to move supplies, and I sent a squad from the Sixth Regiment, the Sixth Regiment suddenly found itself at the front of the line when new shoes were issued. We went so far as to "find" three wagons, courtesy of Wright and McClure Enterprises, which we would loan to the brigade or division when necessary to seize a moment or a load of smoked bacon, as it were. "L'audace, l'audace, toujours l'audace," Napoleon said, and the Sixth Regiment Supply Detail, also known as the Augmented Aaron Burr Mess and Goose Creek Frying Pan Company, proved audacious in ways never dreamed by the Emperor of France.

All of this came to a halt when we were forced out of the trenches at Yorktown and found ourselves heading back to Richmond, serving as rear guard to our column of the army. We backed up for days, getting in a few scuffles, but the Yankees knew we were backing up and knew that if they'd wait just a bit, we'd move and they wouldn't have to push us off. The Aaron Burr Mess took its first casualty in his rear guard action: A. D. Lael was wounded when we backed out of the trenches at Williamsburg. A ball laid open his left forearm from wrist to elbow just as he moved his weapon to support arms. Why no one else on either side of him was hurt we couldn't figure. He walked to the rear, to find a physician.

Finally, we halted and trenched, and waited, and Joe Johnston got himself worked up into a lather and decided it was time, if he wanted to remain a general, to kick McClellan off Virginia soil.

Only trouble was, nobody knew if we could or not.

On May 31, Johnston made his move.

We were now part of Brigadier General R.H. Anderson's Brigade, except we kept getting broken off and assigned here or there because both Col. Bratton and Col. Jenkins had emerged as very dependable leaders. On this day, we found ourselves formed up with the Palmetto Sharpshooters, detached from the rest of the brigade and under the leadership of Jenkins. We were about eight miles from Richmond, just north of the Williamsburg Road, near a village called Seven Pines.

All day, we could hear the booming and rattling of battle south of us. We had no idea what was going on; it seemed maybe Joe Johnston's idea of strategy was to drive right at the Yankees and see what happened.

It was a confusing day. We were supposed to be under Longstreet's overall command, but he was letting D.H. Hill pull together brigades and send them into the fight. That was all right with us; Longstreet was good, but D.H. Hill was from York County, South Carolina, and we all knew he was clever. So was Jenkins; both ran military academies, Hill in Charlotte, North Carolina, and Jenkins in Yorkville, 30 miles north of Chester. And we had Bratton. So we had a good feeling about our leadership, but a really bad feeling about everything else.

We also still had our old smoothbore muskets, effective range less than 100 yards. There still weren't enough rifle muskets to go around, at least in our army; the Yankees seemed to have no problem. We had consistently been forced to leave good positions in our retreat up the Peninsula simply because we were outranged by Yankee infantry.

We were all quite concerned about going into this fight and being shot to pieces before getting close enough to the Yankees to do any good. We were all interested in getting better weapons and making it something like a fair fight.

Late in the afternoon, we finally moved into position.

We were going past a Virginia regiment that had already been in a scrape and come out of it with a bloody nose. Exhausted, stunned men were binding up minor wounds and trying to find their comrades when we marched past, heading north parallel to the line of fighting to the east.

"South Carolina! South Carolina! You started this damned mess! Let's see you put your money where your mouth was!" one bleeding Virginian called out to us. The cry was picked up by others, and we marched into our fight stung by the taunts of Virginians who blamed us for getting them into a war.

Jenkins and Bratton acted deaf.

They formed us up, about 1,500 men, in long double lines perpendicular to a railroad track, Sixth South Carolina stacked behind the Palmetto Sharpshooters. We faced south, and stepped off into a nest of pine thickets, all second growth about 10 or 12 feet high and just as thick as hair.

We'd only moved in about a hundred yards off the railroad when we struck a line of Yankee pickets, who fired a few shots and ran. The Sharpshooters obliqued left a bit, we obliqued right and we pushed on, side by side now.

Jenkins pushed us forward rapidly and we suddenly struck a battle line dug in behind a shallow ditch. We were on them before they knew we were there, despite the warning of their picket fire. We fired when we were only 40 yards out and blew them away. They fired back, and we charged. They broke before we got to them, sprinting through the pine thickets, dragging their wounded.

Jenkins was everywhere. We pushed past their weak entrenchments and were in their camp; men dropped their smoothbores and shed their old cartridge boxes and picked up new equipment from dead and wounded and captured Yankees.

Jenkins gave it about three minutes, then roared, drew us up into another battle line, wheeled us to the west, and off we went again, in good order.

We hit another line of pickets and another line of battle, caved it in and found ourselves in another camp. More men got Springfields, Jenkins roared again and this time we wheeled to the southwest. Another few hundred yards, and we hit another line of pickets, took heavy return fire, and pushed forward into yet a third camp.

We were exhausted, and a lot of men weren't with their own companies or regiments any more. It didn't seem to matter. Jenkins called for one more push.

The pine brush ahead of me was dripping with blood about chest high; other men later said they'd noticed the same thing. The enemy was reeling ahead of us, carrying bleeding men through the thick pines. We could smell the blood through the smell of powder. We could also smell the pines, the wonderful smell that says it's summertime and you should be fishing. We had other business, and for one last time that day, we took care of it.

Tom Wright beat the long roll for the Sixth Regiment and we fell in alongside the pale flag, as best we could, companies all jumbled up, officers jumbled; none of it mattered. We listened, and when Jenkins roared again, we did what he said: We marched at a right oblique, then a right wheel, and found ourselves presently heading due south. We struck another Yankee regiment, at short range, screamed our heads off and ran right at them. They broke and ran, and we stumbled through their camp and found ourselves, suddenly, back in the Williamsburg Road. Cannon began firing from our own lines, and shells exploded among us. Jenkins ordered the battle flags brought into the road and waved, and the shelling stopped.

We formed up, along the road, and suddenly we saw a fresh regiment coming at us from due east, along the road. Jenkins threw the company nearest the enemy off the road into the woods, and ordered all companies to change front and form on that company. Months of drilling paid off, because we moved like a machine. We were in line and ready, mixed up or not, before the enemy got himself uncoiled. Jenkins wasn't content to wait, but hurled us into their midst before they had a clear idea they were up against madmen. They ran off, and we stood panting in the evening heat.

The sweet smell of honeysuckle drifted like balm through the acid stench of gunpowder and blood. Birds began their evening songs, including a couple of mockingbirds that made the dusk chime with song. In the twilight we formed up yet again. The appalling cost of what we'd done became clear when we were all present and could see the pitiful remnants of two strong regiments.

Nobody realized it going through the thick woods, but we had taken extremely heavy casualties. When we finally figured it out, we lost 88 killed and 181 wounded out of 521 men present, for a casualty rate of 51.6 percent — I worked it out after helping the adjutant assemble the numbers for the

Sixth. The regimental commissary sergeant needs to know how many rations to draw — helping get the information was automatic, even though I was as stunned as everyone else by the day's fighting. So I knew how bad it was faster than most — I knew in a mathematical way, rather than just looking around at the wreckage. The Palmetto Sharpshooters lost 20 dead and 202 wounded, out of almost a thousand men. And John Bratton had been captured.

We'd thrashed four separate Yankee regiments from two different corps, and driven through four camps over a two-mile stretch, in a six-hour fight. We'd struck at exactly the right place at exactly the right time to prevent two massive Yankee forces from making contact and driving Johnston off the field. Jenkins had used two techniques to counteract the lack of first-class weapons in the Sixth; he'd put the Sharpshooters in front, initially, with their Enfields. Then, when we struck the pines, the lack of visibility cancelled out the longer range of rifles so many of the Yankees had. The terrain also masked the terrible casualties we were taking, at least until the job was done. Every surviving man had a Springfield or an Enfield by the time we hit the Williamsburg Road, there were still heaps of weapons behind us in the pines, and we had scores of captives, three captured artillery pieces and three stands of enemy colors under guard along our two-mile trail of blood. Jenkins had established himself, at the age of 26, as a military leader of courage and skill. The Yankees had been given something to chew really hard on, because this kind of reckless fighting hadn't happened up to now, when our backs were at Richmond's gates.

And we'd also shut those God-damned Virginians up, succeeding where they'd failed and showing South Carolinians could fight as well as they could talk.

But what a cost.

Darkness put a halt to the fighting everywhere in the area. Some of us went back along the path of horror we'd cut to find missing comrades. We found some, we helped some; others had disappeared completely. The Aaron Burr Mess lost heavily: Fred Babcock is dead, S. H. McWalters, who had shown me much kindness in learning to be a soldier, is dead. Henry McElduff was wounded in the gut; we saw him carried off, but he looked horrible. Our company also lost Capt. J. L. Gaston, killed, and Third Sergeant E.M. Shannon, badly wounded. I am now third sergeant.

I learned all of this from others. One thing I found out on my own.

I went back through the woods with a small group of men and helped the quartermaster sergeant oversee collection of all the weapons and equipment we could find. I tried not to look at the dead and wounded, but I couldn't stop myself from hearing the crying. I just listened to the mockingbirds instead — singing in the moonlight as if there had been no horror that day — got on with the work.

Then I found Lt. Moore. He was propped against the trunk of a big pine, bleeding his life away from a wound in his belly. I thought he was dead, but when I got near I saw his chest heaving and his face contorting. Flies were clustered on his bloody legs. I waved them away.

"Lieutenant! Lieutenant! Moore!" I shook him, and his eyes opened — wild and crazy eyes. He coughed and looked at me and the crazed look went away from his eyes and I saw pure hatred, soul-deep and strong.

"I'm done for, Coleman, and I get you to watch me die? Go to hell," he wheezed.

I couldn't believe what I did next. Here was my tormentor, the man who had made my life miserable for more than a year, prostrate and dying.

"Moore," I said. "I'm sorry I was rude to you at the bank in Chester. It was small of me to be that way. It was wrong."

He just stared at me, and I thought he was going. But he spoke.

"Accepted," he whispered. "But that — it wasn't — that's not ... ." He struggled to say more, but lapsed into coughing that wracked him and sent the blood flowing out over his body. Some musicians from another regiment came up with a litter, and they hauled away Lieutenant Moore, who was still struggling to tell me something. They took him to the field hospital for whatever the surgeons could do to ease his last hours. Gutshot men can take forever to die.

I could feel blackness sweeping over me, foulness as bottomless as the sea, a hole in my stomach that kept opening and swallowing my soul. My knees shook and I leaned my forehead against the pine tree and tried to take stock.

An odd moaning came to my ears. Eerie, soft, not like the groans of the wounded men or the screaming of the wounded horses. I started off in search of the source, and in a shot-torn thicket I found a huge black dog, sitting by a Yankee corpse and howling, softly. I called out for McClure, and we persuaded the dog to come away with us. There was nothing on the Yankee to tell who he is or even what regiment he was from. He had a Bible; it stopped one bullet, but two more caught him, one in the arm and the other in the chest.

Others from the Calhoun Guards who are gone included W.J. Cornwell, wounded; J.H. Davidson, wounded; Henry Duffie, wounded; R.B. Hemphill, my mother's cousin, mortally wounded; John Northrop, wounded; E.J. McDaniel, my classmate at Dr. Watterson's School, wounded in the hand; J.H. McDaniel, wounded in the arm; W.L. McDaniel, wounded in the leg; S.H. McWaters, dead; Howard Morris, mortally wounded; J.C. Peden, wounded; J.A. Rader, wounded; W.F. Smith, wounded; and W.S. Turner, wounded. That was out of 48 men and officers who went into the fight. We fared better than some of the other companies, but it was just luck, nothing but luck. In a big fight, it turns out, there is nothing you can trust but luck, there is nothing you can do but put your head down and go. The Sixth took 550 men and officers into the pines; about half of us came out.

I stumbled through the pines, calling out names, helping men find the way to the rear — to the west, anyway, where the surgeons had pooled their resources and set up a hospital just north of the Williamsburg Road in Seven Pines. We then had to pull our battle line back, giving up some of that hard-won ground, because Jenkins couldn't get anyone to move regiments up to cover our flanks.

We needn't have worried. Next day the Yankees consolidated their lines, dug trenches and chewed hard on the sudden barbed reversal in our direction, from west to east. And we had a new general; Joe Johnston managed to get himself shot, and old Granny Lee, who'd had some regiments digging entrenchments around Richmond most of the winter, is the new commander in chief of our army.

Near Richmond
June 10, 1862

Dearest Elizabeth,

How wonderful it is to get your letters. I treasure them all and read them again and again until the paper wears out. By then, I no longer need them for I have committed your words to memory.

Oh, Elizabeth, if you could have seen us drill the other day! We could do nothing right, we who have drilled for more than a year now and have one of the smartest companies in the whole army here in Virginia! Col. Bratton called out "Forward into line," and all the other companies executed the command perfectly, while we for some reason got it into our heads to do "on the right, by file, into line." So there was the Sixth Regiment in a perfect line of battle, except for our company, which was marching off the field at a right angle! And then the sergeant couldn't remember how to march us back to the right position, because he's new at this and the lieutenant and captain aren't back from the hospital yet. We didn't know whether to laugh or cry, and Col. Bratton asked us if we had just come in from the farm, and then Col. Jenkins cam down. Oh, I can understand how the boys at the King's Mountain Academy must have feared his eye! He singled out the sergeant, looked down at him from his horse and said if we couldn't do better than that we'd need to spend more time drilling. And then he looked down the line and singled some of us out by name and said "Well, Coleman, what about it? Is this the best you can do? McClure? Sullivan?" Elizabeth, how can one man keep track of so many names and faces? But he does.

We stayed for extra drill and kept at it until the sergeants knew all the commands and we believed that he did.

I have shipped a black dog home to mother, by rail. Please persuade her that it is important to me to keep this dog well. She hates a dog in the house, but I am going to presume on her good nature, with your help. I found this dog on the battlefield at Seven Pines, near where Michael Moore got his fatal wounds.

Elizabeth, I know your cousin John is now old enough to join and you have told me how eager he is, but I really don't think we need him. I think he should say home and not get into this. There are enough of us here from Chester. No more need come. Besides, you have heard that the Yankees have been stopped and you may have heard that the Sixth Regiment had some small part in that, and I tell you a true thing, if the truth were known we had more than a small part and I will not say more than that.

I believe it will be over soon, Elizabeth, and I think your cousin need not come help us. Do you understand what I am saying, Elizabeth? Keep him out of this.

Pray for all your brave soldiers from Chester, Elizabeth, who are doing their duty bravely even if they sometimes find they have forgotten the drill.

Your obt svt
William

CHAPTER SEVEN

We had some Yankee prisoners with us the night after Bloody Pines, men we'd swept up while overrunning their positions and camps. We had a little trouble understanding the men from Vermont and Maine, but on the whole found them to be decent men, saddened at their capture and plight and ashamed their regiments had run. Most were disgusted with the general in charge of their army, George McClellan, and said he seemed more interested in getting the Confederate government to surrender to him personally than in pushing events to a military conclusion.

"Next time we'll chase you," a tall New Englander warned us as we settled down near the Williamsburg Road for a night of rest. "We don't see that happenin'," we told him.

The Aaron Burr mess was quickly re-organized; the fight had dropped us down to six men. We took in two men from another mess in our company who found themselves without frying pan or organization after the fight through the pines. We looked after our wounded, buried the dead we could find, and finally assembled to cook a meal, late at night.

Lt. Col. J.M. Steedman told us to take paroles from whatever prisoners we had, for the night, and make sure the prisoners were fed. We took in three in the Aaron Burr mess, and dined well on food taken from the Yankee camps we'd captured. For parole: We asked them if they'd agree to forego escape attempts for the night, inasmuch as we would like to sleep, and they swore they'd spend the night with us unless their own forces mounted a counterattack.

"We don't see that happenin'," we told them again.

We spent perhaps a half hour chatting after our meal of fresh beef and what the Yankees called "desecrated vegetables," which were dried vegetables that regained their normal size and weight after being reintroduced to water. The stories the Yankees told showed us they didn't really have one simple reason for coming down to fight us.

"Everybody else was goin' so I went too," the youngest of them said. The two older fellows — one a fisherman from New Bedford and the other, from a different regiment, a mechanic from Pennsylvania — said they'd been angered when we fired on the United States flag at Fort Sumter, and had made plans then to join up. I explained the theory that we believed the Confederate government had been trying to force Virginia into the Confederacy with a military act that the Union couldn't ignore, with the resulting response something that would make clear to Virginia it was a Southern state.

"Thet would now appear to be revealed in all its glory as a serious miscalculation," the New Bedford man noted wryly.

All three said they'd had no concern one way or the other about slavery until they'd actually marched up the Peninsula, seen plantations with slaves and encountered some slave owners.

"The more I know, the less I like it," the mechanic said. "Them slave owners treat everybody like dirt — they treat people like you the same as their slaves, like you ain't fit to wipe their bum. How can you live with people like that?"

We tried to understand, but fatigue overtook all of us and before we could take the debate much farther, we were all asleep.

The next day we sent the prisoners to the rear, with handshakes all around — how odd that we fight so savagely but treat each other almost as comrades when the battle is concluded. Then we tried again to find our missing boys, including John Bratton. He was gone, swept from the face of the earth. Lt. Col. Steedman took over command of the regiment, but leadership came, clearly and force-fully, from Micah Jenkins, in command of the brigade.

Some thought Jenkins was a bit too full of himself this day, seemingly unaffected by the slaugh-ter the day before and laughing and posturing for visiting generals, who came to inspect our prison-ers and booty. Others pointed out that he'd not hung back, he'd been in front of us leading much of the time, through a storm of fire, and that he was entitled to a little self-indulgent showmanship. He'd paid for it.

Steedman — who had been where he belonged during our advance and was no coward — asked Jenkins why he had taken so many chances. Jenkins just laughed.

"The Yankee bullet will never be made that will touch me," he said. "I know this; they can't hurt me."

In fact, he'd already been shot in the knee at Manassas, a minor wound with no consequences. Perhaps he thought that, like lightning, bullets would not strike him twice?

The end result of Bloody Pines was a reorganization, a quick one. We found ourselves among friends; we were in the Second Brigade of Longstreet's Division, along with the 2nd South Carolina Rifles, the 4th and 5th South Carolina infantry regiments and the Palmetto Sharpshooters, the group formed earlier in the spring by Jenkins when it looked like re-enlistment was going to be a problem. It was a brigade made up entirely of South Carolinians. It felt like a kind of homecoming when we camped together for the first time.

The reorganization served one quick and vital purpose: It put Jenkins at the head of an effective fighting force of almost 2,000 men, units that had earned the right to be called veterans. The 5th and the 2nd Rifles had been "ahead" of us because of the work they'd done at Manassas; we felt we'd pulled up to them by leading the way through Bloody Pines, while they got a lucky draw and had been detached for part of the fight.

The King of Spades, meanwhile, had his own ideas about how an army ought to act. On June 7, Lee pulled Jenkins's Brigade and a lot of other units back closer to Richmond, a few miles northwest of Bloody Pines. We went into camp near Mechanicsville. We were close enough to Richmond to hear the church bells, and wondered if the sacrifice at Seven Pines had done any good at all; we were no farther forward than we had been before the fight. We nursed our wounds, and every day saw a few more men who'd had minor wounds return to the regiment from the hospital in Richmond or the private homes in the countryside where they'd been recuperating. Two of the Aaron Burr mess re-turned, their wounds nearly healed. John Louderman, a farmer who lived not far from McClure, was missing, while young Alonzo Spratt is dead. We found him after the battle, curled in a ball behind a pine tree, in a puddle of blood. Captain Agurs sent a letter to his mother back in Chester.

I try my best to set up some kind of relationship with the farmers in the area, but the simple fact is we aren't expected to be there very long, one way or the other — chasing Yankees or retreating ahead of them. It is difficult to barter our labor for food, and McClure is equally unsuccessful in his nocturnal foraging. It is late spring; there is not much food in the fields. There are no crops except some greens to bring in, only crops to plant. Few seem eager to take a chance on planting a crop the Yankees might harvest. Speculation in cotton, however, is rampant, because the prices are soaring, and people are willing to risk a cotton crop because of the potential profit to be made. We put in one day of work where one of the regiment's companies plants cotton in exchange for some stored hams and dried corn. There is a planter's son in that company and it gives some of the yeoman farmers from his district great delight to see him get his hands dirty. He is not a favorite; even worse, he doesn't know what he's doing, and some of the darkies owned by the man we were working for have to show him how to set the seed at the right depth.

We grind our teeth and take official rations most of the month. We are not allowed in Mechanicsville; the citizens have complained to President Jefferson Davis that the army is rowdy and, even worse, full of fleas. This cannot be denied. We are, on the other hand, well armed with new Enfields. A kind of grand exchange has taken place; we picked up both Enfields and Springfields during our sweep through the Pines, and have turned in all the Springfields to the quartermaster department in exchange for a greater number of Enfields. Wounded men who return to duty are equipped with Enfields, to their delight.

We still are not allowed target practice, even though we now have weapons that will reach out to 500 yards and more. Not enough powder, Jenkins says. He insists we keep our bayonets and not throw them away, as other units have done.

The Yankees, meanwhile, dig trenches and send up balloons; when a balloon goes up, trouble often follows. Sometimes the Yankees send infantry in.

I had taken, in the absence of both the first and second sergeants, half the Calhoun Guards out on picket near Beaver Dam Creek one day when a balloon went up right ahead of us, not 200 yards away. To our astonishment, it is someone we know: Professor Thaddeus Lowe, and his balloon "Enterprise." The last time we saw him was in Chester in the spring of 1861, when his balloon, sent aloft in Ohio, was captured by the wind and deposited near Chester. Professor Lowe is now the enemy, and we can see the telegraph wire linking the balloon to the ground. From there, it undoubtedly connects with Federal artillery.

I was working on a damaged weapon — broken mainspring — when one of the boys pointed out the balloon. The man closest to me was Tom Wright, who had insisted picket duty was what Col. Bratton would have wanted a musician to do when there was no need for music.

"Throw me your Enfield, Tom, and run like the wind to find Col. Jenkins," I told him. "Tell him the Yankees have sent up a balloon and our camp will probably come under fire."

Tom tossed me his Enfield and ran up the hill away from the pond, jumping uphill over tree trunks and tearing through brush. I took his gun and, with the 20 or so men with me, spread out and tried to see if we could pop that balloon out of the sky.

We must have made it hot, because within minutes a couple of companies of Yankees pushed through the brush on the other side of the beaver pond and started firing away at us. We shifted our fire from the balloon and the men occupying its swaying gondola to the blue uniforms less than 200 yards way.

Wright came leaping down the hill behind us, eyes wide and sweat rolling off his black face.

"Colonel say get back, don't bother. He says pull back, leave a picket line, stay south of camp, in the gully. They come, we ready," he pants.

I leave five men there, well up the hill, with instructions to run like hell back to our position if the Yankees came across the beaver pond. The rest of us pull back to where Jenkins and Steedman had concentrated the Sixth Regiment, in a small, shallow gully near the camp.

It all amounts to naught. The Yankees don't shell the camp and don't try their luck with the beaver pond. We stand down, the Yankees stop firing, and they bring in the balloon for good.

The next morning Major General A.P. Hill's division sweeps through our position and tries their own luck getting across the beaver pond. They are torn to pieces, but it blows a cold wind up McClellan's skirts and he pulls his army back.

And we have astonishing news.

Jenkins comes to our mess — he is visiting all the campfires — and tells us our performance at Bloody Pines convinced Robert E. Lee that the army has the will to fight, but lacks the leaders. He made changes; some commanders have been replaced. We will get a chance to fight, to drive back the invader. The men swell up while Jenkins talks. You can see the change, and feel it in the air afterward. They have been made larger by what Jenkins tells them.

Jenkins's ability to move men amazes me. I look at him and see a slightly built, brown-haired young man, admittedly fearless but obviously ambitious. He is a Citadel graduate, a planter's son from Edisto Island whose family plantation is now in enemy hands. He has always followed the military, but I remember him from before the war as a businessman, one who obtained a loan from the Bank of Yorkville to expand his fledgling Kings Mountain Military Academy. Now he is a blooded warrior and a leader capable of inspiring men. My response to him is, I hope, courteous but in no way mistakable as fawning. Others have a different, more emotional response. They want him to like them. I have no idea how he does it. He has now infected the entire brigade, and especially the Sixth Regiment, with the idea that their conduct at Bloody Pines inspired Robert E. Lee to believe that this army of Southerners could beat back a Yankee army more than twice its size.

On June 27, we learn what Lee can do.

Our brigade commander is Gen. R.H. Anderson, an able man. We march a few miles southwest, and form up, with the rest of Longstreet's Division, on the right of a force that is following retreating Yankees pushed out of their position near Mechanicsville. They have halted atop a hill, an open hill. We form on a slight rise a thousand yards away; to reach them, we will have to cross a wooded creek, then mount the hill. We can see the guns at the top of the hill, and dense lines of blue. Gen. A.P. Hill's division has already tried the hill once; the slope is dotted with specks of grey and brown. The afternoon drags on; the warm air carries the odor of freshly turned dirt, a smell that always makes me think of plowed fields. This time, the dirt has been turned by exploding shells, and pine and sassafras trees have been uprooted. The sassafras roots give off a sweet smell — root beer! The sulfurous stench of black powder and the sweetness of root beer. How odd.

Finally, as the sun is hanging low and red, our division starts to move. We rush down the slope and into the wooded bottom, taking only a few casualties from artillery fire. In the bottom, we straighten our alignment, fix bayonets and start up the hill. Hood's Texas Brigade is on our left. They start up the hill, screaming. We are only a few yards into our attack when the Yankees sweep the slope with fire and men begin falling. Our attack falters. Jenkins halts the entire brigade, under fire, dresses all the lines and orders us forward at the double quick, up the hill. On our left, the Texans are moving and men are falling from the ranks. They falter, then move, ahead and it is suddenly different. The Texans have dropped from our sight, into a swale that effectively blocks them from all Yankee fire except dead ahead. They are spared the raking fire that is hitting all the other brigades. And all of us on this part of the hill have orders not to return fire, but to close with the enemy with the bayonet. Anderson and the other brigadiers have seen units already chewed to pieces as they tried to dislodge the Yankees, who have thrown up quick barricades that are surprisingly effective in blunting our fire.

Fortune smiles on us. The Yankee commander has stacked his troops in three lines across the hill, starting midway up and with the final line at the crest. Our entire line is lunging forward, with the Texans hitting the first line hard. It breaks. And once it breaks the Yankees, unnerved by the speed of our advance and by the fact we have not stopped to fire, leave their hasty entrenchments along its entire length, and start up the hill to safety. This blocks fire from the second and third lines, and we move up the hill right at their heels. The second line gives way and joins the flood. The Texans are up the hill and at the crest; through the smoke we can see hand-to-hand fighting. With a scream and a rush we surge over the crest and fire into the running sea of blue. Then they are gone into the twilight, leaving behind wounded and several hundred prisoners, and a few guns trapped as both ends of our line swept around the hill before all the Yankees could get off.

The long, low hill is ours.

It has been a costly victory. Hood's brigade benefited from the geography of their position, but almost half of them are gone, dead or wounded; the price for being first. Hood, blond hair in disarray, sits head uncovered against a tree on the crest of the hill, looking back down the slope at his dead and dying men. He looks like he is weeping. We see Lee ride up to him, he stands and salutes, then we are ordered farther forward on the hill to take up a new position, and we see no more. We have also lost heavily; at least 70 from the Sixth are gone, and many more have cuts, bruises and other injuries that are painful but not serious enough to warrant dropping out. We again dine on captured Yankee rations, a good thing because our wagons are lost somewhere to the rear. It appears that confusion after battle is the expected thing, whether you are the winner or the loser, so we adapt.

The next day we move in behind A.P. Hill's division again, hearing but not seeing or feeling the fighting at Savage's Station, not far from our fight at Bloody Pines.

The following day is June 30, and we are on the move in stifling, windless heat. Jenkins' Brigade is in the lead, moving down the sandy Darbytown Road. Lee rides behind us with his staff; he is joined by President Davis at midafternoon. Shells begin falling among our skirmishers, and we see Davis move to the rear. The Sixth is moved up to push in the skirmishers, which we do without loss. We halt at a fence line; on the far side of the field, on a slight rise, is a line of Federal guns, again formed up, this time in an open hay field with a farmhouse ahead and a Yankee division drawn up around it. Jenkins is arguing with a major general; he salutes and comes up to us. He is in agony as he gives the order to advance across the open field, straight into a line of massed guns. From here it looks like the guns are hub to hub. Other brigades deploy on either side of us. Jenkins is ashen-faced. The orders come. We move out into the field.

Firing begins at 400 yards, and we have plenty of time to think about dying, and plenty of time to die, as we advance slowly and steadily across cultivated fields, taking casualties every step of the way. Somehow we make it across and find ourselves among the gunners, who will not leave their pieces. We pay them back for the horrors we've experienced going across that field, and the officers have to stop some of the men from killing prisoners when they finally yield.

Suddenly Yankee infantry is upon us, forcing us back from the six guns we just captured. We reel back, but not far, forming a ragged line of battle 30 yards in front of the guns and the cheering Yankees. Jenkins rides up and down behind the line, waving a broken sword — the tip has been shot away. He shouts and exhorts and while no one can hear what he says, all know what he wants. Horror competes with pride in my heart and before I can work out which of the two emotions makes the most sense, Jenkins turns the front and spurs his horse at the Yankees. My legs seem to have voted for pride, because I am going in that direction also. So is the rest of the brigade, disorganized as it is — no straight lines, no orderly movement, just a mob of men that goes in, shoulder to shoulder, with leveled bayonets. We are among them, two groups of men fused by a line of screaming, blood and death, but we can't push them out. We hear a roar on our right, and an Alabama regiment throws its weight into the melee. The Yankees give way and move back, in good order, toward a crossroads at their rear. Some of our officers have manned the guns we captured; they turn them into the backs of the Yankees and cut loose. Great damage is done, but the blue mass keeps order. Behind us come two more divisions in grey. They change from line of battle into marching to the front by the right of companies as they pass through our disorganized line, then swing back into line of battle to assault the Yankees. The fighting continues but we never take that crossroads.

We are out of it now. We have nothing left. Frazier's Farm has broken us.

An overwrought Jenkins grieves at our losses but those of us who survive are getting numb to the horror. We reorganize our messes again, and again we dine on captured stores.

Next day we narrowly avoid another fight, being held in reserve while most of the rest of the army bleeds. We are there; we fire at Yankees probing our position; but we are not a part of the madness nearby. We are still numb from Frazier's Farm.

We have been marching or fighting for seven days. While it seems to us to be a confused mixture of noise, blood and fury and wearisome toil, the generals apparently see some sense to it all. Suddenly we are in camp, eating Yankee rations that seem to never run out, and hearing about Yankee regiments steadily marching east much more rapidly than they'd marched west two months ago.

It ends as suddenly as it began. One hot June dusk we form up amid thousands of fireflies in the woods, the sweet smell of honeysuckle thick in the air. We storm out and through thick forest, huge trees, screaming like banshees, and overrun a federal battery posted along the edge of a swamp. They had time to get off one shot, which did no damage because they had, in the darkness, failed to realize the gun was pointed directly at a huge white oak tree only a few feet away. I find Captain Walker — he'd just been Joe Walker, the son of hotel owner James Walker, back in Chester, and he'd been our captain for some months, until he was transferred in the April reorganization. He is bent over the tail of one of the guns. My first thought is that he's wounded, but he's vomiting. Before he gets indignant and orders me away, he says he tripped going up in front of the company, and when he came up he found himself looking into the muzzle of one of the guns in the Yankee battery, watching as the gunner toppled from a wound with the lanyard clutched in his hand. He fell forever, Walker said, and dropped the lanyard just as another inch would have fired the piece. Walker said the worst part was his inability to move; he could see the gunner falling, see the lanyard, see the result coming, but was frozen to the earth, lacking the will to move and accepting the moment and whatever fate it brought. That acceptance, not fear, has now made him sick. I started to tell him that probably it hadn't taken as long as he thought, and that what seemed like a long time was really only a second, and he gets mad.

"Damn you!" he shouts. "I tell you it took forever! Damn you and your cold ways! Get away from me!"

I understand; he is lashing out at me because he is angry with himself for showing weakness in front of me.

We desperately need a break. The Sixth regiment fielded almost a thousand men at Manassas last summer; now we are down to fewer than 300, some of them wounded but still in the ranks, because word has spread that the hospitals are sure death. It is here that we get the only good news of this terrible week, word that John Bratton is alive. He was wounded and captured at Seven Pines, and is awaiting exchange.

The next day we are held in reserve while our tired army pounds itself against more Yankee guns on Malvern Hill. And that brings the hard fighting to an end for now, although we spend two tense weeks near McClellan's army as it sullenly hangs close to its supplies at Harrison's Landing. Then we are pushed into movement again, rushing to Richmond and climbing aboard Virginia Central trains for a thumping ride to the northeast. The land changes, from sand and pine and green briars to red dirt, pasture and chestnut.

We are in bad shape. The fighting since Seven Pines has cut into our already diminished numbers and taken away our good health. We are in rags as we march away from the railroad into the shimmering heat to find another Yankee army, one that is pushing at us from the north. Our shoes are worn out, and many men are barefoot. The active campaigning has worn out both shoes and uniforms, and there has been no opportunity to replace either. Since we are on the move, we have to rely on Richmond for supply or from what we can forage from the countryside. These are our own people, many of whom give us all they can, but it isn't enough. We hesitate to steal — to take food outright, boldly and brutally because we have the power to do so, rather than McClure's sneaky game of pilfering cucumbers and liberating eggs and smoked hams — but hunger is a dictator who can't be denied. We apologize; we do what we do with shame; but we take food as we march north. The officers write out warrants the protesting farmers are supposed to use to get compensation from the Confederate government. Neither we nor they believe it will actually happen.

CHAPTER EIGHT

A letter from Mother has caught up with me. A.J. is now the colonel of the Sixth Regiment Reserves. She says he swooned around for a month after losing the election, then got busy rounding up all the older men and youngsters in York and Chester counties to form a Home Guard unit. She says Obi Jones and William Hollimen, two men invalided out of the Sixth Regiment in June, are now serving with the Sixth Regiment Reserves and telling great tales of their experiences in Virginia.

Jones I can't place; Hollimen I remember as a sickly man who never missed a chance to curl up in some out-of-the-way hole and sleep, and who had the knack of vanishing at the merest rumor of a scrape coming. I am hard put to figure what great tales they are telling, unless it is of measles and stolen hams, because so far as I know neither man ever actually saw a Yankee except for prisoners.

Mother says conscription has caused a bad feeling in Chester, especially the provision allowing anyone who owns 20 darkies to avoid service. The feeling, she says, is that all able-bodied men ought to be glad to fight for their new nation, especially those who were among the loudest in supporting secession when the Legislature voted for it almost two years ago.

Two years! She's right, this fall will mark two years from the election of Father Abraham and two years since our state representatives made South Carolina the first state to withdraw. If things continue this summer as they have gone so far, we may be able to mark our second anniversary of independence with an end to the fighting. I hope so; it is hard to see what, except the prospect of victory, is keeping this army together.

We come off the train at Gordonsville and start marching up the track toward Orange. Jackson has been here ahead of us, and there has been fighting near Culpeper, against John Pope, the man Lincoln sent here to show his effete Eastern generals how the war ought to be fought. Some of the wounded we pass say the Yankees do seem to have their spirits up, even the units Jackson thrashed a few short months ago in the Valley.

When we hit the area where Pope's army had been operating, we are stunned. Dead cattle and pigs strew the pastures, barns have been burned. And the people are glad to see us, and urge us to kill the Yankees. We are cheered as we march through the small towns.

Something has happened here. There is a new and bitter feeling in the air, and it hangs like a cloud of smoke over the region.

We march in mid-August to the Rappahannock; the Yankees are on the other side, and we exchange picket fire with them almost hourly, not to do any real damage, but to keep them guessing and at arms length. Jenkins — now officially a brigadier general — is predicting great things ahead for us. We have heard this talk before; it usually means a bitter fight. Captain Walker is wearing a long face, and it is not because of the sudden heavy rain that has drenched us and made the Rappahannock a raging torrent.

Our position is at Beverly Ford, one of the few places on the Rappahannock where an army can cross without a bridge. The river is not that wide, nor deep; it and the Rapidan, though, are both steep-sided in this part of the country. The difficulty is getting an army, with all its wagons and guns, down to the water, not so much in getting across the water. We learn part of our army had crossed to the north yesterday, in an attempt to hit Pope's flank, and is now trapped there until the water goes down; engineers are attempting to rebuild a bridge. The bridge is built, the fragment of the army is reunited, and there is word that J.E.B. Stuart has conducted another of his exciting raids deep into the Yankee rear.

   Dazzling sunlight brings bake-oven heat. The ground here is amazing. The rain turns it to slick, cloying red clay. When the rain stops, there is a day of mud, then a day when the ground is actually springy and resilient — like nothing in South Carolina. Then it bakes to a ceramic-like finish that grinds down, under thousands of marching feet and wagon wheels, into blinding clouds of red dust. We are issued three days of rations — all coming up the railroad from Richmond now, there is nothing left in this country to eat — and we are marching again, this time to the west and north. Amissville, Orleans, Salem, White Plains — the names go by in a dusty, parched hell of sore feet and sore bellies. I no longer know where I am, except I'm pretty sure we are still in Virginia, somewhere between the white sand of the Peninsula and the blue mountains; the dirt is all red, and it rises into the air in a fine pink dust that hangs above the endless column of shuffling, ragged men like the pillar of smoke and fire that led Moses and the Israelites across the desert.

   There is a dull rumble ahead of us, a rumble we have heard before, and cold fingers of fear grab my spine despite the blazing heat. The pace slows; we are tightening up, closing ranks — we are huddling together. Our instincts are now so strong that even when exhausted we try to get into a compact mass, taking comfort from the closeness.

   We march into the night, always toward the sound of the guns. When the order is given to halt for the night, we stagger off both sides of the road and drop to the ground, not bothering with fires but choking down some of the pork we'd cooked the day before. The only thing that gets us on our feet all night long is the news that there is a clear stream not far away; canteen details are organized, but many men go on their own, throwing themselves face down on the bank of the tiny stream and drinking. We are suddenly, more acutely aware of other afflictions that had been smothered beneath the all-consuming thirst; there are complaints of sore feet, thighs chafed raw by the coarse material of our uniforms, shoulders aching, eyes itching from dust. Despite all this, despite the occasional rumble and clank of a battery going by at a gallop, iron wheel rims striking bright yellow sparks off the stones on the road and drivers cursing their horses, despite the knowledge that a battle is coming, we sleep.

   We are up before dawn, and we aren't up long when we hear the rumble of guns again, north of our bivouac. There is nothing for a commissary sergeant to do. The Aaron Burr mess convenes for a quick assessment; we split an old loaf of bread into six pieces, and share. I fall in as a file closer and the march resumes.

   It is a much more deliberate and focused march today. A cloud of generals rides by, and they seem eager and confident. Nobody knows why they should feel so confident, but it bucks us up. Orders are passed to keep talk and noise to a minimum, and at last we are close enough to the battlefield to see the smoke rising above distant hills to our left. The noise never stops; it drops to an occasional pop and bang sometimes, but it never stops. We are marching up to a thick patch of woods, and as we come closer, we move first into a column of companies and then deploy into a line of battle; we ease into the woods about 50 yards and halt.

   And there we stand for an hour, until the order comes down to stack arms and rest. We can still hear terrific fighting on our left; we are close enough to hear yelling and cheering from time to time, but we are apparently not part of it.

The sun sets. The word is passed from the officers that we are sitting on the exposed flank of the Union army, and that if our luck holds, we will smite the enemy a mighty blow tomorrow. It is mighty big talk, and we are mighty hungry men, so we greet the news with a bit less enthusiasm than our officers seem to think is appropriate. It is a long, hungry night — but in the morning, when the artillery again wakes us up at dawn, there is suddenly something for a commissary sergeant to do.

A long line of wagons comes into view behind us, each bearing rations. The division commissary sends a query to the regiment, asking where Lt. Berry, the commissary lieutenant, might be found. Nobody knows; he has dropped out somewhere on the march. I am sent in his place, and have the pleasure of inspecting and accepting a nice allotment of rations for the regiment. The officers running the commissary ask for numbers on how many men are present for duty; I have the wit to report 400, when the real number is something like 250. I get skeptical looks, but I also get permission to draw rations for 400 men. A group of privates from the Sixth shows up, and we haul the boxes and bags we've been given back to where the regiment is assembled.

Much of what we've got is Yankee rations, captured within the last few days as the armies maneuvered too quickly for quartermasters and commissaries to adjust. The only problem we now face is cooking it; fires have been forbidden. The situation is handled by each man according to his level of desperation. A man who is very hungry takes the salted pork and Yankee hardtack he's been issued and bolts it; a man who is not so hungry makes do with the hardtack, carefully wrapping the salted pork in a rag and storing it in his haversack. In either case, the relief of having both hunger and thirst beaten back to the level of piddling nags that can be ignored, rather than roaring demons consuming all our attention, does wonders for our outlook.

"It is amazing," McClure opines, "what comfort there is in food. I can almost feel the blood singing through my veins again."

"We may be dead tomorrah and et won't matter whether we're hungry or full," Rudy Brandt adds, "but I'd jest as leef be full."

"Or at least not quite so hungry," "Luke" Lucas, ever the truth-talker, points out.

We get a good rest that night.

The guns again summon us at dawn, but there is still no sense of urgency; we are kept in the woods all morning, with nothing to do. Finally, at midday, we are assembled and take arms. It is done quietly — the most remarkable thing about the past 24 hours is just how quiet a force of 20,000 men can be — but you can feel the movement of the entire force, even though it can neither be seen nor heard. We move through the forest like a giant, vicious animal, coiling our muscles for a deadly leap at an enemy we still can't see.

We march by column of companies with the other regiments of Jenkins' Brigade, and now Jenkins is everywhere. We have skirmishers out, and men on both flanks, but mainly to keep us aligned with other brigades — at the right distance, so that when we deploy forward into battle lines, we will not crash into each other. Ahead, surely only a few hundred yards, a battery opens up, followed by volleys of musket fire. The sharp pungency of gunpowder drifts through the woods, setting up a tickle at the top of my throat.

We come up out of the woods and top a vast, horseshoe shape that encloses a flat field like an amphitheater. A Yankee battery had been in that field, and most of it has already left. One gun, with a six-horse team, is trapped; we have overrun the farm road to the north out of the basin, and a creek with steep banks runs down the south side of the field and across its far, open edge, to the east. The Yankee sergeant riding the lead horse on the gun is methodically moving up the creek, looking for a place to get across; men are firing, without orders, from all around the horse-shoe shaped ridge, and you can see the bullets kicking up red dust where they hit all around the gun and its team. The sergeant halts the gun, and we see him rise up and look, with the man on the near horse shouting at him and other men running beside the gun; he then turns the team to the south and rolls full-bore toward a bend in the stream where the banks are lower, and also full-bore toward one of our regiments that has just crested the ridge there. The firing picks up; there is a tremendous splash of water and the gun is across the stream and heading east, pulling away from the thousands of men in butternut who are watching. The firing drops off; the Yankee sergeant stops his team when he knows he is out of range, gets off and calmly checks all six horses and the harness. We give him a cheer, even though we'd been trying to kill him, and he has the wit to turn and give us a tremendous bow, pulling his hat off his head and sweeping it across the ground in front of him. Then he is back on the lead horse and galloping away.

There is another series of crashing volleys to our right, followed by the rebel yell, and we see Yankees in red pants come boiling out of a patch of woods as if the devil is on their tail. All the while, we are moving forward, down across the field where the Yankee sergeant had been; it splits the regiment. Ahead of us, a column of Yankees materializes, deploying into line of battle from a column of march as they come through a fence. We are suddenly running — I never heard an order, but one must have been given — and we are on the Yankees before they are quite ready. They fire and the air is filled with humming and warbling; we fire; they turn and run, right into another regiment stacked behind them. We keep running, but it is uphill and tough work, and we are disorganized. I see Jenkins coming up behind us, then suddenly he is down. Lt. Col. Steedman is holding onto a fence post, with an odd look on his face; there is blood on his hands. The air is still filled with that humming and warbling, the songs of battle that you can hear under the explosions, but I can't tell where it's coming from. Suddenly it stops, as the regiments on our left crash into a Yankee brigade that had been enfilading us as we rushed after the regiment we'd routed. There is another surge of blue flowing east, away from us, with ragged ranks of Confederates chasing them, battle flags flying at the tips of clumps of men that look more like a rampaging mob than an army.

I see no officer from the Sixth Regiment anywhere. I see only a couple of men I know, and we move closer to each other; a soldier's instinct. Somewhere ahead, a drum is sounding assembly, and we move closer, the familiar pale flag suddenly looms through the smoke. Capt. Joseph Walker is there, with Tom Wright, and the regiment is slowly gathering around them. Men begin calling "Sixth South Carolina! Form up here!" We spend 15 minutes drumming and calling, and Walker sends out groups under noncommissioned officers to try to round up stragglers and wounded. It is finally clear we have all we are going to get, and it is grim. Willie McClure has come in with the last group, and he comes over to me as we sort ourselves out. There are 12 men standing in our company, and there are about 150 men left on their feet in the Sixth Regiment.

"We thrashed 'me again, Coleman," McClure says with a tight grin. "Seems like we whoop them like that a few more times and we'll be finished ourselves."

Jenkins is down, Steedman is down, the major is down; Walker is the senior officer left in the regiment, and he sends off a runner to try to find anyone with enough rank to tell us what to do next.

CHAPTER NINE

We were washed up, so far as we were concerned, by Second Manassas. We finally knew where we were when the ragged remnant of the Sixth marched past the Chinn house, which we remembered from the year before when we stood nearby in the rain. We expected to be given orders to head back to Richmond — every other regiment we saw looked as battered and torn as us, with men worn out and shoeless and wearing rags. We felt like we'd been whipped, even though the Yankees had run. I felt like I had nothing left inside, and I was sure we'd make camp somewhere safe and get our strength back.

Instead, Lee turned us north and we crossed the Potomac into Maryland.

Jenkins Brigade is a shambles, barely 500 men on their feet out of 2,000 who went into battle during the Seven Days. Capt. Joseph Walker, who was stunned into noisy protest when he found himself in charge of the Sixth Regiment, was reduced to his usual condition of morose silence when he found out he was also the ranking officer in charge of the brigade, and would lead us into Maryland. He has reorganized us, insisting that we field companies of at least 50 men no matter how many companies a regiment is supposed to have or how many officers and noncommissioned officers have to be reassigned; technically, this makes all of the regiments battalions, but nobody cares. Without this reorganization — done almost on the move, as we head into Maryland — we would have had companies with no officers, companies with officers but no noncommissioned officers, noncommissioned officers without companies, and companies with five privates. What Walker has is a brigade the equivalent of a small regiment, organized into 10 equal companies.

We are all as jumpy as fleas on a griddle. The reorganization was necessary and men can even see where it is a good idea, even a necessary one, but the truth is most of the men don't know anything about Walker and aren't sure what he'll do.

I am first sergeant of a company of 50 men, most of whom I don't know and only a few of whom are from Chester. Willie McCarthy is still here and, like me, still unhurt. We don't talk about that; seems the longer you go on without being hurt, the more likely it is you'll be hurt soon. And we're finding out not all damage is caused by bullets. Yesterday one of the privates just assigned to my company — I think his name is Cooper — began talking nonsense when we formed up for morning roll call.

"Wrangle them a piece," he shouted. "Help them! Help them! Can't you see? Get them out of there! No! No! NO!"

He walked away from the formation, waving his arms and shouting. I went after him and grabbed him by the arm and when I looked in his face, I felt my belly melt and my knees go weak. He was looking at me and not seeing me; he wasn't there, he was somewhere else in his mind, and nothing I did or said had any effect. A chaplain from another regiment came over to see what the uproar was about, took one look at Cooper and told me "I'll take care of him." The last I saw of Cooper he was heading to the rear of the column of march that was forming up, still raving, and letting the chaplain lead him by the hand like a child.

I had not seen anything like it before. Neither had anyone else, and it has shaken us to the core of our souls. Cooper had been a quiet man, the little we'd seen of him, and he'd known his drill and how to make a good camp, and then all of a sudden he just wasn't there any more. He had gone out of his mind, and while I had heard the phrase before, it never meant anything until Cooper did it.

If Cooper, why not me?

I think about this as we trudge northward, breaking out of my melancholy only at the sight of the Potomac. We are crossing at a big ford — I have no idea where we are, exactly, but I am told by the officers that this is the Potomac and when we cross it, we will be in Yankee territory for the first time. Some say Maryland isn't really Yankee territory, that the legislature there would have voted to secede except President Lincoln locked the secessionist legislators in jail so they couldn't vote.

The army, even though terribly depleted by the hellfire summer of fighting and marching we have been through, is still a sight to see as it crosses the river in four broad columns of wading men, men holding guns and cartridge boxes and furled flags over their heads on a warm, bright afternoon. They splash through the water, up to their armpits in places, and some duck their heads completely under to wash off dust from the road. The marching companies go down a long hill to the water's edge in formation, then dissolve into loose groups; when they cross over, they are sent by officers into huge fields on the other side, forming up as they go and unfurling flags of every color; with state flags and silk flags and some of the new, bright red bunting flags, the huge fields look like they are suddenly blooming with wildflowers. There is a ripple of movement and a flash of bright metal, repeated down the assembling ranks, as regiment after regiment forms up, comes to attention, shoulders arms and moves on up the road into Maryland.

It is a good sight; we are weary and grieving for dead friends, and some of us are going out of our minds, but it is good to see just how many of us are left and willing to go on. The sight of the army stretching and then coiling at the river has comforted me. We will take the war to the enemy and end it, once and for all. We all come to believe this.

Maryland had been supposed to be full of men ready to join the Confederate Army; it turns out to be full of men eager to avoid service in either army. There are plenty of men, but only a few have joined us.

The land itself is rich and full and lush, and many crops are coming ripe as we march. We are eating raw, green corn torn from the fields as we pass, and it is good and sweet and cool and juicy. And we are foraging with the blessing of the officers, although we must buy what we take. Since many here are Unionists and consider our Confederate script worthless, we are, in their eyes, stealing the apples, the butter, the bread, and something called apple butter, which I have never heard of before but favor immensely. Somehow, the idea that these righteous Unionists think I am a thief does not bother me so much as it once would have.

There are some here who are sympathetic, and still others who see us as suffering men first and "dirty, scoundrel rebels" second. It is not unusual to find buckets of cool water set beside the road, with no one around to thank.

We march for two days, and finally come to a sizable town. We are told this is Frederick, Maryland, and it seems we are to stay here for awhile. We set up camps in the fields outside town, and some of our wagons finally catch up with us — we have not seen these wagons since before the Manassas battle. Unfortunately, no clothing or shoes have come up. About half the men in the company have shoes that are falling apart. Some men who had no shoes have been left in Virginia.

I noticed today, after taking a brief solitary walk into a bright, green field atop one of the little round hills that characterize this part of Maryland, that we stink. We very badly stink. I walked from one side of the hill back to the side our camp was on, and suddenly was assaulted by the most awful reek, as if a pile of manure had just been turned over. It was our camp. After a few minutes, I no longer noticed. But what must people think when we pass by? How can we be so filthy?

"Ignore it," Willie McClure told me. "So, we smell. We been in these uniforms three months, in the summer. Of course we stink. Who cares?"

He and the others are getting some of the bounce back. The march to Frederick was in easy stages, and the rich food is performing wonderful miracles on us. Even my mood is not so glum. The next day, we swing through Frederick on our way somewhere, and it is actually funny to see townspeople hold handkerchiefs to their noses as we pass; the boys swagger, oblivious to how they look and smell. Some are forced to hang their long shirt-tails out, to cover rents in their britches. Of under drawers most of us have none; wore out long ago or thrown away in the heat of the summer.

We are in David Jones' division, and Walker is in charge of our tiny brigade. We march with Longstreet to Hagerstown, through more of the most beautiful country I have ever seen, with fat cows and ripening fields of wheat and corn, big houses, and huge, stone barns big enough to hold 40 cattle and a winter's worth of feed for them. They keep their cattle in the barns in the cold of winter, different from what we do back home. Some barns are as big as the hotel in Chester, and look to be better built. What wealth there must be in this ground — and, where we are passing through, no plantations with slave quarters. Just farms, worked by families. I think on that.

In Hagerstown, we settle down again. Some giant plan is afoot, and our job, for once, seems to be to wait for it to unfold. We have implemented such plans before, and are glad this time to let someone else have the satisfaction of performing that duty.

All this while in Maryland — 10 days, from Sept. 3 to Sept. 13 — we have not seen a single Yankee soldier. We have kept track of what the Union army is doing, however, through the newspapers. We know the pompous bully John Pope, after his whipping at Manassas, has scurried back to Washington with his tail between his legs, and McClellan has again taken the reins.

Some take our freedom from Yankees as a sign the fight has gone out of the enemy, but I don't think so. I talked one day to some of Jackson's men, who had halted by the road while we marched by. They had fought two days at Manassas, and they said the Yankees came at them again and again and again in that two days. I had two thoughts about what they said. First, I thought we — Jenkins Brigade — had taken terrible abuse in our attack, and wondered whether Jackson's men were made of some sterner stuff, to be able to take two days of steady battle, then find enough left inside to advance with us when we crushed the Union left. Second, the idea of Yankees coming again and again and again — some of them, apparently, continuing to attack after they were out of ammunition — does not indicate that the men are beaten, only that their leaders are not worthy of the men they lead.

They are brave men. That realization also spreads through our ragged army.

The enemy makes his presence known on Sept. 14, when the rumble of guns far to the south summoned us yet again to battle. We march swiftly southward — loping at times — with Longstreet pushing us and pushing his staff to ride ahead of the infantry and find water for us. We hardly stop, finally slowing to a grueling crawl as we head uphill toward a gap in a row of mountains to the east, where a cloud of white smoke at the summit shows us men are dying. We pant our way forward, as the sun sets, past Lee and Longstreet and our old friend D.H. Hill, busy talking and pointing by the side of the road; we turn down a lane and rush through a fine-smelling evergreen forest, emerging into the open again at a small hardscrabble farm — too high up the mountain for good, rich earth. There is no time to catch our breath; we are flung into a column of companies, then wheel right into line, by the inverse because there isn't time to get our proper company positions in the battalion line. We then step forward and take shelter behind stone fence topped with rails.

We no sooner arrive than the roar of firing moves from our right to our left. A mob of butternut rags spills out of the gloomy forest across the small field, and we are overrun by a routed, shattered regiment we can't identify.

"Steady. Steady," Walker shouts. "Let them through."

"They are right behind us," a tattered major with a bloody arm shouts as he hurries past.

"We are ready, sir," Walker tells him.

"You better be more than ready," the major calls back over his shoulder as he hurries after his fleeing men. "They are all worked up."

Walker orders our pale battle flags furled and tells the men to hunker down behind the fence; it is not much protection and in daylight we would have been seen. It is almost full night now, though, and we are hidden. The Yankees burst out of the woods and start across the field, not running, not in good formation, but confident. Walker lets them get within thirty yards, then orders us to open up; we fire by companies, aiming at shadows; there is no way to tell what damage we have done, but the shadows are now scurrying back to the woods. That is it; we huddle behind the split rail fence all night, listening to the wounded moan in front of us and listening to firing elsewhere on the mountain.

Sometime near midnight, Capt. John Gantry — who is commanding the three companies that make up the Sixth Regiment — sends a Chester man from another company, Francis Chisholm, shinnying up a tall tree on a little rise behind our regiment, to see where the enemy is positioned.

"I see campfires — I see campfires from here to forever," Chisholm calls down.

Gantry curses him and orders him out of the tree, then shinnies up it himself. He comes down and won't talk.

Before dawn, Longstreet's staff officers come to us with orders to quietly, very quietly, form up and start back down the mountain. We sneak away, with a battery behind us banging away at nothing to keep the Yankees stirred up and their attention focused where we want it to be focused. We are gone before they realize we are going; we walk away from the enemy, with the rising sun on our backs. We walk all morning and at noon take up a position just east of a little, ugly town called Sharpsburg. We are on a hill, right next to a cemetery.

"They won't have far to carry us," Franklin Knox says with a long face. He is shushed by officers.

We are on a hill, and we have a good view of our army coming in all day, from the north and the east and the west. There is nothing from the south, but the word is that Jackson's men — the invincible iron-men of the Army of Northern Virginia — have captured the entire federal garrison at Harpers Ferry 20 miles away and are on their way, that the whole army will be here by next morning.

So will the entire Yankee army. We can see, hear and feel our men assembling in a vast crescent around tiny Sharpsburg; we can hear, feel and almost see the Yankee army assembling in an even vaster crescent around them, distant dots of color from their battle flags and tiny flashes of bayonets in the bright sunlight showing occasional glimpses of an otherwise hidden foe. The ground here dips and waves in small, beautiful hills, covered in green pasture and green cornfields, but our hill tops all the others around and we can see a long way. To the north, a mile or more from us, there is a great coming and going in front of a large farmhouse, with many Yankee flags and wagons and men and horses. There are men on the roof of the house, and soon signal flags are dipping and waving. McClellan is marshaling his forces, but he has done this before and nothing has happened. We wait. Word comes that two batteries have already been sent across the Potomac, a few miles to our rear, and are ready to cover the crossing if the battle goes badly for us. That Lee would even think of such a thing is a sign to us that we face a desperate battle, even if it is "just McClellan again." But nothing much happens that day — just occasional bursts of firing, five or six muskets at a time, like the first scuttering drops of rain before the storm. The firing punctuates the short night. We wait, arms stacked, just below the crest of our hill, with only a few small fires early in the morning to cook the meager rations that came up during the night. There is a warm breeze rolling over our hill, and it makes the evergreens near the cemetery stir and faintly moan. The smell of evergreen — hemlock or spruce or some other tree I don't know.

At dawn the guns open behind us, to the north, beyond the cemetery. The muskets soon join and we can hear cheers and occasionally officers shouting commands. Then there is a tremendous burst of musketry and the banshee wail of our men going in, more muskets. The white smoke drifts over the hill into our position, and it smells hot. To the east, nothing; to the south, nothing. From the west, nothing. We are shrouded by smoke, but as it ebbs and flows we get glimpses across bright green fields of corn and wheat, dappled with cloud shadows and rippling like water as breezes roll in the same direction as the clouds. The peacefulness of the incredibly rich farmland offends me; men are dying. It should not be such a pretty day, and this should not be such pretty country. I have a dull, persistent headache and, as the hours go by, a sharp, persistent pain in my belly: Hunger. We have been hungry before, often, but this time it also offends me. Waiting to die; why should it seem worse to die hungry than sated? While I am pondering this and wondering why my brain waits for moments like this to bring up such questions, the fighting to the north dies down and suddenly there is another avalanche of noise, from the northeast. McClellan, it seems, will not be able to get around our left and is now moving to the center of our crescent, which means we may soon see action. Tom Wright beats assembly and we fall in and unstack arms; but nothing happens, except the shooting and screaming and confusion has gotten closer.

A messenger on horseback comes to Capt. Walker, and he points at our company.

"Go with this man," he shouts to our lieutenant, Edward Shannon, and we right face and march at the double quick, heading south towards some wooded hills. We go through dips and up small hills, and finally crest a ridge that looks down on a creek; across the creek is a stone bridge. The road on the other side comes across a wide field, crosses the bridge and then turns abruptly to run along the base of our ridge, toward the position we just held. The wooded area below the crest is filled with Georgians, who have scraped out shallow pits and piled up dirt and branches and rocks; they do not quite fill up all the space where rifles can be used to advantage, and it's clear we have been brought in to extend the line northward by 50 more rifles.. We quickly pile up rocks and tear down a fence behind us, adding the rails to our rough-made shelter. Behind us, the fighting is still rolling up and down the center of the line, but we are farther away and have a hill between us and the sound, so it is a bit quieter. We are now on the far right of our defensive crescent. The Georgians tell us there as been no activity yet, just an occasional blue uniform on the far side of the field once in awhile.

We have no artillery; there are about 400 men here. There were other brigades behind the position earlier, the Georgians say, but they were all pulled out and sent to the center.

There is a sudden ripple of movement among the Georgians in their pits; the enemy is in sight in the distant woods, moving on the bridge. The blue line comes into view and firing begins — no organized fire, no commands by officers, just every man picking a target and firing.

"Aim low, aim low, you are shooting downhill!" one of the Georgians shouts "Aim at their feet!" We adjust, and at 400 yards they begin dropping, leaving little lumps of blue behind the slow-moving line. They get to within 200 yards of the bridge, then stop and fire a volley, which as far as I can see does no damage at all. Our steady bang-bang-bang-bang continues, and since they are now standing still, more of them are dropping. Finally they have had enough; they execute a right face, do by file, right, by company and march to the rear in reasonably good order, carrying a lot of their wounded with them. They know they are going to have to do more than that.

An hour passes; the dull pounding to the north is still going on.

A Yankee regiment steps out of the woods and breaks into a run across the field. We begin firing; they begin dropping. They make it across the woods and dive behind a low stone wall that runs between the stream and the field. I think they are going to reform and try to burst across the stream in one rush, then come up the hill, but their plan is different. They start to return our fire. They have not truly gauged their position, however; our ridge curves around the bridge and we are in a crescent above them, while they are in a straight line — a chord across an arc. Those of us on the far right are not shooting at men hidden behind a rock wall, but right down the length of the wall; their targets are in plain sight and are in fact massed together, so a bullet that misses one man will hit another, beyond. Still, the Yankees take it for 15 minutes and put quite a bit of lead in the air, but we take few casualties. Then they pull out — not in good order, but not running; moving quickly, but without panic.

They try it again, and we drive them back again. Ammunition comes up and we are resupplied. On the far wood line, just beyond effective rifle range, we can sense, rather than see, a large force.

I am surprised to see the bridge darken, and suddenly realize it has fallen in the shadow of the trees on our ridge. It is midafternoon. This huge battle has been going on for hours. Every man present knows McClellan is keeping our forces pinned to the north and trying to swing behind us here; first they must take that bridge and so far nothing they do has worked. They have no place to bring up guns and pound us; in this area, any place they put a battery would be within range of our rifles. It is a stalemate — until there is a burst of firing south of us, and word comes that the Yankees have found a ford below us. We are flanked.

The Georgians begin forming up and moving out, and one of their officers runs over to tell us we are free to rejoin our regiment. As we leave our breastworks, we see two Yankee regiments burst out of the woods in column and race for the bridge, where fire from the last company of Georgians still in place sends a score of them tumbling. But they are coming across the bridge and as we go over the crest we can hear enormous cheers coming out of the woods behind them. For a moment it drowns out the rattle of fire coming from the center.

As Lt. Shannon moves us at the double quick across the hills, we see more blue moving to the east; they are coming across another bridge, and forming up in huge blocks of blue.

We spot our pale flag with the bold SEVEN PINES! and WILLIAMSBURG battle honors, and Walker puts us in reserve, behind the battle line that is now formed and waiting for action below the crest of the hill, on the side toward the Yankees. We aren't there long; a staff officer arrives from Longstreet, and we are moved forward, into low ground, a peach orchard; the Yankees are moving up guns, and our ridge position needlessly exposed us. We are now facing uphill, with other regiments on both flanks, and we suddenly realize we can hear the Yankees coming, officers calling out orders and occasional strange crushing and squeaking noises as a battle line hits a cornfield and tramples it; the fighting to the north has died away completely.

The crest of the hill is only 60 yards away, and when the Yankee line tops it, a solid wall of shot hits them and tears them apart. They reel, and drop back; another line appears, and disappears beneath our fire. We scream and rush forward — Sixth Regiment, 1st Rifles, Palmetto Sharpshooters, only about 300 men in all, but it sends the Yankees reeling back. We surge up and over the top of the hill. Then men in our line begin falling; we are taking fire from Yankee regiments that have topped the hill north and south of us and pushed back the regiments on our flanks. We are taking enfilade fire and are in danger of being engulfed by a blue tidal wave that is sweeping up from the middle bridge. Walker orders us back, and we fire as we go. Capt. Gantry is down; J.L.Coker of Chester is now in command of the Sixth Regiment. We fall back, firing the whole time, losing men, losing men. We are pushed back through a battery of our guns and the Yankees surge forward, swarming over them with cheers.

I turn to walk away, and find myself alone in swirling, acid gun smoke. A few steps ahead I see a flash of pink and a patch of dark blue; it's our regimental flag, on the bright, green grass beneath the dead body of Tom Chalk. A flash of that inappropriate annoyance flares up; the damned flag is not supposed to be there, we need it. Someone is going to catch hell! I roll Chalk off the flag and pick it up; the bottom half is red with blood. I keep walking, and while trying to step over the tongue of an overturned wagon that suddenly looms up in the smoke, the sole of my shoe catches, rips loose, and down I go, among strangers who have sheltered behind the wagon and the other shattered debris littering what had been our bivouac last night. I am back on the hill near the cemetery. This is too much: I will not die with my sole in such condition. The pun hits me and I begin giggling. I am overcome by challenges; I can't fix my shoe while I'm holding a musket in one hand and a flag in the other. I lean the musket against the wagon and stick the flag upright, between its spokes; a breeze starts, moving away the smoke and making the pale flag stand straight out. I am very pleased, because it is so pretty, even with Chalk's blood. I turn to wrap a rag around my shoe. Free of flag and musket, it is a job that takes less than a minute. The petty annoyance is finished and I am ready to resume my journey, wherever it may take me. I pick up the musket and wrench the flag upward out of the wagon wheel. It flies up over my head and suddenly there is a clatter of hooves on a flat rock outcrop at the crest of the hill behind me — and there is Lee on his grey horse, his hat in his hand, the afternoon sun behind his head, rimming his hair with golden fire. The horse rears. His staff rides up. He looks at the flag, our regimental identification clear to see.

"Sixth South Carolina! Good, sergeant, this will do. Well chosen. Hold this ground. Do your duty! Your duty!"

I try to tell him I'm alone.

"Hold," he says. "You must hold. Help is coming." He wheels and gallops southward, followed by the few staff officers, one of whom says something incomprehensible to me before racing away.

I am stunned. I am also now under orders, so I again turn my face to the enemy, and see we have been given a reprieve. They are not right behind me waiting for me to fix my shoe, like I thought. A black man approaches from the south; a big black man with a drum.

"Wright!" I call out.

"The general said find the sergeant with the red hair and muster the men," Wright said, grinning. "I found him!"

He stands behind me and begins beating assembly. He is joined by a bugler, who sounds "to the colors" again and again. I stand with the flag atop the wagon wheel, high, where it can be seen, and wait. For a minute, nothing happens, except that those clustered around the wagon first look at me and Tom first with mild surprise and what could be reproach, then begin checking their cartridge boxes and looking to their weapons. Then men come, from all directions, walking, hobbling and in two cases crawling. Some seem to spring up from the ground itself. We form a ragged line below the crest of the hill. Behind us, there is soft talk in an odd accent and a line of bandaged men emerges from an alley. They fall in with us and a corporal comes over.

"Gonzalez, First Texas and some Georgia boys. They sent us from the surgeons."

"Anywhere, corporal, one place is as good as another. Try to build a barricade, and quickly. They seem most anxious to say hey to us," I tell him.

Then Coker finds us, appearing as if out of the sky. He gives me an odd look.

"It would appear you are in charge of the last defenses of Sharpsburg," I tell him.

"It would appear that way," he said, "but that would only be to someone who doesn't realize none of these men are under command any more."

More men arriving, as Lee and his staff comb the town and call them to their duty. Teamsters, white and black, armed with shotguns, faces shining with sweat. Apparently some officers finally noticed the black teamsters had weapons. They go into line. So do the artillery crews from the overrun guns, picking up anything they can find to use as a weapon; there are plenty of muskets lying around.

Tom finally stops beating assembly and the bugler stops his noise. There are perhaps 250 men assembled in a long, wavering line behind rocks, piles of fence rails, boxes, overturned wagons and in one place a rock wall that is in the right spot. Some can't stand, and are propping themselves against the barricade to prepare to aim.

Shouting breaks out from the smoke in our front. The Yankees are moving.

They come up out of the tall green grass 400 yards away and we begin firing. Ammunition has not been a problem today, and neither have targets. We have had plenty of both, but it looks like the balance might turn in favor of targets. It is a sea of blue, coming over the green, and it looks like there are more of them coming than we can kill before they get here. In the end, it is simple math, just like a bank. A ripple of movement goes down our ragtag line, and a hand clutches my heart, thinking they will bolt, but it turns out to be just men hunkering down and setting themselves, twisting their feet to get a grip on the ground and moving cartridge boxes where they will be easy to reach. We are not going to move. We are going to die. I have figured something out. Michael Moore would be proud of me. I anchor the flag in the wagon, pick up a weapon and begin killing.

There is a sudden crackling sheet of musket fire and cheers — our wild, wailing cheers — off to our right, out of sight around the flank of the hill. Again! Again! Now it is one long huge noise, and the ripple this time is in the Yankee ranks, which have shifted to our left — to the north — just as if a big animal on the south end of their line gave it a push and the whole line staggered. Now that big wave of solid blue is showing specks of blue foam, individual soldiers coming from our right, drifting north behind their front ranks. The specks become clots, and soon there is no Yankee line, no blue wave, just battle-driven clumps of soldiers, moving faster and faster until the whole Yankee army is a blue stream flowing quickly north. We cheer, then remember our duty; as they flow by, we kill as many as we can, stopping only when the panting, red-faced, wild-eyed men of A.P. Hill's brigades come sweeping into view, carrying both their own flags and those of the captured enemy at Harpers Ferry.

We spend the last hour before dark going over the battlefield, finding our wounded and dead and bringing them back into their own ranks. And it is now, when my legs begin to tremble and I try to count the number of times I should have been dead today, that I realize that at least part of the time I was as crazy as poor Cooper.

CHAPTER TEN

We rebuilt our defenses that night and got what sleep we could. The next morning we were where we'd been the night before, untroubled by any Yankee probes, and we stayed there all day, waiting for McClellan to attack. He, apparently, had had enough of attacking and had reverted to his Peninsular ways. In the words of the generals, we offered battle and McClellan declined. Since any fool could plainly see he still had us outnumbered at least two to one, the day of sitting and waiting did two things for us: It convinced us McClellan was an idiot, because we were played out and he could have taken us with the fighters he still had, and it built up our spirits. Clearly no one would expect us to attack, so simply by staying and offering to fight we had shown some sand. More sand than our opponents, that was the thing.

That night, after darkness, we built up our campfires and then quietly marched a few miles to the Potomac, where we crossed and slept on our arms. The next morning we started marching south, toward Orange, within site of the east face of the Blue Ridge. It was a beautiful late-summer day, with a high blue sky and fluffy clouds, and everywhere we marched women and boys and old men were bringing in crops from the field — corn, and squash; some wheat; vegetables from the house gardens. We passed wagons loaded with harvest, all heading south with us. More crops were ripening in the fields we passed and fat cattle waddled through rich pasture.

"Yanks ain't getting this," Willie McClure said, grabbing an apple a farm girl tossed to him from her orchard.

They ended up getting none of it. We stayed in that part of Virginia awhile, but the Yanks never came, not even raiding parties. Sharpsburg had been as much as they wanted. Instead of a Yankee army camped in northern Virginia eating the harvest, we had a Confederate army there — a battered army, a small army, but it was wearing grey, not blue, and that turned out to be the real value to us of the terrible day at Sharpsburg. We collected our harvest, unmolested by the enemy.

We also collected our strength.

One bright day late in the month John Bratton came back to us, pale and thin from being in Fort Delaware. He'd finally been exchanged; before going back to South Carolina for a 30-day furlough, he came to find the regiment. He smiled as we crowded around him, then looked around.

"Where's the rest?" he said.

"This is what there is," Willie told him. "This is all of us."

Bratton's face fell. When Bratton had been captured, at Seven Pines, the Sixth Regiment had 550 men and officers. We went into Sharpsburg with 150 men; about 100 of us came out, and a lot of us were cut and bruised from a variety of wounds. We were still dressed in rags; some units were getting re-outfitted, but the only thing the quartermaster had sent to us was a new, blood-red battle flag.

Bratton told us his story.

"Stopped to talk to a Yank captive at Seven Pines," he said. "A lieutenant. Next thing I knew, there were four Yankees drawing a bead on me. Now I was their captive. Thing was, they didn't know where they were or where their lines were. All I could think of was, 'They are going to wander around, run into one of our lines, draw fire, and I will get shot.'"

"They refused to listen to me when I told them where their lines were, they thought I was trying to get them to do exactly what I didn't want them to do," Bratton said. "Finally, I gave up trying to convince them. I tricked them. I told them their lines were due west — of course they were due east. 'Can't fool us, Reb,' they said, and marched us off east. Pretty soon we hit their lines and some fool fired at us and I got this." He rolled up his left sleeve a bit to show us the scar from a bullet wound.

Since then he had been in a federal hospital, then in Fort Delaware, waiting for an exchange. The prison wasn't comfortable, he said; it was on a low, marshy island in the Delaware River near Philadelphia, and was plagued with mosquitoes and rats. Now he was going home.

"I'll recruit," he told us. He noticed the new flag.

"Where's our pale flag?" he asked. Somebody brought it forward — torn, bloodstained, filthy, with six hard-earned battle honors: Williamsburg, Seven Pines, Frazier's Farm, Gaines's Mill, Malvern Hill and 2nd Manassas. I saw tears brimming up in Bratton's eyes.

"I'll take this home. Surely this will move some men to join," he said.

"Will you go through Chester?" I asked.

He nodded.

"The train . . ." he explained. "Fastest way to Winnsboro is on the train."

He agreed to stop in Chester and drop off this journal, which is getting thick enough now to represent a real burden.

He frowned for a moment when I told him who should get the journal.

"She can't read," I explained. "I'm not sure I want anybody to see this, now or ever."

He nodded, and agreed that when he left the next day, he'd take the journal to Sarah Wright.

Sarah couldn't read; no surprise there, most black folks can't read. Tom Wright is Sarah's husband; he can't read, but I'd found out months ago he could do math. We'd been unloading sweet potatoes by the bushel and when I wrote out the chit for the man who sold them to us, Tom Wright came over.

"How many bushels does that say?" he asked, pointing a big black finger at the writing.

"It says he sold us 100 bushels," I replied.

Wright shook his head.

"Only 94 bushels," he replied.

That's how I found out that Pvt. H   couldn't be trusted. He'd been in charge of counting whenever we loaded goods, because he was one of the few men who could add, subtract, multiply and divide. Turned out he was cheating us: Counting as received some goods the farmer actually held back, then sold again. The farmer gave H   a share of the cheat. Pvt. H   found himself assigned to work other than supplies or money at every camp for the next two months, and another private did the counting. It wasn't Tom Wright; we agreed between us that his ability to do math would remain a secret, and he thus became my eyes when I was elsewhere.

"How is it you can do sums and such, but don't know how to read?" I asked him.

"White woman offered to teach me either to read or do sums," he said. "I picked sums. Miss a lot, not reading; miss more, like the right money for a job, if you can't do sums."

"What woman?" I asked, in all innocence and curiosity.

He looked away.

"A good woman," he said. "No need to get her in trouble for teachin' a nigger to count."

Then I realized, it wasn't just unusual for Tom Wright to know how to do math, it was probably illegal. I wasn't sure — I'm still not sure, because I can't even ask the question without someone wondering why I want to know, and doing their own two plus two — but if it isn't actually illegal to teach a black man to read and do sums, it is certainly still an unpopular thing to do most places.

We spent a month loafing and healing, and men began coming back from the hospital and from home — some of the physicians had discovered that home was a tonic, and that men declared mortally wounded might, if told they'd be going home, gather up their spirits and actually heal. Thus the regiment grew again, from a hundred tired and shoeless skeletons to more than 200 men. The healed were joined by the first of something we'd known about and seen in other regiments, but hadn't yet had, for no reason I could figure out: Conscripts. Men who'd been forced to join the army.

All our conscripts were from South Carolina — somebody was making an effort to keep the regiments filled with men from their own states and, if possible, to put them with men from their home districts. So we got seven men from Chester; six, actually. One, it turned out, had put down Chester as his home when he'd been forced to sign up, but he wasn't from Chester, nobody knew him. His name was Smith, or so he said — one of the enormous family of the same name, whose progeny seem to include some of the most notorious outlaws and outrageous sharpers ever to live. The rest of us resolved to keep an eye on Smith, but as it turned out we never got the chance: He was gone, a deserter, the first night he arrived. He stole a pair of new brogans, too, from a new man whose touching faith in his messmates let him think he could leave them near the fire to dry out overnight.

John Bratton came back, bringing 60 new men and 20 convalescent veterans; he marched them in already drilled and ready to fight. And he got tough about camp cleanliness.

Bratton, originally trained as a doctor, was always a stickler for keeping the sinks away from camp, much more so than a lot of colonels who agreed with their men that a long walk to answer a call of nature was an unnecessary inconvenience. Bratton would never let us slaughter cattle near camp, either, on those occasions when the regiment got its meat ration still walking. But now he got fanatical about it. It began the same hour he got back; he spotted a man relieving himself into a campfire, and became furious. He ordered officers' call sounded, and when he had every lieutenant and captain from every company gathered around, he let it fly.

"No man," he said in a low, restrained voice, "will be permitted to be filthy. No man will relieve himself anywhere but in the sinks. Any man caught relieving himself anywhere else will be strung up by his thumbs."

He ordered that anyone handling food had to have clean hands. He then took the officers on a tour of the camp, pointing out piles of garbage behind the lines of tents and shelters we'd erected, stinking piles with flies buzzing in the warm October sun. He got even more furious, and ordered the camp struck and everyone in formation within 30 minutes. There was a great furor, with men searching through their bedding for accoutrements and extra shirts; when we were finally on the line, not exactly 30 minutes later but not much longer than that, either, he kept us standing at order arms for two hours while the officers searched for another campsite.

It must, Bratton ordered, be on a hillside, no matter how slight. There must be a stream close at hand, and there must not be another regiment or a pasture with horses or cattle in it upstream from our camp. The officers finally found such a site about a mile away, and the entire regiment marched off, only to stand at order arms for another hour after arriving while Bratton and a group of noncommissioned officers marked where the shelters were to be located, where the cooking fires would be put, and such. And then we were finally allowed to take to the woods to cut branches to make shelters, stretching what canvas we had and making do with pine boughs where necessary. The leaves starting to fall from the trees made, when gathered up, a fine bed.

Captain Walker — back to being in charge of just our company and enjoying it immensely — later told me what had happened. Col. Bratton had, while at the Yankee hospital, found himself next to a lieutenant from the 79th New York, an odd regiment in that it had a few men and officers formerly of the 79th Highlanders, a regiment in the British army. Most of those men were veterans of the fighting in the Crimea. The lieutenant — himself a native of New York City, not Great Britain — learned from those men how the British army set up its camps, and the reason why.

"Did you ever wonder why human excrement smells bad?" the lieutenant somewhat condescendingly asked Bratton. "It's because that's nature's way of telling you it's not good for you."

Well, of course Bratton knew that, everyone knows that, and besides, we have all been taught, from the time we could understand words, that cleanliness is next to Godliness. The British, however, practiced what was preached, to the degree possible.

The British military insisted on cleanliness, with proper sinks far from camp. The result, the lieutenant said, was a very much reduced rate of all kinds of disease. Filth and disease were partners, he said, and keeping the men clean kept disease at bay. The 79th New York, at the instigation of the officers and men who had served in the Crimea, instituted the same rigorous enforcement of hygiene that the British had used, and had lost far more men in battle than to disease — the statistic that convinced Bratton, for that was unheard of. Both armies lost far more men to disease than to wounds, something like three men dying of disease for every one lost to wounds. The common sense of it all was not lost upon Bratton, either, whose training as a medical man gave him a predisposition to be interested in anything involving disease.

The end result was that the Sixth Regiment found itself forced, under threat of corporal punishment, to keep a clean camp. Bratton went so far as to send patrols upstream a mile every day, to make sure nothing was done to affect our supply of drinking water — no wandering cavalry camping beside the stream, no drowned cattle floating in it, nothing but good, clean, cold water coming down out of the Blue Ridge. We burned our refuse, buried our excrement daily, and men who were by nature slothful and dirty found themselves targeted by the sergeants and corporals, who were under extra pressure from Bratton. And he did punish transgressors — although he didn't actually string anyone up by the thumbs. What he made them do was wear a sign around their neck that said "Pig" while carrying a log from one end of the parade ground to the other for four hours. The sinner's captain and orderly sergeant had to oversee the punishment and were not permitted to leave the parade ground until it was complete. Punishments took place only a couple of times before the men figured out it was easier to do it the way Bratton wanted than to risk the log; the men who experienced the punishment started out cocky and boasting to their friends that the log was not very heavy, and ended weeping and begging for the punishment to be cut short. And their captains and sergeants had the added burden of having to execute the penalty while berating themselves for not doing more to prevent the man from having gone astray.

What I found interesting was Bratton's refusal to make anyone who breaks any rules do extra work as punishment. While miscreants in other regiments might find themselves cutting firewood or digging sinks, that work is always treated as an honest burden to be shared in the Sixth. Those who break the rules get punishment that is purely punishment, something pointless and painful; nobody associates the honest work of soldiering with punishment, as a result.

The regiment's number burgeoned up past 400 again, and our 10-company structure was resumed. Regulations — I have been reading a copy of Hardee's manual — call for regiments of a thousand men, in 10 companies, but everything we do seems to show that 100-man companies are just too unwieldy. Most regiments have from 25 to 60 men in each company.

I also resumed my full duties as commissary sergeant. We were getting rations of all sorts — rice, for instance, instead of just corn meal, and beef cattle, driven up the road to be delivered to each regiment and butchered in the field, along with molasses and vinegar and dried peas — field peas, actually, but good when cooked in a kettle overnight with some pork. But sometimes the brigade commissary claimed it was short, and would only give us half rations of some things and one-third rations of another. I took it without complaining until Tom Wright pointed out that something was happening to the rations between the time they arrived at brigade and the time we went to collect our share. Wright quietly slipped among the black teamsters and laborers who delivered the brigade rations the following week and tracked beans and salt. The brigade had, I knew from checking morning reports, 1,644 men entitled to rations — officers were not included, since they were expected to buy their provisions. For that many men, a week's worth of beans would amount to a bit more than four barrels and a week's worth of salt would be about 3/4 of a barrel, using the tables all commissary sergeants had been given to help them reckon their share of the available rations, so we would know how much we should have given the number of men in our companies.

Wright, unchallenged by anyone as he helped unload wagons at the brigade commissary, located in a guarded barn about 400 yards from the Sixth Regiment camp, reported receipt of six barrels of beans and two of salt. When I went to draw weekly rations, the officer in charge of the commissary, a beady-eyed, sneering man named Snelling, told me I'd only get half rations.

"Why?" I asked.

"That's all they've given me this week. I can't give you what I don't have," he said. He squirt a jet of tobacco juice in the general vicinity of my feet — an expression of contempt for my audacity in questioning his ruling. I admit it annoyed me. I remembered standing in the sunset at Sharpsburg with the same bleeding, desperate men Snelling now proposed should go hungry so he could make an illegal profit. We fight Yankees; we fight our own commissary.

"On the contrary," I told him. "You've got plenty in that barn. I know, for instance, that you've got six barrels of those good beans, and two barrels of salt. What are you up to, man?"

He grinned, revealing a mouth full of crooked, yellow teeth.

"Rations have gone bad," he said, "been condemned."

"Bollocks," I told him, and now I bordered on the dangerous, because I walked over to him and put my nose only inches from his. "You're conniving. Your 'condemned' stores will end up sold on the black market in Richmond, while we go hungry. And you'll put the money in your pocket. I want all those barrels opened, now. You've lied for the last time."

"You're talking to an officer," he shot back. "I'll have you charged with insubordination."

"I'll demand a court martial and when it's held, I'll call you to testify and make sure you get asked about how many barrels of beans you lied about receiving," I told him. "I've got an eyewitness who counted them when they came off the wagon. How does that sound? Sound like something you want? Let's get to it. Provost! Over here! I'm under arrest. I've been insubordinate."

The 5th South Carolina was doing provost duty that day and the corporal of the guard was Miles Blackley, a cousin of mine from Yorkville. I'd often stayed at his house; his mother was my mother's sister.

"Turn out the officer of the day, corporal, I'm under arrest," I told Miles. "I want this — officer — to prove to me stores he's listing as ruined are in fact ruined. I think he's a fraud and a sneak and a thief, and I'm willing to bet quite a bit I'm right."

"Is this so, sir?" Miles asked Lt. Snelling. "It will only take a moment to bring the officer of the day here. Shall I send for him? We can easily prove he's insubordinate by having another officer look at what you have in storage."

Snelling was silent; you could see him working it out. On the one hand, he had the profit he stood to make from holding back the best rations and sending them to Richmond to be sold on the black market. On the other, he had a crazy commissary sergeant who apparently had an agent in the barn. And Snelling had a clandestine operation that wouldn't stand any kind of scrutiny from anyone he hadn't already bribed to look the other way. He had a corporal of the guard ready to bring in officers, and it wouldn't take long for the whole thing to attract the attention of Bratton and Jenkins, who was also back from medical leave and who had command of the brigade — and who had a reputation for honesty. It didn't take Snelling long.

"Just a misunderstanding," he said. "The sergeant didn't understand he was getting full rations today."

We got our full rations and more. I wrote up a complete report and took it to Bratton. When I functioned as a commissary sergeant, I reported directly to him, not to Captain Walker.

"I'm sending my own report up to Jenkins," he told me, "but I'm leaving Wright out of it. That will be our secret."

The upshot of it all is that Snelling is transferred to an artillery unit serving in Charleston Harbor. The boys are resentful that he hadn't actually been punished, but Bratton pointed out to me that proving the allegations would have brought Tom Wright and his valuable skills out into the open, and that we'd not be able to pull the same trick again.

"The truth is, most white men don't give the coloreds credit for any sense, they treat them like the furniture: something that's there when you need it, and that's all," Bratton said. "Snelling will rot in Charleston Harbor until this war is over, picking sand fleas out of his food and wondering every day who snouted him out. And not once will he think it was one of the black laborers; it will never occur to him that one of them could cipher."

"We should be fighting Yankees, not trying to guard against thieves," Bratton added.

The Aaron Burr Mess — what was left of it — was impressed that I'd taken on the lieutenant and won.

"Was that something you thought your way through?" Willie McClure teased. I'm known as a thinker more than a doer.

"Obviously some thought and planning were necessary," I huffed.

He just laughed.

The beans were the best we ever ate.

CHAPTER ELEVEN

We loaf. Well, we call it loafing, even though most people would not. We built log huts, just in case we are ordered to spend the winter here in the lee of the Blue Ridge. It is not much work to build the huts and no great loss if we must leave them behind. The only problem is not enough tools. Had we enough saws and axes, we could build a cathedral. But we do not.

Instead, we found a natural amphitheater near the camp, and use it for church services. We cut down one big chestnut at the base of the hollow and use its stump as the pulpit for the preachers, military and civilian, who pass through the camps as the leaves fall and no word comes of peace talks. More and more men are going to church services, but they seem to find no joy in the going.

We drill — our numbers are up, but included are men who had never been through Charles Winder's grueling sessions. We all must go through everything again, even the basics, and it is a trying time for veterans who already know their drill. But we all must know it if we are to move quickly and effectively when the time comes, and the "old" boys know this, even if the new ones do not. Some of the "old" boys, of course, are teenagers, while the new ones range from teenagers up to men in their 40s. The Confederacy is reaching deep for enough able-bodied men to field effective armies in the spring; another gloomy sign that keeps the boys' spirits low.

I have my own reasons for feeling grim. Among those coming in to replenish our ranks are two I'd rather not see: Elizabeth's little brother John and Ira Moore, the young son of Lieutenant Moore, who bore me such animosity. All of them are 17 — children, with pink cheeks and bright eyes, given permission by their parents to join us and die. John Hemphill we add to the Aaron Burr Mess. Moore will have nothing to do with me. I will write to A.J.; he is still in Chester and can perhaps get to the bottom of this mystery. It galls me greatly to stand convicted of an offense whose nature is still not clear to me.

We are alternately amused and chagrined about Abraham Lincoln's Emancipation Proclamation. Copies of New York newspapers have reached us and we have read the Emancipation aloud and tried to figure out just what it means. Some men are outraged, saying Lincoln means to start an insurrection behind our lines. Others point out that the Emancipation Proclamation has to rank among the greatest hypocrisies ever perpetrated upon a long-suffering public. Its avowed purpose is to end slavery — but only in the areas not loyal to the Union. Slaves in Union states — Illinois, for one — are not and will not be affected by the proclamation.

An interesting thing we have already noticed about slaves and negroes: When the Union army takes over an area, there is initially a rush by many of the slaves to get into Yankee lines. Some stay; others come back. Some slave owners forced out of an area by Yankees have, when the invader was driven away, returned to their land to find many of their slaves already there and waiting for their return. Some of the boys are surprised any of the negroes would believe they'd be better off under the Yankees in the first place; ask those soldiers what they'd do to acquire freedom for themselves, however, and they point out they are risking their lives to preserve it. It gets very confusing, because their freedom includes the freedom to own slaves, which is a denial of freedom.

I try not to ask those kinds of questions; it does no practical good once the season of discussion is at an end, and leaves a residue of dissatisfaction that lingers forever. Others are asking questions, though, about the new conscription exemptions. It seems like anyone connected in any way to a going slave-concern will not be expected to pick up a weapon, while those of us who don't own slaves are going to do the fighting. Those who think about these things are faced with the fact that both their government and the one they are fighting against have, almost simultaneously, taken independent actions that nevertheless work in tandem to make it clear slavery is at stake in this war. But what of the men who volunteered to defend their states and homes? They have gone from warriors defending a new nation to men who fight on behalf of a slave empire, in a matter of weeks. Yet what can we do? We certainly can't quit; if we quit, the Yankees will take over everything and that will be a worse state of affairs than we've got right now. That's what the ministers are preaching on Sundays, anyway. We are still defending our homes.

But it would surely be much appreciated if more of the people whose "property" we are defending along with our own would see fit to put on uniforms and join us here in the piney woods.

Not a lot of our time is spent these days on philosophy. We tend to spend much more time on practical concerns, like finding enough to eat.

Tom Wright has been assigned double duty as an orderly to Col. Bratton. He had, while abroad on some affair on behalf of Bratton, acquired four chickens — a rooster and three hens. He brought them, of course, to the Aaron Burr Mess.

The mess is back to 10 members — newly augmented by the return of Rudy Brandt, who had been wounded at Second Manassas, and A.D. Lael, wounded at Sharpsburg a week after returning to the ranks after recovering from the first wound he got this year, in our initial scrape in Williamsburg. Was that only a few months ago?

The mess consists of Tom Wright, Tom Farrar, Lael, Willie, myself, Bill Lucas, Andy Lindsey, Jack Coleman, John Hemphill and Major Hall, who is not feeling well. The prescription is chicken and chicken soup.

Wright frowns.

"Seems like soldiers are just plain thoughtless," he said. "You can take someone who used to be a right smart feller, worked in a bank and wore fancy clothes and everything, and put him in a uniform and in only two years that person will lose his thinking ability and live like there's no tomorrow."

"There's good enough reason to have that attitude, Tom, but what are you talking around?" twice-wounded Lael asked him, eyeing the chickens.

Wright gave him an exasperated look, then handed him the rooster, trussed by the feet.

"Fry him up," he said. "Rooster doesn't lay eggs."

A great light dawned, one that pierced the fog that comes from two years of immediately eating everything provided for fear there may not be a chance to eat it later.

So it was that the Aaron Burr Mess found itself in the poultry business, a subsidiary of the frying pan consortium. This involved quite a bit of extra work — we built a small enclosure out of woven-together brushwood behind the log hut that was our winter home, where our fowl could spend their days. At night we brought them inside — two years ago, the very idea of sharing my bedroom with a chicken would have made me laugh, but it is inevitable. If we leave the creatures outside at night, they will surely be fried by morning. Sometimes, during the day, we let them out of our enclosure and escort them as they make their way through our camp, pecking at morsels and generally foraging for themselves.

The return on our investment of time is eggs: Two every day, and sometimes three. Not enough for a meal for even one man, but enough to make the cornbread richer and enough, when dropped into the boiling kettle and stirred, to impart the wonderful, rich flavor of egg to whatever happens to be in the pot that day. And our cornmeal — others had mush, some baked it into rough bread, but we fancied that the addition of egg to our water and cornmeal mix gave us "cake.'

We initially afforded much amusement for the boys with our three darlings, but the laugh was ours each day when we ate.

The rooster wasn't half-bad, either, although he was so old and tough he had to be cooked slowly in a pot for most of a day before we could get our teeth into him. We traded half the rooster (cooked) to the fellows from another mess that had a pot, since we had been specializing in fry pans.

Bratton has us scouring the woods and fields for forage for the horses and mules and for us, too. He has gone out himself with a couple of forage parties and brought back samples of items that are edible by either man or beast or sometimes both. One sample of each is hung on the front of the log hut that is his headquarters, and men are constantly coming and going, holding up plants they have found to see if they have a match with an "approved" plant. The side of his hut is lined with other plants, one that Bratton, ever the doctor, says are medicinal. Some of the men, emboldened by his willingness to forage, have told him stories of other kinds of edible and medicinal plants from their local lore.

It works out to dozens of plants and roots and about 17 kinds of edible nut, including some that become edible only with an enormous amount of preparation. But, then, we have the time. There are plants of which the fruits, bark or roots can be eaten, chewed or brewed, ranging from Jerusalem artichokes to sassafras and willow bark. And mushrooms — warm, wet days see us up before dawn, heading into the woods to find the rotting logs that produce, overnight, a crop of mushrooms that can be fried or dumped in a stew. All of it goes to supplement our regular rations, which right now are adequate but desperately boring — salted pork and cornmeal. Next summer, Bratton says, we must be on the lookout for love apples — although some of the men swear they are poison, Bratton says they are not and are in fact wholesome and tasty and known as tomatoes in other parts of the country.

We are, with enough food, good exercise every day from our drilling, and good shelter, healing physically. Spiritually, we are still blighted from the numbing experiences of the summer. We are missing comrades — Fred Babcock is gone from the Mess, dead in the Bloody Pines fight that inspired Robert E. Lee so much that he made desperate odds part of every battle plan. S.H. McWalters died there, too, and Henry McElduff was wounded there and died alone in a Richmond hospital a month later while we were launched into the Seven Days fights. We lost J.R. Peay at Frazier's Farm — really lost him, he simply disappeared. We don't know if he is dead or alive. We didn't have time, all summer and fall, to mourn them properly. Now, in this cold pine grove where the wind moans over our roof every night, there is time to remember them — too much time. Some men seem shriveled by what has happened. Major Hall, ever so full of fun, is silent and morose. He takes to his blanket in the hut and despite Bratton's herbs, lots of food and the care of his comrades, he just fades away into nothing. He is finally taken away to the hospital.

We begin to heal spiritually only when Bratton preaches a sermon late in November. He didn't call it preaching; he was summoned when no chaplain or traveling preacher was available for Sunday morning services, the Rev. Ichabod Barak McCausland having taken himself and his Calvinism to the hospital to confuse the sick with obscure Biblical verse. It wasn't the kind of speech Richmond would have much liked, but it set us back on the road again.

"I know," he began, "that many of you are beset with doubt, that you are worried about your families and worried about yourselves and worried and sick over how much blood has been spilled. We are full of questions about why we are fighting, when it will end, and no one seems willing to give an answer. We are beset not only by Yankees but by fools and knaves on our own side; it goes on, and right now no end is in sight."

"There is no doubt we are in the midst of horror. There is no doubt this regiment has shed and spilled as much blood as any in this army. There is no doubt it will be asked to shed and spill more. I don't know why; I can't figure that out any more, although it seems to me I used to have a reason, maybe more than one. I don't know how long we'll be expected to do our duty. But we are soldiers and our duty is clear."

"I know this: The Sixth has never failed to do its duty. You have never failed; remember that. When ordered to advance, you advanced: Bloody Pines, Gaines's Mill, Frazier's Farm, Second Manassas. When ordered to hold the ground, you held — Dranesville, Williamsburg, South Mountain, even at Sharpsburg, when it looked like there was nothing left of the regiment but a color bearer and a drummer. You held!"

"Remember this, also: You were ready to do your duty when your leaders trembled. We stood in the rain together at First Manassas, the only regiment in the army not engaged, ready to pursue the Yankees to Washington, only to be held back by the fears our of leaders. So we have been ready to do more than asked."

"I think on all this — I look on all that you have done, and done well, and I believe there must be a reason for what we have been through. I believe God is forging us into a weapon, using the hot fires of hell to do it, for some purpose that is not clear to us. How could it be? God's purpose is God's purpose, not ours. We are the instruments of God's will, and trying to understand more than that is useless. We will find out in God's good time, and when we do, when the moment comes and we know it is our moment, that is the time to remember these men."

He reached into the pocket of his frock coat and pulled out several sheets of paper, covered with writing.

"Fred Babcock, Bloody Pines," he began. He continued reading, slowly, for 10 minutes, a list of all the Sixth Regiment dead that started with poor Fred and ended with Alfred Zimmermannn from Company G.

He finished, folded the papers and put them back in his pocket.

Bratton's quiet voice carried to every part of our natural church, in a hushed silence that could almost be touched.

"Did they die for nothing?" he asked.

Then he just walked away.

Someone down in the front began singing "Amazing Grace," and soon the pines filled with the sound of hundreds of men singing. When we finished, there was silence — it was a still day, with bright sunshine filtering into our amphitheater in the pines, and it was warm.

One of the fifers got to his feet and turned to us.

"Enough of that; some of this," he said, and launched into "Wait for the Wagon." Others joined;

Tom and other drummers got their drums and joined in. They swirled through all the songs familiar to us from two years of marching to music — "Soldier's Joy," "New Tatter Jack," "Hog-eye Man," "Ole Zip Coon," "Duke of York's Troop," and on. And the song men have been marching off to war to the sound of for nobody knows how many years, "The Girl I Left Behind Me." The sound rolled out across the hills, and soon men from other regiments — and more musicians — were hurrying into our grove, drawn by the sheer volume of sound.

They brought songs new to our musicians. One of them would play a song through on the fife, then they would start over and all would play it — after two years, most of our musicians are very good at quickly picking up a melody. We soon had a dozen drummers and two dozen fifers in our grove. Someone brought a cornet, and then an entire band assembled.

They played all afternoon and into the warm night, when a bonfire lit up the scene. The melodies were endless; the ones that made me want to stand up and dance like a savage were the wild Celtic tunes, the ones that made me feel reckless and brave, so that I hunched down deeper against my tree lest anyone see me so affected by mere music. Willie McClure looked at me and laughed.

The drums made the air tremble and the fifes were like a rampart of sound surrounding us. Hundreds of men stood, sat — just let it wash over them.

They played "Bonnie Blue Flag." It apparently got youngster John Hemphill thinking, for when it was finally over, sometime near midnight, and we all headed back to our huts, he said, "Why does the song say 'band of brothers?' Most of us are not kinfolk."

"It's from Shakespeare, Henry V," I told him. "It's an allusion the songwriter put into his work."

"Why?" he asked.

I was surprised to find out I actually had an answer — it just came out as natural as if I'd been thinking about this for a long time.

"Because Henry V was an English king in the 1400s who won a battle against overwhelming odds, just like those faced by the new Confederacy," I said. "The allusion is meant to inspire us with his example."

"But if I don't know the allusion, I don't benefit?" the boy asked.

"True enough, but a lot of people do know the allusion," I replied. "They spent their youth in school learning, rather than haring off to join the army at 17."

"I still don't understand," he said.

"Henry had about 900 men left in the army he'd invaded France with," I said. "They had captured a French town, and were making a long march back to meet their fleet when they found themselves cut off by a French army of 12,000 knights and men-at-arms, near a place called Agincourt."

"One of Henry's generals said he wished for more men from England, and it prompted Henry to make a speech."

"I still don't understand," Hemphill said. "What was the speech? Why would you make a speech then? Shouldn't he have been looking to his ammunition trains?"

I reached deep and surprised myself again. Long ago I'd been forced to memorize soliloquies in Shakespeare's works and this was one of them.

"Henry rebuked his general," I said, "and then went on:"

> If we are mark'd to die, we are enow
> To do our country loss; and if to live,

The fewer men, the greater share of honour.
God's will! I pray thee, wish not one man more.
By Jove, I am not covetous for gold,
Nor care I who doth feed upon my cost;
It yearns me not if men my garments wear;
Such outward things dwell not in my desires.
But if it be a sin to covet honour,
I am the most offending soul alive.
No, faith, my coz, wish not a man from England.
God's peace! I would not lose so great an honour
As one man more methinks would share from me
For the best hope I have. O, do not wish one more!
Rather proclaim it, Westmoreland, through my host,
That he which hath no stomach to this fight,
Let him depart; his passport shall be made,
And crowns for convoy put into his purse;
We would not die in that man's company
That fears his fellowship to die with us.
This day is call'd the feast of Crispian.
He that outlives this day, and comes safe home,
Will stand a tip-toe when this day is nam'd,
And rouse him at the name of Crispian.
He that shall live this day, and see old age,
Will yearly on the vigil feast his neighbours,
And say 'To-morrow is Saint Crispian.'
Then will he strip his sleeve and show his scars,
And say 'These wounds I had on Crispian's day.'
Old men forget; yet all shall be forgot,
But he'll remember, with advantages,
What feats he did that day. Then shall our names,
Familiar in his mouth as household words-
Harry the King, Bedford and Exeter,
Warwick and Talbot, Salisbury and Gloucester-
Be in their flowing cups freshly rememb'red.
This story shall the good man teach his son;
And Crispin Crispian shall ne'er go by,
From this day to the ending of the world,
But we in it shall be remembered-
We few, we happy few, we band of brothers;
For he to-day that sheds his blood with me
Shall be my brother; be he ne'er so vile,
This day shall gentle his condition;

And gentlemen in England now-a-bed
Shall think themselves accurs'd they were not here,
And hold their manhoods cheap whiles any speaks
That fought with us upon Saint Crispin's day.

"My God," Hemphill said when I'd finished. "Now I understand. You talked your way around it, but Henry summed it up: 'He today that sheds his blood with me shall be my brother.' You say he won the fight?"

"I am not William Shakespeare," I pointed out.

Hemphill frowned in great concentration.

"What does Shakespeare have to do with this?" he asked. Laughter broke out around the camp-fire and Hemphill's face flushed. "You were talking about Henry and now you're talking about some-body else. What about Henry? Did he win?"

"He won a great victory," I said.

Lael wouldn't let it sit, taking up the role of court jester left vacant by Major Hall's absence in the hospital.

"This King Henry, did he face Yankees with Parrott guns and a fleet?" he asked.

"He faced knights in armor and his ragged army was sick, underfed and barefoot, just like ours is a lot of the time," I said.

"And did he pitch into the Frenchies with his barefoot, sick hungry men?" Lael persisted.

"No," I acknowledged, "for Robert Lee was not among his generals. What Henry did was taunt the French, goading them until they made an attack on a position he chose for defense. The French had to attack uphill across a muddy field. The mud slowed down their charges and the English archers picked off the knights on horseback, starting at 300 yards. The French also were squabbling among themselves, too, so their attacks went in separate, not all at once."

"Just like Yankees," Lael said.

"Much like Yankees," I acknowledged.

"Was Shakespeare in that scrap?" Hemphill asked.

"No," I said. "He wrote much later."

"He was safe a-bed in England on St. Crispin's Day, then?"

"Pretty much," I said, acknowledging the point and seeing no need to clutter up his analysis with mere dates.

"Did Henry really say those things?"

"That's a good question. Seems like Shakespeare said them, for sure," I said.

"Well," Lael said, cheerfully, shifting his tobacco from one cheek to the other and spitting, "It appears from the amount of blood shed that this band of brothers called the Army of Northern Vir-ginia is a mighty big family. I'd just as soon not get any more brothers that way. And if we're havin' our druthers, I'd rather be a-bed on St. Crispin's Day or any other day."

On that note, in good spirits, we retired for the night. The next morning we got orders to form up in heavy marching order; the Yankees were making a move near Fredericksburg.

CHAPTER TWELVE

We played almost no role at Fredericksburg, but we learned much about the value of a stout stone wall. Other South Carolinians were there where the worst slaughter was done, and they told us a few days afterward, when our brigades chanced to meet and pause together at a crossroads, that the fields in front of their hill looked like a shambles.

"But," one greybearded sergeant noted, "they kept coming, stepping over their dead and wounded each time. They came twelve times before they finally give up, and each time they went back the field was a deeper blue."

Young Hemphill listened raptly to the tale of Yankee soldiers slogging across a frozen field, again and again, attacking an enemy inviting the attack. He looked at me with his mouth slightly open and awe in his eyes. The idea that we are in very good historic company has not been lost on anyone, although it is very difficult to think of knights in armor while scratching fleas. Lael wondered, just about then, what a knight would do if he had to scratch fleas. Men roared with laughter — proof enough that all their minds were pretty much on our Shakespeare conversation.

We'd spent the fight behind the lines, in reserve for once, hearing the battle, smelling the smoke but not firing a single musket. We just stood in the cold and shivered.

Col. Bratton seemed content to miss the honor of participating, and content with the outcome.

"No one but a fool can miss the implications of this fight," we overheard him saying to Brigadier General Jenkins afterward.

The Fredericksburg fight concentrated the army for a time and we soon had stripped the countryside bare of provender. Even our three chickens — caged on a regimental supply wagon by a teamster who shared our mess so long as he preserved our precious poultry — were hard-put to find forage. The Yankees had gone into winter camp across the river. They had a supply line pouring food into their camps; we had a supply line with a broken railroad to Richmond, not enough wagons and worn-out horses. We spent January and February near Fredericksburg, building stout shelters of log, but each day less food found its way to the army and each day the area stripped of trees for firewood grew until we began to get some idea of what the Biblical plague of locusts had done to ancient Egypt.

It was clear to everyone we'd soon be starving if something weren't done. Late in February our brigade, along with some others in Longstreet's Corps, was ordered south, below Richmond. But it was not a hasty march; we almost dawdled, and some in our company ran into trouble when we got too close to the attractions of Richmond.

I am not sure I have conveyed the enormously boring aspect of most of our existence as soldiers. One may stand guard detail only a few times before the novelty wears off; indeed, everything we do is, once learned and mastered, certain to eventually lead to a sense of boredom so deep that the boys will often let their desire for diversion overcome their good sense. In the height of battle that boredom seems extremely attractive, compared to the prospect of death, but once in the grip of the safe but mundane routine of camp life, even battles start looking good.

Besides, what is the threat of punishment to men who live in the presence of death?

A detail of 10 men, one from each company, was sent to Richmond to pick up overcoats we'd stored there in the spring. It came back three men short, including Alfred R   from the Calhoun Guard. The Corporal of the Guard reported his absence to me, as the only person with any rank higher than his whom he could immediately find from our company.

"He is not yet absent without leave," the corporal said. "Their passes were good until midnight tonight, and it is now 7 p.m. But the others said he scooted off into a saloon; he'll never make it back and the Richmond provosts will sweep him up in the morning out of a gutter somewhere. If he's lucky he won't be robbed and murdered."

The corporal then cheerfully went back to the guard tent, whistling.

Alfred, a Chester man who'd worked as a baggage porter at the railroad station, had been itchy for quite some time. It looked like the itch was going to get scratched, but the thought of him swept up by the Richmond provosts, who had a bad reputation for exercising more authority than they had the natural intelligence to handle, did not sit well. What I should have done was find the captain, but the thought no more than surfaced than I found myself, to my surprise, shoving it aside. This was something his chums should handle, not the officers, not the army, not the provosts.

Tom Wright had heard what the corporal said, but just walked away. He returned a few moments later with a bulky package, wrapped in brown paper.

"Sergeant," he said, "You have a problem. General Lee may have paid attention to you in the shadow of Sharpsburg, but nobody in Richmond is going to pay a lick of attention to a sergeant. What you need is — " and he pulled up one corner of the paper to show me a grey uniform with gold braid showing on the sleeve — "a colonel of infantry."

"How did you know I was going to tackle this myself?" I asked him. He just smiled.

What Wright had produced was nothing less than John Bratton's new coat, specially made for him. It was a dress coat — not what he wore in the field, which was a simple brown frock coat with a colonel's three stars on the collar. This beautiful grey coat was for when he wanted to make an impression someplace other than on a battlefield.

It was a wonderful coat, it was just what we needed, and it unfortunately was exactly tailored to fit Bratton, who, while he has a large heart and an even larger reputation, is in stature somewhat smaller than the average man.

The Aaron Burr Mess was summoned to "fall in for a special detail," and a quick check, done in a barn with the doors shut and guarded against intrusions, was that the jacket would fit Tom Farrar, one of the new men who joined the army and our mess after Sharpsburg.

"You're going to go far, Farrar," I told him.

"Have I been breveted, then?" he asked, with a smile.

"Battlefield promotion, limited duration," I told him. "Don't get that dirty or I'll skin you."

"How will I know what to say? I don't know all the things a colonel might say."

"This is a special detail escorting the colonel on a search for a . . . a staff officer who is masquerading as an enlisted man," I said, making it up as I went along. "He has information about enemy intentions and may have been forced to keep his head down and stay in his enlisted man role because . . . because enemy spies may have him . . ."

"Where he can't change back without giving the game away?" Farrar volunteered.

"Excellent!" I told him with relief. "I'll give the marching commands and such to the detail, that's nothing a colonel would bother himself about. You just look aloof and impatient and chip in when you see a good time. Remember, we may have to bluff provosts, Richmond police . . . who knows?"

The first job was to get out of camp, which could have been the end of the ruse. No pickets had been set this far from the front lines, but camp guards had been posted to check passes. We could have snuck out, but this gave us a chance to try our scheme; if we got found out, I'd count on convincing the guards we were just having a joke.

We formed up, a dozen men, mostly from the Aaron Burr Mess, with me as first sergeant and Farrar marching by my side in the spot where the captain would normally be. We picked a guard post as far from the guard tent as we could find.

We approached and the challenge rang out.

"Who comes there?"

"Friend!" I answered.

"What is the countersign?"

I, of course, had no clue. We kept marching toward the sentinel, who held his gun exactly as prescribed, arms port.

"What is the countersign?" he asked again.

"Do you want me to shout it?" I asked. "So everyone hears it?"

That kept him thinking until we were upon him, whereupon "Col. Farrar" walked up to him.

"Do you know who I am?" Farrar asked. This, I thought, was pretty brazen, but Farrar turned out to be a better judge than I of his fellow man.

"Yes, sir," the sentinel said, returning his gun to shoulder arms, with a look on his face that revealed he had no idea who it was but wouldn't admit that for the world.

"I am taking out a special detail," Farrar said. "We have a job to do and might not be back for some hours. You are to inform your relief — and no one else — that we may be returning and we may be in a hurry. You do know your standing orders require you to take orders from the noncommissioned officers and officers of the guard detail, the officer of the day and the camp commander and no one else, correct?"

"Correct!" the sentinel snapped.

"See to it then," Farrar told him. He turned to me.

"Sergeant?"

"Detail, forward, march," I told them quietly. We tramped off into the night, trying hard not to snicker. I quietly asked Farrar whether he was officer of the guard, officer of the day or camp commander.

"Which one do you need right now?" he asked.

The walk into Richmond took only a few minutes. We passed stately homes, then storefronts, then brick buildings rising three and four stories into the sky. When we got near the Virginia statehouse, it started to get noisy. Saloons and bawdy houses competed for our attention, with saloonkeepers plying us with noisy admonitions about the purity of their beverage and bawdy house hucksters touting the purity of their wares as well. Pianos and fiddles added to the din. The boys discussed whether some of the establishments should be "saloons with girls" or "bawdy houses with drink to supplement sin," and concluded that it was a distinction without a difference. What one of them actually said was "I guess you can get satisfactorily drunk and diseased in either."

We began our search for Alfred R   and it did not take long to pick up his trail. Even in a part of town where having a good time was the point of being there, R   's exploits had attracted attention.

"Short fellow with blond hair and brown eyes, his eyes blink when he talks," we told the saloon-keepers.

"His eyes blink when he sings, and when he shouts, and when he fights," the proprietor of Old Jack's Lair told us. "He left here five minutes ago, heading for Millie's."

We got directions to Millie's — Millie's Emporium of Feminine Delight, according to a flier we found in the gutter — and marched off. The businesslike demeanor we exhibited — along with our fixed bayonets, indicating a detail on some serious provost duty — cleared the street ahead of us. A lot of people, it seemed, had no desire to get mixed up with provosts. When we got close I halted the detail and went ahead to scout — to look in the window, actually. Someone came at me from an alley, and I lurched backward.

"Mister, don't go in there, I've got what you want," a female voice whispered. "Come on back in the alley and I'll fix you up."

I praised the inadequacy of Richmond's gas lights, because I blushed.

"Not what I'm here for," I stammered. Even in the dim light I could see her eyebrows rise.

"That's all there is, here," she patiently explained.

"I need to get a man ..." I began, and she stopped me with a hand on my forearm.

"No man can do for you what I can do," she whispered. "Come on, two dollars."

I blushed even more. I was sure she could feel the heat coming off of my face and I suspected my face was as red as my hair.

"No, not ... I need to find one of my men ...." I stopped. It would not do to explain to her what was really going on. "I'm leading a provost detail," I said instead, and she pretty much vanished in front of my eyes.

"Dirty sneaking bullies," she hissed from the alley.

A peek in the window showed men and women in a kind of drawing room. R   was not in sight. A reconnaissance around the building showed three doors. I went back to the detail.

"We thought we'd have to send out a search party for you, next," Farrar joked.

"I don't see him," I reported. "But this is where he's supposed to be. Let's keep this going — four men in each door, one man stays on the door to keep everyone inside, the other three search the building. Farrar and I will set up in the parlor. Search it room by room. If anyone asks what you are doing, answer nothing, and if they persist, refer them to Colonel Farrar here."

It wasn't much of a plan, but it seemed like the kind of thing a provost detail might do, looking for deserters and such, so we put it into operation.

Through the doors we burst, and such a covey of quail exploded out of the shadowy thickets that the air was filled with color and movement.

"Stand fast," I shouted. "We are looking for a deserter."

Our men went in every direction, upstairs and into the basement. We could mark their progress through the seemingly vast building by the shouts and shrieks in the various bedrooms. Farrar strode around the room and came back, looking thoughtful.

"All privates and noncommissioned officers, no officers," he murmured.

A formidable apparition now strode into the room, a strapping, tall woman in a purple dress, with her green eyes blazing.

"You sons of bitches. I paid Godwin. This has got to stop. These women are on their backs 12 hours a day and we still can't make enough to pay off you bloodsuckers."

I had no idea what she was talking about.

"Madam, we are here to look for a deserter," I replied.

"Sure you are," she sneered. "Sure you are."

The men began coming back down. R＿ was not among their number.

"Lord, Lord, Lord," Rudy Brandt said, shaking his thick blond German head. "The things I've seen tonight. My oh my oh my."

All the men were grinning.

"See?" she said. "Why do you even pretend?"

I hesitated, unable to figure out what to do next. Farrar stepped into the breach, but I was immediately unhappy that he had.

"Miss Millie?" he inquired, giving a small bow. "I believe we have business. It will be the usual."

That prompted a string of profanity from the now red-faced woman in a purple dress. She walked out of the room into an office and came back in a moment with an envelope, which she gave to Farrar.

"But I am goddamned if we will service these pigs tonight," she sputtered. "You'll have to come back tomorrow, when there aren't paying customers." And she concluded with another string of profanities, such that I expected to see the varnish peel from the woodwork.

"Doesn't Godwin usually enjoy some refreshment?" Farrar asked her. I was ready to dissolve into the carpet.

"I told you, not tonight," Miss Magnificent Millie replied.

"Duty calls us," Farrar told her, smiling urbanely. "If you will give us two bottles of your best, we will forgo the pleasures of the flesh."

Millie swore again, left and came back with two bottles of ... something. Farrar took them and bowed.

"Au revoir," he offered, and then gestured at me.

"Outside, form up," I told the men. Out into the street we went.

"What was that?" I asked Farrar. He looked at me with surprise.

"Coleman, you erudite moron. She thought it was a shakedown — you do understand that prostitution is illegal and only exists because authorities are bribed to ignore it? — anyway, she expected she'd have to give us something, and who are we to disappoint such a lady?" He beamed and thought himself quite clever, which I suppose he was. A bit too clever for my taste.

"All right, what is in the envelope?" I asked.

He opened it up and gave a low whistle.

"Coleman, we are in the wrong trade." He held up $200 in Confederate. Plus two bottles of whisky. I scowled, not knowing what we should do. I took the money and the whisky, putting the money in my jacket pocket and tucking the whisky inside my jacket.

"Let's keep going," I said. "We still haven't found R＿."

We resumed going from saloon to saloon, with no trace of our erring brother. After an hour, near the Spotwood's bright lights and loud noise of politicians and generals making merry, we heard a disturbance around the corner and, in it, a familiar voice. We doubletimed and deployed in a short line of battle, finding R   , much the worse for wear, being pinned to the cobblestones by a group of Richmond toughs.

"Charge bayonets!" I yelled, and the toughs scurried off into the shadows, to be replaced instantly by a detail of Richmond provosts. Real provosts. I could feel sweat trickling cold down my spine. The detail was in the charge of a captain. He had a brass badge on it that said "Provost." Trumped.

"Seize him," the captain told his men, pointing at poor R   . Two men stepped forward — hard cases, very similar in appearance to the toughs we'd just sent scurrying away.

"You will not," Farrar said, stepping in front of R   . "This man is our responsibility."

"He just assaulted some citizens. He is under arrest," the captain said. "You have no authority here."

"Do you want to go see Mr. Godwin and make sure of that?" Farrar asked the captain, taking a step toward him and putting himself squarely between R   and the provosts. The captain hesitated. I gestured for the men to step forward and take R   . The captain made up his mind.

"You have no authority here," the captain said. "He is ours. Hand him over or we will arrest you all. Soldiers are not to be in Richmond with their arms, and you are the queerest excuse for a colonel I've ever seen."

Farrar for once was speechless. He looked over to me.

"Captain, a word, please?" I cajoled. "Can we have a private word?" We walked off to one side, into the shadows.

"Captain, the colonel is on a special detail of some delicacy. The young fellow is the son of an important officer. We really could use your cooperation in getting him out of this," I told him. I reached into my pocket, pulled out some of the money, and, groping in the dark, found his arm and put the money into his hand.

He counted it. "Well, it's important to know where duty lies," he muttered, making the wad of bills disappear somewhere inside his coat. "Still, some respectable citizens claim he assaulted them."

"You mean the vultures who were trying to rob him?" I asked, filling his again empty hand with a bottle of whisky.

"You're right," he said. "People like that are not to be believed."

He sneered — maybe he was smiling — and went back to his thuggees.

"We're done here," he said. They dissolved into the shadows of Richmond.

"How?" Farrar asked.

"I'm a quick learner," was my response. "Let's get out of here."

We stepped off, with two men supporting R   and the rest marching at port arms as if guarding a prisoner being escorted. We again moved through the streets without difficulty, and soon found ourselves confronting our brigade sentry line. Our attempts to congratulate ourselves on a job well done were premature. The guard had changed, and the gullible chump who had let us out was no longer to be seen.

"Halt!" came the cry. "Who comes there?"

"Friends," Farrar called back, quietly.

"Advance one with the sign," the sentry called out.

I went forward.

"Manassas," the sentry whispered.

"Soldier, the sign has been changed since we left."

"Then I must call up the officer in charge," he replied.

"No, wait, don't do that," I said, stepping forward into the faint light so he could see me. "We've got a situation."

He looked at me apprehensively, then back over his shoulder.

"Sergeant, you don't understand," he whispered to me. "I have to call out the guard."

There was a bustle and stir nearby, and Col. John Bratton stepped forward, along with several officers. Grand rounds. Our bad luck.

"And what situation might that be?" he asked me.

I saluted. He returned it.

"Sir, we are reporting in with one of our men who was — ah — well, he was misplaced." Behind me, R   began singing a bawdy song.

"Misplaced? Equipment can be misplaced. A misplaced soldier. Would that be the loud baritone?" Bratton asked.

"Yes sir," I said.

"Move the detail forward."

Farrar did his best to hang back, but the sentry was poking up his fire, and with more light Farrar found he couldn't hide. Shortly after becoming visible he became conspicuous.

"What is this?" Bratton asked sternly. "Private Farrar, have you been promoted? Where on earth did you get that uniform?" His face lit up with knowledge. "Ah. Indeed."

Farrar did the smart thing. He just stood there, at attention, and said nothing.

"Sir," I said, desperately. "Sir, if we can just explain."

"I doubt that is remotely possible," Bratton said. "Don't even try." He turned to the sentry. "Call out the guard," he said.

"Post Number Two! Corporal of the Guard!" the sentry called out, and our goose was cooked. The corporal called the officer of the guard, who called out the guard, who took our weapons, ordered Farrar out of Bratton's uniform, and marched us off, Farrar in his shirt and drawers. The only thing I managed to do in the confusion was leave the rest of our "payoff" money under the whisky bottle on the ground near the fire. We were kept under arrest for three days — not able to participate in any soldierly duties during that time and restricted to one part of the camp. R   awoke the next day with no clear recollection of anything that had happened. His lack of information was pointedly and repeatedly remedied by his friends, who told him what he'd gotten up to and how it had led to their present condition.

We never heard what happened to the money and the whisky. We did hear from the Rev. Ichabod Barak McCausland, who has lost weight under the rigors of our campaigns and is now but half the man he was before. He compensates for the reduction in ballast with a bigger cargo of admonitions.

"It's the Book of Job for you, Coleman," he intones as we ride out our punishment. "Very appropriate. Job 31, verses four through six."

"Doth not he see my ways, and count all my steps? If I have walked with vanity, or if my foot hath hasted to deceit; let me be weighed in an even balance that God may know mine integrity."

We were not sure how it applied to our condition, but we knew a question would produce only a new onslaught of verse, so we remained politely silent, hoping our politeness would be mistaken for contriteness.

CHAPTER THIRTEEN

We did not stay near Richmond long after that. In February we moved out, with much of the rest of Longstreet's Corps, to the southeast. Army rumor had it that we were moving off to relieve the burden on northern Virginia, where provender had been picked clean by two armies operating for two years. The area near Suffolk was rumored to have both a modest number of Yankees and sufficient victuals to keep us in style. The cavalry moving with us was sent farther west, where good grazing was reported. A lot of our artillery went there as well.

We eventually found the Yankees. While there weren't many of them, as these things are counted, they were very well dug in, like ticks. Longstreet's response was to issue shovels and start us digging in as well. He then occupied the works with enough men to repel an initial assault, and used the surplus to launch what amounted to raids and sorties into areas where neither Yankees nor Confederates held full control. It soon became clear that we lacked sufficient force to drive the Yankees into the sea, and they lacked sufficient force to clear us out of their front. Stalemate, while the winter wound down and we filled ourselves on the region's stored foodstuffs, supplemented, again, by what we could take from the area's abundant streams. And, occasionally, from the Yankees. While the "campaign" lacked the wholesale resupply we'd gotten after some pitched battles, we still picked up some useful items, including leaking metal canteens.

While the whole canteens we took from Yankees were useful for carrying water, the leaking ones, when split into two halves over a fire that melted the solder that held them together, were also quite useful. We used them as small fry pans, as makeshift shovels, as small bowls, as dinner plates. The Sixth was in pretty good supply — after the shameful incident at Dranesville, we never again shucked our packs prior to a battle. As a result, we never again faced a time when we were without the basics necessary to support life in the field with some degree of comfort. Other units lost heaps of knapsacks by stripping to fight at Sharpsburg. Not us. Still, a Yankee canteen half turned out to be a welcome addition to our camp kit, and we stayed on the lookout for them. Our issue wooden canteens were only good for carrying water.

We are in pretty good shape so far as our uniforms go, as well, although we will never grace the pages of Godey's. From somewhere the army has supplied us with coarse trousers and jackets of jeancloth — part wool, part cotton, apparently. It is not particularly strong, it frays easily, but it is quite warm. Shoes are still a problem. Anyone who ever saw a cobbler's bench was taken out of ranks for a time this winter and put to work in brigade workshops making shoes, but to make shoes you need leather, and to have leather you need cattle. We appear to have run through quite a few cattle; fresh beef is a very scarce item, and we subsist on all the parts of pig known to gourmands and some that are not. We are told of civilians making shoes out of dogskin; surely not. It is certain that our armies consume copious quantities of horses, mules and cattle, and the question has to be asked: Is the supply running out?

We are not running out of gunpowder, however, and it is now, for the first time, that we get some actual practice at hitting targets with our weapons at various ranges. The Palmetto Sharpshooters have done this routinely since they were first organized last spring, and they are often called out to drive away artillery or push a crowd of Yankee officers away from an observation point. A few of their better shots can, using the standard Enfield, hit a man 800 yards away. Most of our fighting is done at much closer range; indeed, some of it has been done so close that no sight adjustments were necessary. The advantage of being able to hit targets farther away is pretty obvious — especially from an entrenched line of works with an open field of fire across 180 degrees of view, extending several hundred yards. Longstreet — much grimmer now than when we first served under him, he's changed — is telling his generals that the plan must be to maneuver into strong positions and force Yankees into rash attacks — much as they did at Second Manassas, where Jackson held a strong defensive line for two days against repeated attacks. True, it about wore him out, but he held, until we unleashed an avalanche on the Yankee flank that swept them back to Washington. Again. And Fredericksburg — our Agincourt — has made an indelible stamp on a lot of minds.

Longstreet's generals see no glory in this, we hear from men detailed to work on division staff, but this is his Corps and they will do as he asks, because he has led them to victory after victory. So we learn to dig, and we learn a bit more about shooting. I am, with my weak eyes, better with a shovel than I am with a rifle, but even I improve after a time. We set up damaged barrels or stack crates at various distances and use them for targets. We learn to estimate the distance, set our sights for the right range, and actually hit the targets.

A.D. Lael, who has been wounded twice so far, is especially keen for practice in shooting. According to him, we've been wasting a lot of shots with the wrong range.

"These guns are trickier up and down than they are sideways," he says cryptically. I ask him to explain.

He frowns and has McClure hold up his Enfield, with the rear sight all the way up, extreme range, 1,000 yards. Lael then takes a ramrod and holds it so the small end is resting on the front sight and the other end is resting atop the rear site.

"See that?" he asks. "You're looking through the notch at what you're going to hit, but the barrel of the Enfield is pointing up over it. That ball has to go up in the air pretty far to come down and hit what you're looking at."

"How much?" I ask. "These sights are set for a thousand yards. I can't even see a man at that distance, the muzzle of the thing blocks out the target."

"Yes, well, a thousand yards is a bit much, might be the Enfield company is showing off," Lael acknowledges. "At that range the ball would be at least twelve feet off the ground at five hundred yards, so it would come back to man-height at a thousand yards."

"Why?" I ask.

Lael shrugs. "I'm not sure. But remember all the times we've gone back through where we fought and found the trees over our heads all full of bullet holes?"

He's right. Some of us never do get the hang of estimating the range accurately, but many of the men work it out. Perhaps they can keep the rest of us up to the mark, although my sense is that once the shooting starts things pretty much go to hell.

I have had a letter from Elizabeth. I asked her to speak with Thomas Mantour about why Lt. Michael Moore came to the bank the day I enlisted. Maybe Moore wants me to figure something out about his bank business, not this war.

Elizabeth's letter only added to my confusion.

She was now employed at the bank — doing, in fact, my job. That news was in itself disquieting — who ever heard of a woman good with numbers? — but I'd set my reservations aside last summer when that news came to me in one of her previous letters. I asked her to check through the files to find out what she could of Moore's business. She found a loan authorized to him, but never collected.

I must know more. I apply for leave, but before my request can be decided, we are ordered to move back to Richmond. There has been a huge battle near Fredericksburg, the Yankees have been thrashed — again — and they are heading back to Washington. Lee and Jackson whipped them without two-thirds of Longstreet's Corps. Now the far flung units of the Army of Northern Virginia are being recalled for another summer of campaigning. We are united in hoping that this summer's campaign will be decisive — the summer that the Yankees finally realize they can't beat us and might as well call it off. Michael Moore's question will have to wait. The Sixth South Carolina has work to do.

My recollection
of the War of Secession
or the War Between the States

By Miss Hanna H. Coleman

In '63 my brother William procured a furlough and came to see us, it was a joyful home coming, mother looked ten years younger. he brought us a chicken that he had, had in camp, he called her Susan Jane. Susan Jane was a little chick, when a soldier who had been on a foraging, expedition captured her. brother bought her and every night she slept under his bunk; when she grew larger, (our soldiers were then in winter quarters,) she would lay an egg every other day, which meant, muffins for breakfast, when she came to us, and saw chickens for the first time, she took to her heels and ran as if the enemy were after her, sure enough.

CHAPTER 14

We are assigned to George Pickett's division, but something has gone wrong. We marched up quickly from Suffolk. May became June, and we have been, despite our haste, sitting in camp. Corse's Brigade and Jenkins's Brigade are still in Richmond; the brigades of Garnett, Armistead and Kemper are nowhere to be seen, nor is the rest of the Army of Northern Virginia.

Micah Jenkins, our brigadier, has come storming back to our new camp near Richmond twice in June, almost but not quite treating his fine horse savagely in his bad temper. He has been to see Adjutant General Samuel Cooper, the top ranking general in our army, Jefferson Davis's adviser. He has even, some say, been to see Davis himself.

Jenkins' is insulted that our brigade is apparently to be left behind on whatever campaign is taking place this summer. Camp gossip has it that Lee got permission for whatever it is he is doing only by promising to leave two strong brigades behind to safeguard Richmond from a surprise attack up the Peninsula. That would be us.

Davis and the Confederate Congress didn't much like the way Lee had been taken by surprise by Joe Hooker in the Wilderness around Chancellorsville. Yes, it all turned out well — if you call losing Stonewall Jackson on the day of his greatest victory a good thing — but nobody was too happy about the way Hooker had, early in May, taken his huge army and moved it 30 miles undetected. Had the Yankees not lost their nerve after Jackson fell on them like an Old Testament curse, some say, we might be seeing them in Richmond's streets right now.

Men are of several minds about our fortunes this summer. This Lee has made a name for himself — and for our Army of Northern Virginia — but the name has been bought with our blood. We are glad to be victors time after time. That is certainly preferable to being the vanquished. But there is some talk that Lee is reckless with our blood.

I have received more letters from Elizabeth. Her talk of home has kindled a fire in me to see familiar places.

In the first days of July we get wonderful news — our army is in Pennsylvania and has routed the Yankees again. No sooner have Richmonders begun celebrating than more news follows — after a three-day fight, our army is in retreat, with heavy losses. By the second week of July trains filled with wounded are making their way into Richmond, destined for Chimborazo, the huge hospital set up in tents and hastily erected frame barracks. Word circulates that at last the army met its match: Yankees defending their own land demonstrate even more valor than we have already seen, again and again, in Virginia and Maryland. And this time they were well handled, at least after the first day.

We have mixed reactions to news that the other three brigades in Pickett's division played a major and costly role in a massive three-division assault on the final day. The numbers are chilling: two brigadiers dead, Kemper not expected to live; seven colonels dead, six wounded; half the men who started the assault either did not come back or came back wounded. There are stories of a stone wall, of Yankees standing and cheering when our attack was turned back, shouting "Fredericksburg! Fredericksburg!" across a bloody, torn field strewn with broken bodies.

We would have been in that assault. We debated the "what ifs" late into the nights. To Jenkins, it is all perfectly clear: Had we been there we would have carried the day. He does not envision failure. This despite the loss of 13 colonels in Pickett's division alone.

The body of the army — what is left of it — is still well north and west of Richmond, between Richmond and the Union army. We, however, remain near Richmond, a fact that agitates Jenkins. He tries mightily to get us sent to an active command. It seems not much will now happen in Virginia the rest of this year, with the army greatly needing a period of recuperation and the Yankees, apparently, content simply with driving us out of Pennsylvania. Jenkins wants us moved west, to recover Vicksburg — the other great defeat of July.

Late in July Jenkins is galvanized by a message from Lee, one he reads to each regiment at morning parade.

> Dear General Jenkins,
>   I regret exceedingly the absence of yourself and your brigade from the battle of Gettysburg. There is no telling what a gallant brigade, led by an efficient commander, might have accomplished when victory trembled in the balance. I verily believe the results would have been different if you had been present.
>   Sincerely Yours,
>   R.E. Lee

Jenkins is quite puffed up by this, and word circulates — one never knows the source of these stories, but they are always plausible — that Longstreet has also publicly spoken of the absence of Jenkins's and Corse's brigades in terms that make it clear he wished we had been there.

Those who have been with the Sixth Regiment since Sumter — there are still quite a few — note that this is the second time we have missed out on a chance to strike a meaningful, possibly decisive blow. The regiment arrived late at First Manassas and was, at the time the Yankees broke and ran, the only unfought regiment on the field. At that battle, any unit that saw combat was so disorganized as to be incapable of effective action, regardless of the outcome of the fighting on any part of the field. We were, therefore, perfectly positioned to march hard on the heels of the fleeing Yankees and perhaps galvanize the rest of the army into pursuit. And we were exceptionally well drilled for a regiment in the summer of 1861, thanks to the relentless ministrations of Charles Winder, later killed serving under Jackson. We were instead kept on the field, in rain, doing nothing except contemplate the wreckage of humanity that littered the field.

Others say the war does not permit of decisive blows, that the time when a nation's destiny could be changed by one day of fighting — Agincourt, Hastings — are gone forever, that nations are now like terrible machines grinding away at each other. It makes for interesting discussion around the campfire, but most appear to have missed the significance of both Lee's and Longstreet's remarks: Both men are aware of the brigade and see it as having potential. This is good news if you are Micah Jenkins and pursue glory; it is not so good news if your desires flow more toward preserving body and soul intact. The portent is that we will see action.

On August 10 I get leave — 30 days. I use four of them just traveling. One can draw an almost straight line running southwest from Richmond to Chester, and find railroad tracks following that straight line. Unfortunately — for me and for anyone else wishing to move merchandise, people or troops — there are four separate railroads involved, each with its own width of track. This was apparently designed to protect each railroad from the acquisitional urges of its neighbors, and is duplicated across much of the South, a Hobbesian approach to free enterprise. The advantages to railroad owners may be obvious, but the disadvantages to travelers are equally obvious.

I am but a soldier, with a blanket roll. My arms and accoutrements are left behind with the Regiment, so I'm traveling light, just me and Susan Jane, one of our chickens. She had stopped laying, we believe just for the summer, and the Aaron Burr Mess had decreed that Susan Jane should also get a furlough, to restore her morale. It is a simple matter for me to jump off the train in Danville, walk across town to the other train, and get back on board. For a man and a chicken, this is nothing. For those traveling with belongings, however, the problem assumes large dimensions.

Many of those on the move appear to be women and children, not accompanied by men. This makes sense, given that so many men are with the armies. Many of the women and children are accompanied by trunks and chests, most of them bulky. This means that every time they must change trains, they need to hire porters and wagons to take their belongings from one station to the other — they are almost never nearby. Then they must arrange to purchase their tickets, and they sometimes find that a train is full, or that it won't run until the next day. They also find that some employees of these little two-bit railroads are not above making special arrangements — for a steep fee.

None of that affects me. I am on furlough, but Col. Bratton kindly gave me orders directing me to report to the commander of the Sixth Regt. Reserves in Chester for special duty — it means I travel at government expense, and with some degree of authority. I get priority in boarding. Even so, I don't abuse it; like most soldiers, I've become a master at finding comfort in small niches and quite a craftsman at the job of staying out of the way. No woman with children stayed behind on a baggage platform because I took her space.

The towns rumble past; I rattle from Richmond to Burkeville to Danville, losing a day in Danville because the only locomotive available was held up by a mechanical problem. Then it is on to Greensboro, North Carolina, and another change of train to get to Charlotte. Then — things are looking more familiar now — there is another delay before there is finally a train to Chester. I'm aboard, and we wait hours for it to start, in stifling heat. Finally, it wrenches itself into motion with a sickly howl from the whistle, which sounds like it has caught a case of croup. We lurch south, jolting across the bridge over the Catawba near Nation Ford and rolling finally into the familiar fields and forests of South Carolina. There are interminable delays to shunt boxcars onto sidings — this is a mixed train, with both freight cars and a couple of passenger cars. Finally we reach Chester, and the wheezing old engine, leaking steam and hissing frightfully, shudders to a halt. I leap to the platform and wonder for a moment if I have come to the wrong town.

The station is crowded with people, travelers who surround the train's conductor and batter him with questions. There are mounds of baggage. Below the station, in the modest switching yard, there are piles of boxes, crates and barrels, and sentries. There are tents; Chester is now some kind of depot for military supplies. I walk across the tracks — the smell of hot iron and hot rocks. A warehouse has been taken over and turned into a hospital — there are dozens of sick and wounded men inside, apparently men taken from the trains because they were too ill to travel any farther. Inside, a man in shirtsleeves is tending to a groaning soldier sitting in a chair, and a girl with hair glowing copper in the sun is holding out a swatch of white cloth to him; a bandage. I've found a trackside hospital, I've found old Da Vega who isn't a doctor but runs a pharmacy, and I've found my little sister Hanna. I'm torn between delight at seeing her and horror at where I've found her.

"Hanna!" I bark. She turns, and Hanna is no longer the 12-year-old tomboy I remember but a young woman in her early teens. When she sees me the tomboy comes back and she races across the warehouse and hurls herself into my arms, shrieking and laughing.

"Brother William! Oh, brother, what a sight you are! Don't you know Colemans are supposed to stay out of the sun? You are a red and sunburned mess!"

And she bursts into tears, still laughing.

She notices Susan Jane.

"What? What are you doing with a chicken?" she asks.

"Surely you are confused," I tease her. "This is a golden goose."

I get the old look of exasperation from her.

"Eventually you'll tell me," she says. "Let's go find Mother."

We walk across the tracks, through the station and onto the streets of Chester, up the hill, past the triangle, heading to the northwest. Home. Still some magnolias in bloom, their sweet smell coming strong and true through the dry tickle of dust and the musty smell of "inside" coming from the open doors of houses we pass. Then we are turning onto the walk and then going through the door into the coolness of the brick house. Mother's shawl and bonnet on the pegs by the door. The smell of wax and polish. The ticking of the clock in the parlor. The smell of cleanliness. The smell of chicken roasting in the cookhouse outside. It rolls over me like a wave, and suddenly I realize I haven't eaten in more than a day. Home. I find myself trembling, and kind of float into the dining room and into a chair, where Mother find me. She gasps and calls out "William?"

I turn to her.

"Might I have some of that chicken?" I ask.

***

Hours later I am alone in my old room, trying to get comfortable on the too-soft bed and trying not to knock over anything. The room seems too small, too filled with things, many of which seem likely to break. It is home, but it is very strange and I feel very out of place. I cannot get used to the bed and finally spread a blanket on the floor and, filled with chicken, rice, cooked greens and about a gallon of milk, I sleep through the afternoon and evening and night.

***

I awake to breaking dawn and for a moment I'm annoyed with myself for waking up before musician's call. Then something stirs beside me. I open my eyes to see Susan Jane's beady black eye regarding me solemnly. I bestir myself to find the household already up and preparing breakfast. I also find that my uniform has disappeared and some of my clothing from before the war has been laid across a chair.

Hanna tells me that after I collapsed — her word — they attempted to put Susan Jane in with the rest of the chickens in the pen behind the house; she squawked and tried to get away from them, and after a few moments of uproar they decided it would do no harm to put her with me. I explained that Susan Jane undoubtedly exhibited the contempt of the front-line veteran for the stay-at-home militia, but Hanna said it seemed more like terror.

While I am finishing breakfast I hear an odd clicking and wheezing, and an enormous black dog comes into the dining room.

"Rover!" Hanna cries, and gives him a hug. "William, this is the Yankee dog you sent us after Seven Pines."

The dog eyes me cautiously and takes a step away.

Mother comes into the room.

"William, that dog is very well mannered for a Yankee. He has been a good and loyal companion to us and he also has produced this."

She brings out a vest, beautiful, black — as black as the dog. I give Mother a questioning look.

"We had him sheared, and I had the hair spun. Astonishing, isn't it?"

Indeed. The vest is as fine as anything I've ever seen, and promises to be warm. And it doesn't smell a bit like dog. I am instructed, for a time, in the use of dog hair in clothing, in wood for making shoe soles, in the making of bone needles — a hundred household stopgaps undertaken to deal with the shortage of manufactured goods and cloth, all stopped by the Yankee blockade. The only thing no one seems to have found a satisfactory substitute for is coffee. Coffee is coffee and nothing else will do.

My brother John now comes into the kitchen and Hanna and my mother leave, on some domestic errand or another. He has grown and is almost a man, but fortunately he is still 17 and not eligible for conscription. He is eager to join, but Mother has heeded my letters and exerted all her power and guile to keep him home and safe.

"I wish to smite the Yankees, brother," he tells me as I linger over breakfast.

"They smite back, John," I joke.

"A nation of cowards," he retorts.

I feel myself turning red — a relative thing, of course, because Colemans are some shade of red at all times. I am surprised to feel anger, and even more surprised when it seizes control.

John's arm is suddenly in my grip and my face is close to his.

"You speak as a child," I hiss at him so the women in the next room don't hear. "They are as brave as us. They believe in their cause as we believe in ours. We are butchering each other and when we are not doing that we are sickening and dying in camp, both sides. War is stupid, and you are a stupid boy, although it is not your fault you are stupid. Listen: The Yankees attacked us 12 separate times across the same ground at Fredericksburg, they lost 5,000 men in an afternoon. That was stupid, but it was brave. Was that the act of cowards? They aren't afraid to fight and they've shown us again and again and again that they are no more afraid of dying than we are. And dying is what we are doing best. Sometimes I think this war will not end until we are all dead. It goes on because both sides have lost so many lives that they can only justify the loss by going on."

"War is stupid. You stay out of it. One Coleman is enough, Mother and Hanna need you. Stay home. If you come to the front I'll break your Goddamned arm and you'll be sent home."

He is shocked beyond words to find the gentle brother he used to know converted into a scowling madman with a grip of steel — two years in the army have changed me, mentally and physically. John backs out the door, still trying to find words. Finally he just turns and bolts.

The day brings a steady stream of visitors, including some soldiers recuperating from wounds, seeking word of friends with various regiments. Few ask about the conduct of the war. What they seek is word of their friends and relatives.

Finally the stream of visitors halts. I find a coat that still somewhat fits — all seem to be too tight across the shoulders and chest, I'm disappointed at how they have shrunk — and I head next door in search of Elizabeth. Her housemaid informs me she is "at work, at the bank," which of course I should have realized. My mind has played tricks. It has accepted the news that she holds my old job, but it has not then extrapolated that knowledge in any kind of useful way.

The walk through Chester fills me with odd emotions. It is good to be home, but home seems different. Even acknowledging that I, myself, am different, there is still more. Chester is slightly shabbier than it was. There are former soldiers in town — men who have lost limbs, whose service is done. I find myself avoiding them. There are also more strangers in town and I gradually realize, from their demeanor and from bits of various conversations I overhear, that these are people from distant regions who have been displaced by the war. That portions of the land had been made uninhabitable, I knew, but, again, my mind did not carry that knowledge forward. What happened to the people who used to live there? Obviously they went somewhere else. One of those places, it turns out, is Chester, which is just about as far from all the fighting as any place in the South.

The door to the bank is before me, a massive oak barrier that nevertheless opens silently and easily at a touch. The inside is much as I remember it: Polished dark wood, white walls, high windows with sunlight streaming in, dust motes floating in the air, and a general air of coolness and hushed, subdued discussion from the various tellers and clerks and customers.

And in the midst of all this decorum and order and church-like solemnity sits Elizabeth, her chestnut hair tightly bound up, consulting with Thomas Mantour. He, like Chester, seems different to me. Smaller, for one thing. And — furtive? He seems to be having difficulty looking me straight in the eye. It occurs to me that if this man ordered me to advance against an armed enemy, I'd wait to see him out in front before moving. It is a marvel to me that this man once gave me orders. Even more marvelous: I once coveted this man's approval.

"Coleman," he says, advancing a hand toward me. "How marvelous."

I nearly laugh out loud, but stop just in time and adopt a look that I hope is neither obsequious nor stern. I take his damp hand and give it a firm shake.

"Mr. Mantour."

"Coleman, you know the Widow Gifte? She has taken over many of your duties. Surprising how a woman can do that, but, you know, we haven't had much choice. Look around. Mostly women, with all you men gallivanting off to war."

"Yes, well, sir, as I recall, some of us were gallivanted. I recall a receipt for women's underpinnings," I tell him, and he turns white.

"Well," he harrumphs, and a crafty look comes over his pudgy features. "Well, we must not hold Andrew's youthful excesses against him," he says, looking at me from the corner of his eyes. From this I take it that Andrew is to be blamed for the petticoats. I don't believe it.

"And how is Andrew? I understand he commands the Sixth Regiment Reserve," I say. Mantour fidgets.

"Um, no, well, he does, but he is in Spartanburg, recruiting. He wants to go back to Virginia," Mantour snorts indignantly. "The boy does not know where his best interests lie."

"The boy," I say, emphasizing the term, "stopped being a boy on a December day in Dranesville."

Elizabeth intervenes at this point.

"William, how wonderful to see you alive and unhurt after all you've been through. Perhaps you would like to escort me to the hotel for dinner? You may be able to explain some things about this job I find puzzling."

I bow stiffly to Mantour and, when Elizabeth has collected her bonnet and a basket, give her my arm. It is but a short distance to the hotel, where Elizabeth asks for a corner table, away from the crowd. With a silent apology to Susan Jane, I order chicken again.

Elizabeth is all business.

"I have figured something out,' she says. "Mantour is a scoundrel."

She lays a letter on the desk.

It is a letter from Michael Moore, the gist of which is that he has enlisted in A.J.'s militia company, at Mantour's suggestion, and is again seeking a new loan, not just to set crops, but to buy more land and to retire his old mortgage as part of the transaction. He noted that his brother, John, was his partner in the expanded farm — almost a plantation — he hoped to establish with the money. The letter is dated shortly before the day I dismissed him in favor of dinner — the day I left the bank. It appears I am not the only person who joined the militia under pressure, and it appears Mantour used more than petticoats to try to feed his ambitions for his son.

"Well," I tell Elizabeth, "at least his family got the benefit of the money. I never found a use for the petticoat."

She is shaking her head.

"The money never changed hands," he said. "Mantour didn't keep his end of the bargain. Moore's family was ruined that summer, they had no money for seed, they had little crop, and the bank took the farm for the unpaid mortgage."

Moore's animosity is finally explained.

My recollection
of the War of Secession
or the War Between the States

By Miss Hanna H. Coleman

   Our town was filled with the military all of the time, Hoods
entire force, passed through here, from the West, going to reinforce Johnstone. I saw most of the prominent generals, had bows,
and sometimes words from them, as they passed by our gate. Beauregard, Hood, Longstreet, Cheatum, Joe Wheeler, Bragg Joe. Johnstone,
Nat Evans, Gen. Morgan etc., they were fine looking men, Beauregard
I thought exceedingly neat and dignified, and Joe Wheeler handsome
and dashing looking with his crimson sash waving and black plumes.
Gen. Cheatems men stayed several days, meaning no disrespect, the
Gen. took aboard a little more than he could carry, and was inca-
pacitated, for a time, when he came to himself the alarm was sounded, to arms! and the men came rushing to ranks from all quarters.
One soldier was in the barbershop, and fell in ranks with one side
of his face shaved. They soon left, to catch up with their comrades
already on the march.

CHAPTER FIFTEEN

The days pass, slowly at first, then more quickly. I find that beneath the veneer of bustle and activity, Chester is still the same town I remember; fewer young men, women more in evidence than ever. There is a new section in the cemetery. These are soldiers who have died on the trains, or men who have died in town after being dropped off the trains as too seriously wounded to continue traveling. Old Da Vega is keeping a list of their names and which graves they are in; there are about 30 so far. I visit Capt. Obadiah Hardin's grave — he is the only Chester soldier whose body has been sent home. Of course he died a hero, holding the flag at Dranesville after the color bearer was wounded, and he died in December of 1861, before the pace of killing increase so dramatically. Now there just isn't time to ship all the bodies home. The rest of Chester's dead soldiers are waiting in distant Virginia graves. Someday more may be brought back to Chester, but some will surely stay where they are. It troubles me that some graves are unmarked. No one will ever be able to put flowers on those graves. That is grievous for the families of the dead men; it is as if a husband or brother or son simply disappeared, rather than died.

Elizabeth won't talk about Michael Moore's land, saying only that she has just about convinced old Mantour that he must make amends. The desire for a confrontation with the old scoundrel still burns in me, but I have learned, along with how to sleep on the ground and how to make lobscouse, how to be patient. I spend a lot of time with Elizabeth, when her duties at the bank do not occupy her. I am content to eat chicken, tomatoes, rice and cheese and all the other food that two years in the army have made me appreciate. I am content to laze about, to have the old men of the town buy me drinks, to tell polite lies about how fine we have it in the army, to catch the amused looks of the other veterans — those who are home because they have lost an arm, a hand, their eyesight — when I tell these polite lies.

Near the end of the month a dusty boy on a dusty mule arrives in town, looking for me. He bears a note from Col. Asbury Coward, the commander of the 5th South Carolina, based in nearby Yorkville. Coward is home, sadly enough, to bury one of his children. Odd to think of death occurring other than in the army, but it does.

> Coleman: Stay in Chester, do not return to your regiment. Find others on leave from any regiments in the brigade, or in Hood's Division; tell them the same. Send word to me here on how many you find. More instructions to follow. I act on Jenkins's authority, and now so do you.

It is signed, as is his whim, A. Coward, Yorkville.

I derive two points from this: We are now somehow involved with Hood's Division, and there is to be some movement of our brigade, and rather soon, that would move it from where I expect it to be on Sept. 1, when I am supposed to report back.

Nothing for it but to do my duty, and in not much time I find there are three men besides myself who meet Coward's specifications. The dusty boy on his dusty mule is on his way back up the dusty road to Yorkville within an hour, chewing on the last of four fried chicken drumsticks we fed him for dinner after listening to his growling stomach.

Elizabeth frowns when she learns of Col. Coward's summons, for surely that is what it will be.

"William," she says as we sit on the swing on Mother's porch. "William, how long have we known each other?"

"All our lives," I answer truthfully.

"And how long have we been spending our time with each other?"

"Before I joined the Sixth we had been in each other's company quite frequently," I respond.

"Could it be said we have an understanding?" Elizabeth asks, not looking at me.

"I have often hoped that could be said," I respond, surprising myself with an answer that might actually be clever.

She stamps her foot.

"William, the expectation of every resident of Chester is that we shall be married. Are you aware of that?"

In fact I am not, and being somewhat preoccupied with trying to think about what Coward's note might portend, I am caught moving by the flank by her volley, and quite enfiladed.

"I have not been in Chester for two years," is my response, while looking for good ground upon which to rally.

"Let me assure you that this is the case. I invite you to ask any person walking by what they think our understanding is," Elizabeth persists.

Reinforcements arrive, in the person of a corporal with horrible scars on his face, one of Hood's men, seeking me out in response to the inquiries sent about because of Coward's note. With great relief I take him across the street and chat with him about where he can be found if there is an urgent summons.

"William?" Elizabeth begins when I return to the porch.

"Did you see that man, Elizabeth? His face?" I ask. "Could you love that man? I believe our understanding should remain an understanding until this war is finished."

She is shaking her head.

"It is very hard for the women who do not have a man," she says. "You do not know. There are the women who have husbands, sons, brothers and fathers at the front. Then there are those whose husbands remain at home. Then there are those like me, women who have not married or who lost their husbands so long ago — everything that happened before the war almost seems like it is ancient and happened to someone else. I am regarded as a single woman, William, and in addition to being attended by prospective suitors, I sometimes find myself approached by others whose intentions are less than honorable. This war has changed much, including manners."

I feel the heat rising in my face.

"Who?" I ask, furious.

She shakes her head.

"That is not the point. Thrashing such a person is not the answer I seek. There will be others."

The war has changed much, indeed. For a woman to almost solicit a proposal of marriage would have been unthinkable two years ago.

"Elizabeth," I begin, taking her hands, "it was of course my understanding that someday we would be married, but surely you have left out one category of woman: Those who impulsively married when war broke out, and who are now widowed, or caring for men who are crippled in mind and body. Surely you will not risk that?"

"I would risk it," she whispers, turning away from my eyes.

I feel the waters of the Rubicon splashing on my ankles.

"Elizabeth, will you marry me?"

"Oh, William, what a nice surprise!" she has the audacity to respond, smiling devilishly and making me a curtsy. "Of course I will marry you."

And so it was, with arrangements made with haste but not unseemly haste — wartime marriage has become somewhat of an industry in all our towns, it seems, and certain conventions have been abandoned and replaced by expedients justified "because of the war" — that on Sept. 9th, 1863, I find myself married. Elizabeth's home becomes my home, my belongings are carried there by a still-cold John and a giggling Hanna, my mother gives me a hug, and for one night I am a married man, the details of which I am not committing to this journal. Convention may have gone to hell because of the war, but there are limits ....

Only one night, because on Sept. 10th, Col. Coward and a makeshift detachment of Yorkville men swing into town at noon, just as the first of what will be dozens of troop trains rumbles into Chester, taking thousands of men — including Jenkins's Brigade, which Coward says is indeed now part of Hood's Division — west to join Joe Johnston somewhere outside Chattanooga. The Chester contingent is assembled and Coward arranges for one boxcar from the Chester rail yard to be attached to the first train, to accommodate us and others from Longstreet's Corps who have been gathering here from other points in South Carolina. We will not wait for the brigade, but will proceed to the final destination and do what we can to make things ready for the brigade's arrival; Coward has been in touch with Jenkins and Longstreet by telegraph, and this is the plan.

It is sudden — there is one hour to say good-bye to everyone, to see to the Chester men who are going, to try to find some food to take with us, for we are thinking like soldiers and that means we are thinking about food. It is all done at a terrible fast pace in blinding midday heat. There is no time to do what I have been putting off doing, confront Mantour about Moore's family — it will have to wait. The last clear image I carry with me is of Mrs. William Coleman standing on the platform at the Chester station, bravely waving a handkerchief at me as the train lurches west. The black dog is beside her, still regarding me with a coolness I find disconcerting. Does the beast's tail never wag?

CHAPTER SIXTEEN

We rumble and clank across South Carolina and into Georgia, picking up more men along the way. We also pick up rations — this is a massive logistical undertaking, and someone has gone to extraordinary lengths to create what amounts to a huge pipeline, with men and supplies pouring into it in Virginia and coming out the other end in the railroad depot in Atlanta. In Atlanta, however, things change. We have moved out of the jurisdiction of the Army of Northern Virginia and the arrangements made by the Confederate high command, and into the jurisdiction of the Army of Tennessee, Braxton Bragg commanding. His arrangements appear not to have been made; the gush of men and equipment into Atlanta begins to build and swell, and there is no planning nor provender to move us to the Army of Tennessee itself, many miles away somewhere between Chattanooga and Atlanta.

Longstreet arrives with the second train and immediately gets into a fracas with Bragg's quartermaster over a variety of issues, including the lack of horses. It apparently was understood by Longstreet that horses from the Army of Tennessee would be provided to his artillery, thus sparing the need for more trains to transport horses and their forage from Richmond to Atlanta. This was not understood by Bragg.

Those of us who traveled with Coward, a diverse group from many regiments, are put to work as runners and workers until our own regiments catch up. I am content to shift bags of rice, but Coward remembers that I am good with figures and literate and have commissary experience, and I soon find myself assigned to Longstreet's staff as a clerk and general factotum. It is an interesting job. Having served, as it were, on the "retail" end of the supply line with the regiment, it is an eye-opener to me to see what goes into finding, tracking, collecting and dispensing the food and equipment for an entire army — the "wholesale" end.

It is interesting, also, because of the proximity to headquarters. We have never been under any illusion that our military leaders are anything but men like ourselves, but this close-up daily view of generals leads me to understand that, yes, they are men like me, but with somewhat of a different take on things. It is very important to maintain protocols, apparently, with significance attached to whether one general sends another general his "respects" or his "compliments" as a prelude to a communication. A subordinate respects his superior; only a superior can issue a compliment. This is more important than casual thought would suppose, because it helps keep straight who is giving orders and who is taking them — a critical issue when men's lives are on the line. It is the same as an enlisted man saluting an officer — you do it to signal acknowledgment of different roles in the hierarchy that is the army. But these salutes, physical and verbal, are also critical to some egos, who have confused the use of courtesies as signals for something valuable in itself. And egos are clashing among the generals, who seem these days to be learning from the French at Agincourt rather than the French under Napoleon. Right now there is some tension between Bragg and Longstreet; Longstreet is clearly supposed to report to Bragg's army, but just as clearly considers himself the equal if not the superior of Bragg in stature if not in position or rank. There is not much exchange of compliments and respects taking place between Longstreet, momentarily in Atlanta, and Bragg, somewhere near Chattanooga. The natural competition between two strong men is made worse by Longstreet's belief that the lack of support for him to move his divisions forward is a deliberate slight by Bragg. It is supposed by headquarters wags that Bragg is somewhat miffed at the idea that the Army of Northern Virginia may be seen as coming to his rescue after he gave up Chattanooga without much in the way of a fight.

Be that as it may, for those of us exposed to the operations of a headquarters for the first time, the waves of troops leaping from the trains and quickly forming up for a fast meal at the depot, arranged by the civilians of Atlanta, is an inspiring time. And, truthfully, the lack of foresight by Bragg's commissary is not an immediate problem. Every regiment moving by train found itself assaulted in every town by civilians eager to feed the army; there is a sense among these people that this massive move by rail is unprecedented, something that could only happen in our modern age, and they want to share it. There is also a sense that this much energy is not being expended for nothing, that a thunderbolt is aimed at the Yankee armies somewhere to the north and west — that many of the brave boys jauntily riding atop the boxcars are destined for blood and death. The civilians are trying to pay a debt that will soon be owed by flooding the boys with food, and the regiments are, as they leap off the trains, encumbered by sacks of food. That they have been given more than they could eat on the trip is unusual, given the usual practice of soldiers of eating everything they can as soon as they can. The last-arriving regiments are surfeited as fully as the first: just astonishing, for thousands of boys are involved in this movement.

We move Longstreet's headquarters forward into the field, with Bragg, somewhere in the north of Georgia — I'm not sure where I am and it doesn't much matter. There we find that an attack is planned, that Longstreet is to command two divisions from the Army of Tennessee — that Bragg, who did nothing at Chattanooga for long weeks, is now moving before all of Longstreet's troops are up. Word has come in that Yankees pushing at our line have fallen back and are now moving north, back toward Chattanooga. This would appear to be a slender reed upon which to base an assault, but what does a mere commissary sergeant, even one working at what amounts to corps headquarters, really know?

September 19th is spent in confusion, but, for us, no fighting; it is taking place somewhere in the forests off to the east. I am pressed into service as a courier — given a horse, despite my protests that my riding skills are nearly nonexistent. It is a day of pain and confusion for me, of hanging on desperately while galloping up and down the road back toward Atlanta, trying to find commands and deliver orders, being cursed by colonels, having suggestions thrown at me for what to do with the horse from soldiers who laugh while watching my desperate attempts to avoid being unhorsed. Nevertheless we move forward, and arrive in the middle of the night. Longstreet, Bragg and other generals I don't know spend a long hour meeting to decide what to do.

At dawn on the 20th there is hell to pay, and not from the Yankees. D.H. Hill, in charge of a division, did not attend the meeting and could not be found by couriers sent to him in the middle of the night by Bragg, and as a result a planned dawn attack did not occur. Hill, it turned out, was at his headquarters, asleep in an unused ambulance; it was simply that no one knew where he was. Such a thing — a mere quirk of fate, that a tired man should seek the relative comfort of an ambulance instead of the ground — is enough to darken a reputation. A furious Bragg reportedly insulted Hill in front of his staff, and there is an unspoken insinuation in the air that Hill was showing the white feather. Words were exchanged — which must have in itself been interesting to hear, as Bragg has a squeaky and plaintive voice and Hill sounds like a crow with the croup. Hill is furious at the never-quite-spoken insult, and the fury spreads to his men. At 9 a.m. they assault the federal line in their front, break it, and drive into the federal rear, spreading chaos in their wake. The assault is finally halted when the federal commander shifts brigades to get in Hill's path, but the resulting confusion on the federal side gives us a remarkable opportunity.

We go into the fray, in support of Hill; Hood's division, what there is of it, finds a hole in the line where a federal brigade has apparently been pulled to stem Hill. Hood's regiments pour through the breach, crumbling the blue regiments still in line on each side. They break, and run. Longstreet seizes the moment and hurls all the troops under his command forward, all in columns of companies moving through thick woods, deploying into explosive lines of battle when they break into the Union rear. He then sends word back to Bragg, taking care to note that "Harvey Hill has blown a hole clear through their line and the road to Chattanooga is open." In other words, giving credit to an Army of Tennessee general, and to a man Longstreet respects.

Bragg falters, but the corps commanders do not, pressing forward along the line despite opposition that stiffened as the route forward narrowed and federal reinforcements were pressed into our front to slow down our advance. There is savage fighting, in heavy timber and brushy fields, much of it face to face, and because I am still a courier, I see much more of it than usual, even though I am not called upon to take part in any of it. I am merely required to keep from getting killed so that messages can be delivered. This conjoining of parallel interests — duty and personal safety — I find to be a most comfortable fit. Darkness falls, and couriers from along the line are sent back to the headquarters commands with news that the federals who had dug in across our front at the end of the day are pulling out, heading toward Chattanooga.

Bragg does nothing. We — couriers brought to Bragg's headquarters by our respective commands in the event orders must be sent out as a result of this post-sunset meeting --hear voices raised in argument from the grove of oaks where the generals are meeting. The gist of Bragg's position is that his army is used up and must be brought back to order before an advance can be made. Longstreet and Hill and others I don't recognize are upset, and argue that failing to follow up robs the victory of its value.

As they argue, there is a disturbance in the air on the road from Atlanta. Something is coming — the soldier strewn on the side of the road sense it, they are getting to their feet and looking south.

And into view, gleaming silver in the bright moonlight that would make pursuit possible without the confusion of trying to maneuver in darkness, comes Micah Jenkins, at the head of his brigade, moving swiftly and in good order up the road. There are more brigades behind his — the rest of the Army of Northern Virginia troops, thousands of men, all combat veterans. They are disciplined, unfought, somewhat tired but available for immediate duty. It is exactly the orderly, competent, battle-ready force Bragg says he needs. The hair stands up on the back of my neck; There is power here.

The generals come out of their grove to see what the disturbance might be. Jenkins, spotting Longstreet, trots over, dismounts, salutes and asks a question. Longstreet smiles — long since we have seen that — and takes Jenkins over to Bragg. Bragg keeps his same expression — as if he had bit an unripe persimmon. There is more acrimony. The generals have lowered their voices, but there is no disguising the venom. One general puts himself within inches of Bragg's face; the fury of his posture makes words superfluous. Bragg turns way and folds his arms. Longstreet's shoulders slump. Bragg refuses to believe that the Yankees have really left the battlefield at Chickamauga Creek.

The column passes; in the quiet that then settles down, the mockingbirds take advantage of the moonlight and fill the air with mimicry. It is as if we are surrounded by every species of bird on the continent, but really it is just a few mockingbirds.

All the next day we are idle. Regiments are advanced a few hundred yards, then pulled back. Longstreet is beside himself. Jenkins is frantic with disbelief. In the midst of all this I am released from Longstreet's headquarters, and report back to the Sixth South Carolina. I am greeted warmly and barraged with questions, but a quiet word from John Bratton keeps me mum on much that I have seen. I regale them with tales of red tape. I do not tell them I am now a married man, and I do not know why I keep silent.

The next day we cautiously, oh so cautiously, move the army north toward Chattanooga. We move through the debris left by an army that is defeated — abandoned weapons, mountains of supplies, wagons left behind with horses or mules still in harness, unburied dead. Dead who died crawling away from us, crawling as far as they could get before being taken. There are terribly wounded Yankees along the road. The foolishness of our hesitation is clear to every man in the ranks: This Yankee army, with the exception of a few brigades, was utterly defeated.

We creep up into the heights overlooking Chattanooga and the Tennessee River — beautiful vistas, with the Yankees clearly visible and crawling like busy ants about their business, far away. Longstreet's two divisions, now united, are on the western flank of the Confederate army, on a height aptly called Lookout Mountain. We can look down from here and see just how the Yankee army has got itself corked up tight — we can have a chokehold on their supplies, because Chattanooga is easily cut off.

We have a month of relative ease, simply putting up some basic earthworks. The position is not easily defended. It is in fact impossible to defend, although I would not have said so without two years of soldiering behind me. The mountain is dreadfully steep, but it is huge — long. There are not enough of us to defend all of it, it is heavily timbered and cut by ravines, meaning there are just too many rat holes for us to hope to plug them all. We put up defenses at the approaches, but each is too far from the next to be mutually supportable. A fast, strong attack could overwhelm any one position. The belief of our generals is, apparently, that the impossibility of advancing on the mountain without being seen will give us ample time to shift forces to the threatened point. That is not our concern; we bask in the autumn sunshine, enjoying the sight of leaves on the mountainsides turning gold and red, savoring the smells and crispness of weather that is pleasant. There is a vague feeling that we ought to be exploiting the fine weather by maneuvering, but we are content to wait for our quarreling generals to decide on a course.

There is some kind of flare-up between Evander Law and Jenkins. Law moved his entire brigade into the valley below Lookout Mountain, then left to visit Hood. Hood was wounded at Chickamauga, the second major wound in two months, and there is doubt he will survive. Jenkins — acting as temporary commander of Hood's Division — discovered what Law did, and moved his brigade back with the rest of the division, touching off a fury of accusations. The problem appears to be vague instructions from Longstreet and even vaguer orders from Bragg, who is wont to be vague so that he can then claim his subordinates failed to carry out his orders, if things go awry. Which they seem to do quite frequently in the Army of Tennessee. This is all just fodder for the fighting between

Law and Jenkins — any opportunity for a misunderstanding is an opportunity for a fight. The end result is more bad blood between Jenkins and Law, who have been feuding for some time. Both want command of Hood's Division. It is difficult for those of us from South Carolina to reconcile this feud with the former friendship of the two men. Law was at one point an instructor in Jenkins' Kings Mountain Academy, the military school in Yorkville he founded prior to the war. The thoughtful point out that our generals seem most prone to fighting with each other whenever things are not going well in the field. Vicksburg, Gettysburg, and a squandered, bloody victory at Chickamauga Creek surely make "not going well" a vast understatement.

This feud becomes an issue for all of us when the two men are given an opportunity to cooperate in a key venture, but fail to do so.

The Yankees, with two armies combined in Chattanooga and a Confederate army sitting on its best supply routes, are starving. Desperation breeds resourcefulness. The Yankees, showing the kind of alacrity that Stonewall Jackson would have praised, in late October pry open the pantry door by hurling two brigades across two river crossings in one night, brushing aside a force we had at Brown's Ferry — a force under Law's command — and digging themselves in very deeply. They are embedded like ticks in the landscape, and are halfway to setting up a shortened and much more efficient supply route back to the end of their pipeline 25 miles to the west in Bridgeport, Alabama. They control the river up to Bridgeport, and now from Brown's Ferry back to Chattanooga. All that remains is Lookout Valley and a notch through Raccoon Mountain, the next mountain to the west. We can spot them moving troops up from the southwest, but the valley is five miles wide; our artillery can't command the route. It is a task for infantry.

Our high command seems to believe itself outdone by the Yankees in the area of night operations, and eager to prove we can also work effectively at night. On Oct. 28 we are called to fall in at 6 p.m. A small Yankee force has been spotted separated from the rest of the newly arriving federals and Hood's Division has been given the task of capturing them and severing the supply route through Lookout Valley. Jenkins will attack the camp, on the south, with Bratton in command of Jenkins' brigade, backed by Benning's brigade in reserve; Law, by virtue of his better knowledge of the terrain from earlier (botched) assignments, will set up a blocking line to pen up the main Yankee force, which has marched up to Brown's Ferry and is camped there. Robertson's small brigade of Texans, staunch veterans but one of the units torn to pieces at Gettysburg, will be Law's reserve.

Night operations are something of a rarity, since so many things work against their success. Presumably a night attack is to be a surprise, meaning noise must be kept to a minimum. But noise — the commander's voice — is the only means of communication at night, when our flags can't be seen and when our eyes can't pick out the alignment and take the direction of march. Since we will probably be attacking through forest — most of the valley is wooded — there is a fair likelihood that this will be a mess.

"It is just as dark for the Yankees," McClure observes before we set out.

"But they will be setting still. All they have to do is defend," I point out.

"We will get them up and moving, then we'll see," McClure says. "It seems to me we need not be organized to perfection, only more organized than them. We can do this."

I shrug, but in the gloom I doubt he can see it. It is not a time for expressing doubt. It's a time for having faith. McClure has it. I'm working on it.

We check each other for noise by the simple expedient of standing in place and jumping up and down. Anything that will make a noise is easily located and dealt with. Canteens are filled up, tin plates and cups are wrapped in our blankets or in rags in our haversacks, and the musicians are simply ordered to leave their drums and fifes at division headquarters and fall in at the rear to help the surgeons. We have one brigade bugler, who will be at Jenkins' side; all we expect to hear from him is basic calls, especially "advance," after we have quietly gotten ourselves lined up in something like close enough proximity to the Yankee camp.

It is a slow and tedious march, but it is, much to my surprise, done fairly quietly. And — a variation on McClure's concept of relative efficiency — it is not necessary to be absolutely quiet. The Yankees are on the move themselves. A certain amount of movement is what they expect to hear, because their own troops are still arriving and sorting themselves out on the road from Raccoon Mountain to Brown's Ferry. The key will be launching our assault before they realize their peril.

Luck favors us. The Yankees have not extended their sentinels as far forward as they should. Every veteran knows the sentinels are posted according to a simple formula: How much notice do you need to get your own main force on its feet and in line of battle before the enemy arrives? You calculate the time needed, convert it into distance according to terrain and visibility, and make sure your sentinels are that far out. And if necessary you have defensible picket posts that can slow up an enemy, to get you more time to plan a response. Careful probing by our scouts shows, however, that the Yankee sentinels are close to their camp, not more than 50 yards out in some cases. This is the mark of green troops, or at least a green commanding officer, and as the word whispers its way down the line we take heart.

We shuffle into the darkness, and our officers quietly try to line us up generally perpendicular to the direction we're going to go when the word comes; we lie down to wait. We are sweaty from marching and the night is chill; it gets cold. Finally, at 1 a.m., word snakes down the lines to rise, load, and fix bayonets, quietly. It is done. A bugle somewhere to the rear sounds 'Advance.' We rise and silently walk forward into the darkness. The order is "No shouting," since that will tend to disorder our movement and make it impossible to hear commands. We still have about 200 yards to go, but it is impossible to gauge distance in the darkness. Finally, to the left, sentinels call out challenges, and a few fire their weapons at the advancing shadows. We steadily surge forward; the sentinels in our front have fled, shouting an alarm. We break into an opening — a field — and see, in flickering firelight, a Yankee camp in the most incredible turmoil, with shouting and swearing and men trying to take their weapons from the stacks.

"Fire, fire on them, and advance," comes the command, and up and down the line we open up.

The Yankee confusion settles and then takes the form of movement away from our line, which is actually a line formed instinctively as the men broke out of the woods and into the open. It is a loose line, but it is a line. We are advancing through the camp. And advancing. Past blankets and dog tents and smoldering campfires and strewn haversacks and knapsacks. And still advancing through the camp.

It is a very large camp.

I am gnawing on this thought when a volley goes off in our faces and men fall on both sides of me. Another volley, to the left. Two more to the right.

Bratton is among us.

"Lie down! Return fire!" he shouts as he runs down the line. We are down, we are firing, but the return fire is terrific. This is clearly not the small force we had expected. There are thousands of

Yankees here. Their failure to extend pickets was not inexperience, it was arrogance: They never expected anyone to attack such a large force.

We have moved them, but we have not scared them. Not yet. Three of Bratton's regiments are on the ground in the Yankee camp, pouring fire into their position only a hundred yards ahead. From the right we see, by the flash of muzzles, another of our regiments extending around their left flank. Firing from the left moves ahead and seems to wrap around the Yankee position. It is the maneuver of an officer who knows himself to be in command of overwhelming force, or it is the maneuver of an officer with overwhelming confidence. I hope the Yankee commander thinks it is the former and I hope he is prone to panic. We are one regiment away from surrounding this huge Yankee force. Word comes to press forward, and we advance, firing, compressing the Yankees and threatening to lap around their rear.

No word is given, no command spoken, but suddenly our attack halts and we begin pulling back, disengaging first from the flanks. As we pull back we hear firing coming from our rear. The Yankees make a few pushes toward us, but their pursuit is half-hearted. We form up as best we can to march by the flank, and when we strike the railroad along the base of Lookout Mountain we deploy again into battle line, as the dawn breaks and we try to sort out what happened.

We never learn for sure what went wrong — secrecy increasingly surrounds our failures — but what we in the Sixth South Carolina come to believe is that we bit off more than we could chew and faced what almost seems like treachery at the same time.

We were not attacking a regiment, as we'd thought, but one of Geary's 12th Corps divisions — veterans of the Army of the Potomac sent west by train (taking a page from our book, this time) to reinforce the Yankees at Chattanooga. We were attacking a force four times our size — and almost succeeding, except that Law inexplicably failed to block another Yankee force sent out from Brown's Ferry when the din of our attack reached their ears. It was that force — another division — that fell upon Benning in our rear and prevented him from sending up the reserves. Even then, Jenkins reportedly sent word to Evander Law to advance his brigade and help save the day, which Jenkins believed was still possible given the enormous confusion. Law refused, and it is widely, if quietly, reported that he said "I will not win Micah Jenkins his major generalcy."

This is what it has come to: Jealous generals would rather see each other fail than the army succeed. There are reports that a court of inquiry will be held into the affair at Wauhatchie Creek, but the night's work plunges me into black despair. I am unscathed, and indeed the butcher's bill for this battle is not exorbitant, but that is a relative thing and a mark of just how much I have come to accept death as a normal part of existence. Many good boys are dead, and for nothing. So that two young hotspurs can add more braid to their kepis?

My recollection
of the War of Secession
or the War Between the States
By Miss Hanna H. Coleman

After Dr. Babcock came home (he had been promoted and was one of
the surgeons of the 6th Reg.) then was in a hospital in Richmond he
saw so many sick and wounded soldiers there, exposed to the weather, and unable to get home, he decided to get a vacant house and
open a hospital. He procured houses on a lot in front of our house,
the property belonged to the estate of my Uncle Richard Kennedy
and had been used as a carriage factory, there was one very large
building with a upstairs, this was filled, up and down stairs with
cots, procured from the Government supplies packed away here. And
these cots were soon occupied with the desperately sick, and men
whose wounds had been so neglected, that many an arm and leg was
amputated. The smaller houses on this lot were used, one for the
doctors office, the other for commissary stores, and another still
for a kitchen. Dr. Babcock did noble work for the soldiers, the
out houses on his own place were filled with cots, and many a poor
fellow found a quiet and comfortable resting place. As soon as the
critically ill who were in the hospital were convalesced, they were
sent to a private house, Young Gilmore Sims, a son of the author,
was taken by Mrs. Anna Kennedy and nursed back to life.

My mother had the furniture moved from one parlor and had it
fitted up for her boys, she asked for the friendless and poor, and
the room was never vacant. One poor little fellow from Georgia was
so grateful, when he left, he took my mothers hand and wished her
much joy, and that every hair in her head might be a tallow candle
to light her soul to glory, it was a poor speech but the best he
could do. Another little boy was from Marion, S.C. he was a mere
lad, 14 or 15 years old, and was pitiful to see, so thin and white
and covered with vermin, mother took a servant and bathed him and
cut his hair, putting fresh clean clothes on him, he was real pretty, after his ablutions, as he lay back on his pillow, his forehead so white and his eyes so blue. The poor fellow died, there was
no strength to build on. Still another of her boys was a skeleton,
named Jolly, poor Jolly was always cold, and would stay in the
kitchen, by the fire, the servants would get very vexed for, he was
neither neat, or particular.

Mr. Lester was Dr. Babcock's clerk, I think he spent most of his
time at the window looking out for me, He became very intimate with

our big dog Rover, and many a package of sugar Rover brought me, it was tied around his neck. Once Mr. Lester was sick, I wrote on a piece of paper, "how are you" and gave it to Rover, he came back after awhile with a long note.

There were two other hospitals in Chester, one in charge of Dr. Preileau, the old Academy, the building now used by Mr. Joe Walker as a private residence, this hospital too was filled with the sick and wounded.

Quite a number of brave soldiers died here, Dr. Babcock had them buried, at the cemetery, and had their graves marked, with the names of the soldier and, the company he belonged to. On each memorial day, now, the graves are strewn with flowers, and some day we hope to have a monument, bearing the name of each of the Chester men who wore the grey, and were so brave and loyal to the Confederacy.

CHAPTER SEVENTEEN

October becomes November. The weather turns from gold to grey, with dark clouds close enough to touch. We wake up twice to find ourselves in fog — so much for visibility from the top of Lookout Mountain. We extend our sentinels farther down the side of the mountain, trusting to Providence to give them time to scramble back to our lines if the Yankees make a push. But they appear to be content to occupy the valley and Chattanooga; they have a strong force in the valley, and have positioned a fortified battery to command the best descent route for troops down off the mountain.

When the weather turns even worse, we are given orders to march. We come down off Lookout Mountain on a night lashed by storms — shrill winds push drenching, cold rain on us, turning the steep roads into mud chutes. Two men in the regiment are hurt when they lose their footing and fall off the road into rock-strewn gullies. We reach the bottom, and wearily turn toward the northeast. An all-night march brings us to a railroad, but there is no train. There are also no rations, and we starve for three days, utterly at the mercy of Bragg's commissary, for there are no farms here, no civilians to beseech for food. The few civilians in the area of what we learn is called Tunnel Hill were all related to the railroad some way or another, no farmers, and have long since left. Soldiers from both armies plundered what little remained well before our arrival. Two divisions of men under Longstreet, 12,000 men, wait in hunger for a train that finally arrives, and we begin climbing aboard. The train takes us up the track about a hundred miles to Sweetwater, Tennessee, up the valley of the Tennessee River. There we disembark, and the trains go back for more of Longstreet's boys. At Sweetwater there is a rail yard, and in the rail yard are boxcars and in the boxcars, we happily discover, are rations. Soon the rail yard is filled with the smell of wood smoke and frying pork, and we are relatively happy. Arriving regiments are quickly issued rations, while we, Bratton's Brigade, South Carolinians being "first" again, are formed up and marched through the town, taking the road to the northeast that continues to parallel the railroad.

The Sixth is out in front, forming the advance guard for the entire march to the northeast, where we expect to find and cross the Tennessee River. We have two companies forward, well in advance, deployed as skirmishers, and a company on each side, deployed as flankers, a long thin line parallel to the road on each side. Six companies are within this "U" shape, on the road; behind us a half mile or so is the head of the main column, with the rest of Jenkins' brigade in the lead. The purpose is to find or trigger ambushes the Yankees may have put in the path of our march; since we have some of Gen. Joseph Wheeler's cavalry even farther out front, scouring a much wider area than our regiment can cover, an advance guard is somewhat of a formality. But it is a different kind of duty and makes the first part of the march more interesting. It also gives us first opportunity for some fast foraging before the rest of the army moves through, although there is precious little left to harvest in this high, wide valley. We snatch what we can — measly pumpkins, some overlooked ears of dried-up corn — on the fly. We are moving rapidly, and there is no such thing as stopping to pick a field clean or check out a spring house.

We make a meager bivouac that night, in weather that has turned fine. The next morning we are back with the brigade and the Palmetto Sharpshooters are in advance. We hear there are formidable fortifications at Loudon — which we built to stop the Yankees, but it didn't work. The Yankees now hold the town, which was where, until this summer, one of the biggest railroad bridges in the hemisphere was located, being more than 500 feet long, across our old friend the Tennessee. We are not looking forward to an assault on fortifications, but we need not have worried. Longstreet throws a feint towards Loudon then goes west six miles and crosses. The Sharpshooters told us they ran the final quarter mile, were thrown into a handful of boats, crossed the river upstream a short distance from a crossing point, and stampeded the few Yankees there. Our engineers quickly extend a pontoon bridge across the Tennessee and the rest of Jenkins' brigade is flung across the river. By the time the Yankees come back in some force to see what we're all about it is too late, we're across and on the move. We skirmish for several hours, but Loudon is ours without a real standup fight. The Yankees did have time to take up their own pontoon bridge at Loudon, put it on wagons and haul it up the road toward Knoxville.

Knoxville, it appears, is our goal. We learn from prisoners that we are up against Burnside. Some of us — a mere handful — remember Burnside from our brief attachment to Cobb's regiment above the stone bridge over Antietam Creek a year ago. Yet another army has been moved by rail from one side of the country to the other.

Jenkins is impatient; Knoxville may be the goal, but he has his own goals. The Yankees are moving toward Knoxville, not in panic, but in a determined, organized way. Jenkins pushes us hard and, by using cavalry, forces the Yankee rear guard to deploy several times to hold us back, to give their main body time to reach a defensible spot and throw up some earthworks. We are dealing now with mud — it has rained again — and it is exhausting and nerve-wracking work, over several days. We capture some of their guns, and they abandon wagons filled with supplies, apparently harnessing the teams to guns and caissons to move them more effectively through the mud. Since our own commissary is not functioning too well and since the landscape is scoured as thoroughly as any plague of locusts scoured Egypt, we are grateful for the effectiveness of the Yankee commissary. We pick up a good many wagons as we lurch through the mud toward Knoxville, but there is never any sense that we have inspired fear in the Yankee host. Since they are retreating toward their base, the loss of supplies is not serious to them.

Finally we think we have a good part of the Yankee force pinned, and the brigades of Hood's Division, commanded by Jenkins, launch an assault aimed at keeping them pinned while some other force turns them and takes them from their rear. It does not work — the other force is somehow misdirected, the jaws of the trap fail to close and the enemy, after delivering serious blows to our brigade, continues his march to Knoxville under cover of darkness. But there is a story within the story.

Evander Law somehow misdirects one of his regiments and his entire brigade collides with Robertson's brigade, throwing off the whole attack — an easy enough error in unfamiliar terrain that is covered with brush, where visibility is limited, and an attack made as the sun was setting. Jenkins, however, pitches a hissy fit for all to see. Word comes down the line, as we regroup from our failed attack, that Jenkins viciously chastised both Law and Robertson with no regard to whether the rebukes could be overheard by soldiers. This is a stinging insult, these generals see their image as part of their stock in trade. No good can come of this. The boys all know that we are going to be the battleground of competing ambitions and, while we respect Jenkins, we also wish he were not so relentlessly pursuing glory. And there is suspicion, again, about Law's ability to affect every move

Jenkins makes that might reflect credit on him. Longstreet does nothing.

We grimly march on and finally find ourselves contemplating Knoxville as late November shrouds us in purple twilight, heavy clouds and wet, cold wind. The Yankees have fortified a number of hills around the town. We encircle them — not really, for we do not have enough men to ring them with steel. But we lay siege, we cut off their easiest supply routes. The only vulnerability of their position is that it straddles the Tennessee River, part of their force on one side, the rest on the other. This is not a problem for them so long as their pontoon bridge, the one they transported from Loudon, is in operation. A plan is set in motion to use heavy rafts, released upstream, to break up the bridge. The Yankees have foreseen this and run heavy cable across the upstream side of the river, blocking the rafts so they can be snagged, pulled to shore and dismantled. There are days of sparring with the Yankee outposts, and moving our entrenchments closer. Finally an assault is made against Fort Sanders, the highest of the low hills, the one that, if taken, would command the next two in the chain. The Yankees are aware it is a key position, however, and have strongly fortified it.

The attack, supposed to be a surprise with no prior artillery assault, is launched at dawn on November 29th. Bratton's brigade is not involved in the assault, which is a disaster. Someone failed to get good information on a moat in front of the fort; when elements of two brigades hit it, they found it much deeper than expected and many floundered and were shot down. Those who broke through the ice-covered water and somehow made it across found they could not scramble up the earth parapet, which had frozen solid and was slippery as ice. And they had no assault ladders.

The assault was further complicated by two things we haven't seen before. The cleared area in front of the moat was covered with telegraph wire strung haphazardly between stumps, tripping men and disrupting the movement toward the fort. It gave the Yankees just that much more time to pick targets, by slowing the advance. Then we see our boys huddled in the moat, under the Yankee line, being shot to pieces, and also being assaulted by hand-thrown artillery shells. The Yankees have lit the fuses in the shells and tossed them among our men, causing terrible carnage. Our boys can't do a thing — the shells are too heavy to pick up and throw back over parapet, which is 12 or more feet from the waterline.

They were mowed down until Burnside stopped the carnage. What happened next is so significant of the hopelessness of the assault that it is almost unimaginable.

It is one of the conventions of war, we have learned, that the side getting the worst of it in a battle is the side that asks the other for a truce to remove wounded. Asking for a truce is very much a concession that the day has gone badly. In front of Fort Sanders, however, it is Burnside who stops the carnage with a flag of truce. He sent it out after the attack faded away, with several hundred of our men, mostly wounded, still in the moat. We think of Burnside as a compassionate man — one who put convention aside to avoid needlessly slaughtering a clearly defeated foe. Men who would have bled to death or froze to death in the moat instead surrendered. A few who were unhurt were exchanged, on the spot, for some prisoners we had grabbed days earlier.

We believed this was the end of the day's disaster, but we were wrong. Word comes down that we are to send out work details to build scaling ladders, scrounge rope and make grapples. We will make another assault, this time with artillery support to keep the defenders pinned to the earth. Jenkins has convinced Longstreet it can be done. We are not so sure, and while the boys do as they are told, it is clear that the sight of hundreds of men shot down in 20 minutes is not inspirational.

We have built our ladders, tested them. We are formed up and given the special instructions. The artillery will pummel the ground where the telegraph wire is strewn, to try to break it up, but it is expected that the area will still be a mess. Therefore we will not attempt to hold any kind of battalion formation once we reach that part of the field. Companies will release from the battalion and sprint across the ground and through the moat, each with its own scaling ladders. Our goal is to breach the fort's walls, to get inside and stop the terrible artillery that rained triple-shotted canister down on the first assault. Regiments coming in our rear will attempt to keep formation and order, and, once in the fort, will be charged with pushing out into the enemy's rear and rolling up the works to each side that connect Fort Sanders with the next forts in line. Artillerymen will advance in this second line, without guns, to try to turn the fort's batteries around and use them on the Yankees.

It is a desperate plan, and men are praying and writing letters. Willy McClure is sweating, despite the cold day. His faith is wavering. We have not quite been in a situation like this before, seeing our goal in front of us and knowing it to be a fortification that some very good troops failed to take once already. Jenkins, however, is smiling — this despite three dead colonels in the moat. He will go in with Bratton's Brigade in the first part of the attack. We admire his bravery but think him foolish as well. He is foolish, but not completely crazy. When we form up for the attack, he is wearing a nondescript jacket and hat. The only way to tell he is an officer is the sword he is carrying — and the fact that every man in the division knows him. He will at least not attract attention by wearing his dress uniform. That has turned out to be a mistake for others, and Jenkins is one of the general officers who has decided to profit from their hard-won lessons in war. The philosophy of each side is that the men will not function without officers. It was only a short step from that belief to the decision that officers should be special targets. Now the page has been turned and our officers, some of them, are doing what they can to not stand out quite so clearly as part of the leadership cadre.

All this is just thoughts to keep from thinking about wire, canister, icy water and a 12-foot-high icy slope. The day moves on and gradually the realization spreads that we will not be making the assault.

Couriers have arrived from Chattanooga; Braxton Bragg has lost both Lookout Mountain and Missionary Ridge, our supply line back down the Tennessee River is now gone because he will be pulling back toward Atlanta. We are cut off in a barren, hostile wilderness. The ammunition and provender we have may be all that we get for quite some time. Longstreet has, without doing a thing himself, been converted from aggressor to defender. Late in the day, word of events around Chattanooga reaches the Yankees. We hear them cheering, then they fire every gun in sequence around their ring of fortifications, in a salute to their comrades a hundred miles to the southwest and a boast that they have ammunition to spare while we now must count every shot.

We linger around Knoxville for several days, but it is clear we are gathering up whatever we can gather preparatory to a march, in some direction. We sidle and leapfrog around Knoxville and are finally assembled to the north; we march north, toward Virginia.

CHAPTER EIGHTEEN

Even when we are forced to move, Longstreet is moving aggressively. We find a Yankee force ahead of us as we move northeast, and Longstreet attempts to bring them to bay near Bean's Station, which we were surprised to find was not a railroad station but an old Indian agent station. The move comes to naught — something about McLaws men not having enough to eat — but we do pick up more wagons and more supplies that the fleeing Yankees left behind.

With that behind us, we are apparently done with war for this season. Longstreet's two divisions are spread out around the valley of eastern Tennessee. We have thrown off all connection with the ill-tempered Braxton Bragg and the ill-favored Army of Tennessee. The East Tennessee and Virginia Railroad stretches northeast away from us, back toward Virginia; there are bridges to fix and guard, but a pipeline back to Virginia is set and rations and supplies are moving again. The many wagons we confiscated on our hurried march toward Knoxville are still with us and help bridge the gaps that exist between the railroad and our camps.

This is a land of Unionists. We feared a bleak trek through barren hills, but the only bleakness is among the people. The land is bountiful — a valley filled with food, both stored for the winter and still in the fields, for the climate here is such that some farmers set out their greens and onions in the fall, to have them already started in the spring when the soil is too wet to work.

They make a fine addition to our rations, as does the butter, the milk, the cheese, the hams, the stored potatoes — all the richness of a region not seriously touched by a hostile army. Union troops had been here before, sweeping through from the Cumberland Gap down to Knoxville. We are a different story entirely for the local Union sympathizers, and it is with great delight that our officers issue them documents that will allow them to be paid — in Confederate money, and when they take the documents to Confederate authorities in Morristown, where Longstreet has set his headquarters for the winter.

Our camps here are elaborate and comfortable. This is the third winter of the war — the third winter! We are expert in making do with what we have. The Sixth Regiment is a regiment of moles. Our standard winter abode starts with a hole in the ground, on the side of a hill with good drainage. We mark out an area the size we want — 10 feet wide and 14 feet long seems to be the size usually arrived at, and the reason seems to be that any bigger requires more serious engineering and bracing than we have at our disposal.

After digging the hole down four feet, we line it with logs cut from the abundant forests that spread across the parts of this valley that are not farmable — the rocky spots and the low spots along the streams. The logs run up out of the hole two feet or more. We then erect a roof, using more poles to outline it and stretching canvas over the poles. Some have improved upon canvas, using boards stripped from abandoned Unionist barns and homes to create a kind of clapboard roof — shingling using planks. Each shelter has its own fireplace, made of rock or brick held together with mud and clay. The fireplace is usually in one end, and goes through the log wall, so that the chimney can go up the outside gable wall without any complications caused by going through the roof.

On the inside we use limbs and saplings to stack beds along the walls, three high. These are planked if possible but if not some care is given to making a latticework of limbs and twigs. Upon this we put mattress ticks — some of the bags used to ship rations, or something made from pieces of canvas too small to be used for roofing, sewn together to make long, narrow sacks. These are stuffed with leaves, straw or, best of all, pine needles, and make a luxurious bed, being warm and also smoothing out the lumps of the latticework and softening the hardness of the plank beds. Luxury, of course, being a relative thing. This is indeed comfort for soldiers, and we thrive for a week after setting up our camps, resting from the strain of the campaign we have just concluded and eating everything we can eat as fast as we can eat it.

We spend a week building our camp, and a week enjoying it, and then the winter's work begins. Like Roman legions of long ago, Longstreet's divisions go to work as their own supply depot. Those called out the previous year for shoemaking details are again brought forth, sent to the various big barns appropriated for the purpose and set to work producing shoes. This army is harder on shoes than anything a civilian could imagine, a good pair won't last 90 days on campaign. We have all become somewhat skilled at repairs — using cord to re-thread the torn stitching to keep a pair of shoes intact until replacements can be issued. The big problem continues to be the stitching, not the leather itself. Mud gets into the stitching and abrades it; when it lets go, the shoe essentially unravels. Our shoe depots set to work not only making new shoes, but repairing those that can be repaired. Dozens of men are involved in this, and others are rounding up every bit of leather the valley can produce. Tanneries within 50 miles of Morristown are stripped of leather, and not just for shoes. Artillery harness, wagon harness — all is in need of repair or replacement.

While some barns are being used as shoe factories, others are designated as wainwright shops, blacksmith shops and general repair shops. Wagons, caissons, limbers, gun carriages — all get attention. This valley has some coal, and we both use it ourselves and see it moved north and east to Richmond, for use in the factories there. The forges run for as long as there is daylight to see.

The coal goes to Richmond, and from Richmond comes uniforms, some of them quite natty. The Union blockade appears to be not as effective as they would like, because some wonderful uniforms are coming to us from England — dark bluish-grey wool, very well made.

The coal does not move without some preparation. Again, like Caesar's armies, we are put to work restoring the rail line heading northeast into Virginia. Burned bridges are rebuilt, using timbers cut on the spot. Damaged track is replaced — sidings are looted of usable rails. It is interesting work, but just as maneuver is for the rank and file only an arrangement of basic commands like "left wheel" and "by file, right," so too engineering is little more for us than shovels, axes, saws and lifting. It is just a series of small tasks arranged according to a plan that results in a useful structure. It is very satisfying to be sent on details that produce something besides death, and no one complains at being so tasked. Each bridge rebuilt, each embankment restored, each loading platform constructed, each wagon road firmed up and repaired increases the flow of supplies from Richmond.

The flow of supplies is steady, and it includes ammunition. We are not sure what to make of this, but there appears to be a plan. The regiments are taken out regularly for target shooting. Until now we have not done much of this, save for the fellows in the Palmetto Sharpshooters. They, having been equipped with rifle muskets before anyone else, in the first months of the war, had undergone some training in how to use them. The rest of us have received instruction in loading, and one period of instruction in shooting last year during the "siege" of Suffolk, but the excuse used to explain the lack of actual shooting practice has been the lack of ammunition.

That is no longer the case. We explore in detail what it is our weapons can do. We have some surprises.

The first is that some men are natural shooters and others are not, and this in no way necessarily corresponds to what might have been presumed about them before they actually stepped up to a line, alone, and tried to hit a target varying distances away.

We shoot at 100, 200 and 300 yards, and we shoot singly, for the purposes of correcting our technique and for individual instruction, and we shoot in all the ways that we have always shot: by company, by file, by rank. We use a variety of objects as targets — we are not so flush with material goods that we would think of wasting good canvas or stout planks as targets to be shredded by Minie balls, but there is a debris of broken boxes, barrels and old, fraying canvas around every army.

The second thing we learn is that our weapons are somewhat peculiar. The Enfield just shoots high; even at 50 yards, the ball goes in eight inches over the spot being aimed at. It's different at every distance, and we find that it is important to use the sliding sight and properly estimate the range in order to hit the target. Again, some men are better at estimating distances than others, and we regularly compete by trying to guess the distance to a tree or a post and then pacing if off to see who came closest. I am not surprised to find that McClure, who is a pretty good judge of most things, is an excellent judge of distance.

Our weapons are, when used properly, formidable. After two weeks of practicing our shooting in the cold Tennessee winter, the regiment is mustered in front of a long row of target material set 200 yards away. We are told to adjust our sights to 200 yards and we then hear the rarest of all battlefield commands — fire by battalion. There is a five-second burst of firing as each man aims at a specific thing, and then there is a faint cloud of white smoke drifting away, and 600 men peering through it. We are released from ranks to examine our handiwork, and it is impressive. The boxes and barrels and old tents are speckled with holes.

We reform and march up to 100 yards from the target, and once again we fire by battalion. This time the results are spectacular: We can see wood splintering and barrels falling apart, poles holding old canvas snapping apart under the impact of the lead.

We shoot once a week after that. To my surprise, I become a pretty good shot. I must wear spectacles to read easily — the type in books tends to blur. But I can see clearly at a distance. I can see the sight at the end of the barrel and I can see the target. The notch in the sliding sight tends to blur a little on me, but if I really concentrate, I can put the sight right in the notch and right on the target, just as we are being instructed by our officers. We gradually extend our range, until some of us are regularly hitting targets at 400 yards and a few can reach out to 600 yards and connect at least some of the time.

Shooting at targets gives us much to think about and much to realize about the possibilities of our weapons. We have always known they had greater range than the old blunderbuss muskets we had at the beginning of the war, but we have never really taken much advantage of that, except on one occasion when the Palmetto Sharpshooters were used to drive off an enemy battery.

Thus, warm, snug, well fed and gainfully employed, with bushwhacking Unionists our only worry, the men settle in to pass a winter. If only our officers could be similarly kept busy we would not be treated to the unseemly spectacle they offer.

The feud between Evander Law and Micah Jenkins continues. We of course take Jenkins' side, but even we wish they would just stop. Jenkins has filed reports blaming Law for his failure to accurately direct his brigade in the scuffle we had with the Yankees before we got to Knoxville. As is so often the case in these affairs, Law's mistake is seen as costing us a great victory. Since the opportunity was lost, no one actually knows what would have happened, but the finger of blame is pointed his way. Both Law and Jenkins want Hood's division, which Jenkins has been running ever since his brigade was attached to it after Gettysburg. That rankles Law, who was with the division much longer and who was one of Hood's favorites.

Nor is that discord the only strife among the officers. Lafayette McLaws has also been accused of failing to do his duty by none other than Longstreet. Longstreet is indignant that McLaws would allow a trifling thing like hunger to stop him from attacking a clearly disarrayed enemy like the one we faced at Bean's Station. There is some indication that McLaws failed to carry out the attack at Knoxville properly, also. We hear through the medium of camp gossip that the official language used to describe McLaws' shortcomings is "lack of confidence," which seems to us an astonishing indictment of what is, considering the odds we always face, no more than common sense. Only an idiot would have any confidence that our plans would have the desired outcome. McLaws, in turn, is blaming Jenkins for failing to bring the enemy to battle before we ever got to Knoxville, saying if Jenkins had done the right thing it would have made a battle at Knoxville unnecessary — another opportunity to win the war lost, of course.

And Longstreet has asked to have Jerome Robertson, a brigadier with long service in Hood's Division, removed from command.

The word is that Laws is resentful of Jenkins, and that McLaws is, for lack of a better word, lazy, while Robertson is incompetent, ineffectual and prone to skulking with his entire command just as some privates will try to skulk and avoid battle. Robertson is accused of trying to demoralize his own men with whining about lack of food, shoes and intelligent leadership during the campaign from Chattanooga to Knoxville. Whether that is whining, or whether he did not wish to appear to be a moron to his troops by telling them that they were actually eating food, wearing shoes and winning battles when their experience was obviously to the contrary, is quite the question in camp.

That some generals are weary and discouraged, if not actually discontented, does not sit well with the patriotic fire-eaters, led by Longstreet. They are moving for court-martials and courts of inquiry — what next, a Committee of Public Safety and then a guillotine for those who do not display enough zeal?

There is only one alarum for us in the months of winter, and it gets us out of camp for only a week, to track down a rumor of Yankees moving to our south and west. It amounts to nothing, and we are back in camp the better by a couple of geese picked up along the way.

We learn that one of the rivalries that plagued us all fall is resolved. Neither Jenkins nor Law will take command of what was Hood's division. General Charles Field has recovered from wounds and has been assigned to command of the division; Jenkins resumes command of his brigade. If he is disheartened by this blow to his ambitions, he does not let it show. He is the same young fighting cock he ever was, highly visible in the camps of our regiments and showing the same old flare for remembering names and incidents. For awhile, anyway. Then the malaise finally gets to him, too.

There are other changes. McLaws disappears, some say to a desk job in Richmond, and Joseph Kershaw — another South Carolinian — takes charge of his division. Jerome Robertson is sent back to Texas to organize reserves. Evander Law resumes command of his brigade, but only after a court martial at which Jenkins testified against him. The leaders in Richmond seem to take Law's side, and word goes around the campfires that Jenkins has been accused of unseemly ambition — of trying, with Longstreet's help, to get Evander Law eliminated as a rival for a major generalcy.

This takes a toll. Jenkins seems to shrink. He is frequently ill, doesn't eat well, and becomes even sicker as a result. Bratton frets over him, but Jenkins remains ill, to the point where he is sent home in March to recuperate.

Of Field we know little. He is a quiet man, seemingly fond of food and rest, and does not come into our camps. We see him only at the occasional morning parade, where he silently observes, double chins puffed above the hard edge of his coat collar, and then leaves after speaking only with the field officers. His appointment produces no change in our daily routine.

So we pass the winter, eating well (as these things go), remembering lost comrades, writing home and gradually recovering our good spirits.

We end the winter with more new uniforms, enough to equip all 500 or so men in the Sixth with new jackets and trousers. They are dark English cloth. In March we begin to move northeast, parallel to the railroad and sometimes on it, in a series of marches that takes us to Bristol. We then say goodbye to Tennessee; well equipped and in good spirits, Field's Division, Kershaw's Division and Alexander's artillery are transported by rail, in relays, to Charlottesville, and by the middle of April we are again part of the Army of Northern Virginia. We have a couple of weeks of watching the apple trees blossom and of enjoying the rest of the army cheer our return as we move past them from bivouac to bivouac.

Then, in early May, Field's Division is moved north of Gordonsville and we soon find ourselves in the vicinity of Chancellorsville, where the terrible fighting took place last May. There are reminders: torn trees, bones occasionally sticking up through the leaves of the forest, burned homes. We hear the sounds of battle distantly, but we are not engaged. We watch the mayflies swarm over a tiny creek, and bask in the dappled sunlight coming through the rapidly leafing trees.

Jenkins has rejoined the brigade, but he is still gaunt and sick. He rides in an ambulance.

That changes early on the morning of May 6, when we deploy on both sides of the Orange Plank Road and see hundreds of our men coming through the woods at us, in good order but clearly pressed and withdrawing from a fight. Jenkins leaves his ambulance and mounts; he seems cheered by the prospect of a fight. His cheer spreads, and he exchanges a joke with the Rev. Ichabod McCausland, who has a new brown coat with satin trim and who has been greatly in evidence the last two days.

We deploy on the left of the plank road and must advance while allowing the retreating men to continue; "to the front by the right of companies" is the command, and we try to keep order as we plough through scrubby trees and some tangled undergrowth.

"Trouble up ahead," a retreating Virginian tells us. "Just a bit too much for us."

"That means it's time to turn it over to the South Carolinians," one of our wits shoots back. "We're always cleaning up your messes."

There is more as the two forces pass each other, all in good cheer — even those retreating are simply moving back, not scared, just acknowledging a battlefield reality. But we all know that battlefield realities shift, almost from moment to moment.

We then go back into line of battle, a little ragged because of the forest and undergrowth, but a good line. The enemy appears — in tangled groups. For the first time in months we fire, picking targets as they come clear of the brush. Their attack stops immediately. This is more like it, and when the order to advance comes, we are happy, and move quickly forward for half a mile, when our skirmishers reported earthworks ahead. They do not extend very far to our right, however, and a plan is worked out to take three brigades — not ours — farther to the right to turn their line and make a frontal assault unnecessary.

After a couple of hours, that flank assault unfolds — Longstreet's trademark, another Second Manassas — and we see the shudder in the enemy line. We hardly need the order to advance, and we are up and over their works with fixed bayonets in a couple of thundering heartbeats. There is some booming of guns, and we are briefly among them, capturing a few not quick enough to get out of our way. There has been some small amount of hand to hand fighting here, but since I was in my post as a file closer, it was done before I got over the crude breastworks the Yankees had thrown up.

Longstreet is behind us, roaring us forward, and the forests are alive with men swarming in pursuit of fleeing Yankees. They are fleeing, however, the way our men fled: They are moving back because they know they have the worst of it right here and right now, but they are not taking off as if their next stop will be Washington. But they are moving, they are being pushed.

We halt, reorganize and are marched up the Orange Plank Road to redeploy and, presumably, resume the assault and turn the withdrawal into a rout. The Sixth finds itself in the lead in the gloomy shade of the forest, with Longstreet, Jenkins and Kershaw and their staffs on the road ahead of us. We can hear the generals talking, at least bits and pieces of it.

"Their baggage can't be far behind," Longstreet is saying. "Once we push them that far, they'll break for good."

"Just don't let anyone stop us," Kershaw urges. "We are a division strong and organized — we can break them. We have the edge, and what's more, they don't know we're here."

Jenkins agrees.

Rev. McCausland catches my eye.

"It appears a moment of destiny may be at hand," he says. "This may be our hour."

We lunge down the road, and never did the regiment feel more like a single wild beast. We march in perfect order, and we march fast, relentlessly, moving down the road where the flank attack already crossed and aiming for the distant, fleeing backs of the Yankees we pushed out of the works. I look back down the long column — left, right, left, right — the entire body of men moves as one. It is an awesome and humbling sight — a killing machine moving toward its target, barely leashed power pulsing through its movements. The hair goes up on the back of my neck.

We come around a turn in the road, confident and moving as swiftly as any of Jackson's men ever marched. Men emerge from the forest on our left and right; it is of no concern, they are our men, part of the force that turned the enemy's flanks. We see them halt, and some are pointing at us; shots ring out and then there is a ragged volley. Longstreet is down, Jenkins is down, Bratton is hurling our company forward into line and screaming for Lt. Col. Steedman to bring up the rest of the regiment. Suddenly Kershaw is riding toward the men in the woods, hat off, blonde hair streaming, screaming, "They are friends! Friends! You are shooting friends!" and he whirls and rides back to us, "Friends, don't shoot them, they are friends, it is all a mistake!"

Bratton halts us and puts us back on the road. The long line behind us shudders to a halt.

Longstreet is down, we can see bloody froth around his throat. Jenkins is down, head bloody but talking, calling out for us to "Drive them, drive them!" Field is sent for and Longstreet manages to let him know he is in charge. Bratton is senior colonel within Jenkins Brigade, and he is now in charge of the brigade. He looks at Steedman, and Steedman knows he is now in command of the 6th Regiment.

Doctors call out for stretchers, then ambulances, then a guard. Our company — lead company in the regiment — is pulled out of formation, and we are told to escort the ambulances to the rear, clearing the road as we go. Many officers and brigade noncommissioned officers who were riding with the generals have been wounded, two killed. Longstreet and Jenkins are so badly hurt the ambulances can't travel quickly, but without our help they will not move at all. Orange Plank Road is choked with men, horses and guns, all waiting to move forward.

We have a moment before our special task begins, and some of the men who fired on us approach, stunned and seeking forgiveness.

"You looked like Yankees," one weeping Virginian from Mahone's Brigade explained. "Those dark uniforms, and the way you moved. And you had no flag."

We are too preoccupied to be angry — and it is not the first time we have been under fire from our own troops. Bitter memories of Dranesville come flooding back. But the soldier with tear-streaked cheeks is right. We did look like Yankees. The normal condition of a Confederate regiment is to have a motley collection of uniforms — enough at each new issue to refit the men in the worst shape, never enough to outfit everyone. We'd been outfitted down to the last camp cook in dark uniforms. And our flag was still around the corner, in the middle of the regiment with C company. Having figured it out, I felt better, but I also know better than to explain it to anyone. They won't care and will think me strange. Besides, what difference does it make? And now what? What of the attack? Is that not what should be happening? Shouldn't Field be moving ahead with Longstreet's plan, which is what Lee himself expects?

Company A starts back down the road ahead of the ambulances, shouting people out of the way and shutting off the little farm lanes that feed into the Orange Plank Road. It is effective, but it also telegraphs the news that Longstreet is down. You can feel the change in the air, just as if a storm were nearing. Where we pass, stillness follows. The troops move out of the way and then stand silent as we sweep past.

CHAPTER NINETEEN

Jenkins died at 5 p.m. on May 6, the day of the fight. Kershaw was with him. "No Yankee bullet will hurt me," Jenkins once boasted, and he was right. Jackson, Longstreet and Jenkins, all shot by their own men.

Longstreet is badly hurt but the surgeons we overheard discussing his wounds seemed to think he would recover, although whether he will ever be able to speak again is in doubt.

Kershaw finally notices us and sends us back to find the regiment.

"There is no sense being silent about this," he tells us. "Just tell them two of South Carolina's bravest and brightest were struck down today, and that we must trust in God and continue."

The road is less clogged than it was during our mad dash to the rear a few hours ago, but there are still brigades on the road, and they should have been somewhere else by now. Our progress slows, for everyone wants to know more — word spread up the line before we passed, of course, but all are eager for details, and everyone seems to know we are from Jenkins Brigade.

We finally find the brigade, a half-mile farther up the plank road than when we left them, and settled in behind a rough breastworks of logs, brush and red soil. Steedman adds us to the reserve, 50 yards behind the line. We learn that the delay to take care of the wounded generals, and the delay in sorting out the confusion and having Fields try to figure out what was expected of him, gave the Yankees time to stop and throw up yet another line of works. With darkness falling, no attack was made. The pendulum has stopped swinging; it now hangs straight down, with neither side having any momentum or movement.

It is a dark, bleak night, one that matches our thoughts. I will not dwell on it, except to note that in addition to the inevitable sadness, there are two other emotions evident: anger and frustration.

We spend the day behind our works, with skirmishers thrown forward. The Yankees are actively probing all parts of our line, continuously, trying to find out who we are, where we are and whether we intend to stay. Their probing stops about 5 p.m. At 9 p.m. the order comes to move out, and we move southeast, through the forest at first, then along the railroad cut that turned out to be the key to the success of yesterday's flank attack, then finally on a good road. We halt for a few hours, and are on the move again at dawn. We break out of the forests of the Wilderness and into farmland about 7 a.m.

At 10 a.m. we find Yankee cavalry between us and a small town visible across the fields ahead of us. Bratton whips us into a three-regiment battle line, two regiments behind that, and the cavalry moves off, without a fight. We pass through the town — Spotsylvania Courthouse — and take up a position on the eastern side. Almost immediately we are given new orders by Field, and we change front forward to the left on the Fifth and move northwest, where the sound of firing can be heard.

The ground here is all fields and hedgerows and small hills and crests and valleys. The visibility in any direction is limited by the terrain — an enemy could be on the other side of a hill only a hundred yards away and no one would know. We see a brigade ahead of us, and move to its right, extending its line and finding ourselves engaged with an enemy probing forward with a heavy skirmish line. They stop and fade back behind hills and hedgerows, out of sight. They come out again a short time later, in full line of battle, and aim to our right, where they know our flank ends. Bratton prepares to throw his two reserve regiments in that direction, but only gets one in place when more of our troops appear behind us and extend to the right, snapping into position at exactly the right time to give the Yankee a nasty surprise. Their attack again fades away, leaving a few dark blue blotches on the bright spring grass. The Palmetto Sharpshooters, sent out as skirmishers, halt when the order to deploy is given. They deploy, and then move forward. This is not what is expected, and Bratton is concerned. He sends a runner to Col. Walker, commander of the Sharpshooters, to find out what is happening. As firing breaks out along the still-moving skirmish line, word comes back that Walker isn't sure what is happening, he gave no order. The line disappears from view, the firing intensifies. We suddenly see men in blue coming back toward us, but it is almost immediately apparent that they are under guard. The Sharpshooters — Jenkins' Sharpshooters — come back out, take up the skirmish line at its normal distance, and send back more than 120 prisoners they seized out of the retreating federal force. The brigade gives them a roaring cheer, and we set to work building breastworks.

We pass a quiet night — rations are adequate and we are comfortable and tired and glad to rest. The next morning we are moving again, to our left, across a road, and we throw up more rough breastworks. We are getting good at this. We lay down logs, rocks, sticks, in a line that marks where the works will go. Then we dig behind it — bayonets to loosen the soil and pry up small rocks, then cups and tin plates to move it. The dirt goes on top of the logs and brush. It does not take very long to create a ditch behind which you can shelter most of your body. If there is time, we find logs and put them atop the piled dirt, then clear out underneath most of their length; we can then put our musket barrels through the opening, and have quite a bit of protection for our heads, as well. We can have a rough breastworks up — maybe only thigh-high, but effective shelter — in less than an hour.

Nothing happens all day, and we spend the time deepening our ditch and raising our rampart higher. Saws are brought up and we reinforce our ditch with log walls in places.

Finally, on May 12, there is a sudden, tremendous assault on our line. Bratton lets them get within 50 yards of our works before allowing the regiments to fire, and we drop them without mercy. They break almost immediately, and we shoot them down as they run.

The firing continues to our right. On the left of our line — where we are — we can see several Yankee regiments to our right, in front of part of our line but hidden from direct view by a small crest of ground. They are "in defilade," out of our range and hidden from those of our boys who are within range. Bratton calls for a battery to fire on them; the battery commander can't see them, but Bratton, from our front, can. He signals back to direct the fire, and it seems to be effective — we can see disorder and men firing. The battery commander is uneasy by this novel approach to artillery fire, however, and refuses to continue to fire at something he can't see.

Bratton, frustrated, waits an hour — the fighting is still roaring hugely to our right, and Bratton wonders out loud if "by some happy mistake they are fighting among themselves." Finally he can't stand it any more, and pushes our two right regiments (the Fifth and the First South Carolina regiments) up over the crest that is between them and the hidden enemy. Their skirmish line goes first and when the men come over the hill, they find the enemy before them in great force, but firing away at something to their left that we can't see. Our skirmish line opens and when both regiments top the crest, they lunge forward instinctively and the enemy immediately buckles. As they break, some run across our front, finally coming into range, and we bring a number of them down. Our men return, bringing in 40 prisoners, and again there is rousing roar for them from the rest of the brigade. Some of them doff their hats in acknowledgement.

We have done well. We have fewer than a dozen wounded in the entire brigade, and we've captured almost 200 prisoners and left the fields in front of our positions heavily covered with blue. But now we are given orders to move again, over to the right, where the firing has been taking place all day. There we find horror.

It seems we have been only playing at war on our part of the line. Here is where the noise of battle originated, and here are its results — bodies everywhere, broken men moaning in the darkness, others staggering about looking for friends or for surgeons, or for their units. Blue uniforms are among the brown and grey of our men, mostly all dead. We are put in line, brigades on either side us of tightening their lines to make room, and we set to work, in the gloom of night, to build up the hasty trench we find scratched along our position. Fire comes from a hidden enemy; we don't bother returning the fire, we simply crawl and dig, and are shot as we do. The worst for me comes when we must move a body to extend our part of the ditch. It is a familiar face, someone who has been with the Sixth since Sumter, but I can no longer remember his name, and this troubles me. Maybe I never knew his name? Does anyone know his name? I ask, but no one does. We roll his body to the rear, and I hope someone misses him from the ranks and can tell his family. We pass the night, and see battered regiments pulled out from our front. They pass through our lines silently, the order being given to keep quiet and not let the enemy know what is going on. We have no idea what is going on, either, but we remain quiet and pass the night without fires.

At dawn we abandon our line and move to the rear another 500 yards, to find a line of our works already dug. We are held to the rear of the line, a kind of reserve; at midmorning we are sent back to the left, to Fields, who also puts us in reserve. Then we move to the right — we are doing a lot of moving. We spend five days moving about Spotsylvania, occasionally building works. Finally we move out and discover that we are the rear guard of the entire army. Yankee cavalry is at our heels — they never get close enough to force us to make a stand, but they do, as McClure observes, a wonderful job in keeping our stragglers on the move.

We cross a river, using a railroad bridge. The next morning we burn it, stacking tinder and timber and straw torn from a nearby barn under the part of the bridge that extends over dry ground next to the creek. It blazes and roars, and the bridge itself begins to burn. When it starts to collapse, we move off, with Yankees sending spiteful shots in our direction.

We march, then halt and dig a line, then march, right through the end of May. The skirmishing is sharp, with a seemingly endless supply of Yankees constantly feeling and probing our line, looking for a weak spot. They do not find one, but we lose men steadily.

One of the techniques that is now evolving is the snatching of pickets from their post. Both sides are trying to find out exactly what force is in front of them, to find out whether the other army is on the move or sitting still. We sometimes find a picket post empty when the relief is sent out; the men have been snatched by ambuscade. I'm told we are doing the same. It seems a piffling way to fight a war.

The piffling turns to wholesale death the first week of June, when the new federal commander — it is Grant, he who captured Vicksburg — tries a frontal assault on our line near Cold Harbor. We are not engaged, but we hear the furious sounds. The attack is beaten back, with heavy losses.

Our sliding movement to the right continues, and in mid June we break our endless series of camps and entrenching and marching by crossing the Chickahominy. We find ourselves on familiar terrain: This is where the Sixth was first really blooded, the battlefield at Seven Pines. The buildings are all burned, the fields are for the most part not tended. It is a desolate scene, and again we find bones washing up occasionally through the pine needles of the area's forests. I expect to see that black dog standing over poor Lt. Moore. We are silent as we pass through the battlefield, the place where Jenkins' military career suddenly shot up. Elan, drive, courage — ambition. Now buried in South Carolina, and not even at his family home on Edisto, but on strangers' land. The Yankees hold the sea islands, still.

Richard Anderson is in charge of Longstreet's Corps. Field only commanded the corps a day or two; he is regarded by Lee as a division commander, not a corps commander. We find him to be a competent leader, but not a flashy one. He runs the division as if it were a vast business. His relations with the brigadiers are courteous, but he is not approachable. Bratton seems to have had no trouble adapting to his new rank, new responsibilities and new leader. Like many of us, he is hoping we will soon find an opportunity to use our now very apparent expertise as soldiers to end this thing, to strike one blow that will be decisive. But for now it is just march, dig, eat, stand picket, march, dig, eat .... We never completely stand down from the Wilderness to Cold Harbor, some parts of every regiment are awake, fully equipped and ready to fall in every single hour of every day and night for six weeks. It is grueling, but we prove to be up to the challenges this new type of relentless warfare is presenting.

Lee seems to be aware of our abilities. There is a sudden lunge by the Yankees to the south, across the James, and troops are shifted everywhere to meet the threat. Field's Division is whisked out of its latest line of works and hurled southwest; we cross the James near Drewry's Bluff. The Sixth is again in the lead, and we find ourselves advanced as skirmishers. We move up to a line of our own works, which are empty, and move in, and halt for the night, the familiar fireflies of June flickering in the darkness. Dawn reveals that our own line on both sides of us is occupied by Yankees. Our troops that had been there have been pulled out and sent even farther south, to Petersburg, and the Yankees have cautiously moved in. Too cautiously, and in too weak a force. Our generals are meeting somewhere, and field officers leave to a bugle summons, presumably to find out what the plan might be. To our front, we can see regiments in blue moving toward us, and we send word back. What follows is quite astonishing. It is apparent to all of us that we will be better off in possession of the line of works, and that our plan will be to assault them. It's also apparent that there aren't many Yankees in the works now, but there will be shortly — we can see them coming, and apparently others can, too.

Field's entire division simply moves forward, led by a regiment near the middle of the line that suddenly forms up in plain view and begins marching in line of battle toward the works. It is all line officers and enlisted men — captains and privates, not a battalion commander or brigade commander anywhere in sight.

There is some firing from the Yankees. Since we are in the works already, on the flank of at least one of the Yankee segments of the line, we push to our left and begin prying them out of the works. The Yankees are veteran troops, they know their position might be strong but they have too few troops to hold it; they begin moving back. We can see their officers trying to rally them, but the men move off resolutely. Once again, they are not running. They simply know the limits of their position, just as our men knew the strength of ours. The works are ours, almost without loss.

Bratton and the other generals rush up, drawn by the outbursts of firing and the cheers of our men as they sweep into the entrenchments. They are surprised by what happened, and pretend to be angry and try to find out who ordered the advance.

"Why, we did, General," one private tells Bratton, and Bratton bursts into laughter.

"You will put me out of a job," he tells the man. "What kind of a soldier gives himself orders to advance against the enemy?"

There is great satisfaction, but the Yankees are not finished. After two days in the entrenchments taken in what we now call the Soldiers' Fight, we move southwest, passing through Petersburg and into a new line of hasty works southeast of the town, thrown up near a redoubt that houses a battery. It is a terrible place — the Yankee lines are close, and they appear to have gotten the edge on us in entrenching. They are dug in deeply and can bring fire down on our section of the line from two directions. We are out on the front of a bald hillside.

Our entrenchments are in poor shape. We must dig or die, but it appears we will do both.

Bratton does the best he can. Companies are sent out into the darkness to dig rifle pits a hundred yards ahead of our main line; we hear them working, and so do the Yankees, who send shots into the darkness on a regular basis all night long. They also send over raiding patrols, who attempt to snatch our men out of the shelters. It is a night of whickering bullets slicing through the darkness, the blinking of muzzle blasts dimming the work being done by the fireflies.

While some are busy on the rifle pits, others are working on the main line of works, trying to put in transverse trenches to provide shelter from the fire coming down our line from the left. It is slow work in the dark and with no real tools. The warm June night is rich with the smell of freshly turned earth — almost as if it were planting season. There is also the sweet pungency of pine and sassafras roots that we hack our way through when we come to a patch where there used to be a hedgerow. And while all that is taking place, some of us are armed and alert and ready — doing the more traditional work of a soldier, not this new grubbing in the dirt that has marked our efforts since we came back to Virginia.

When dawn comes, we stop work and try to find places to rest in our ditch where the probing Yankee rifles can't find us.

"Now I know how a possum feels," McClure jokes as we scrape holes for ourselves in the side of our ditch one morning. "Sleep all day, roam all night. Never thought soldiering would be so much like being a possum." He has, in the middle of all of this, in a landscape increasingly barren of even leaves, managed to find straw to put down between us and the red earth.

We go through two days of this, and finally our works are a real protection. We can move about with some degree of safety if we are careful. The safest places are, by design, up on the firing line itself. Real tools have arrived, and with them we cut and peg and fasten logs hauled from a nearby wood lot by mule — under cover of darkness — to keep our earthworks intact. Then we start work on more deep ditches, ones that zigzag their way back up the slope behind us and over the crest, emerging into the open behind the hill where the Yankee guns can't find us. Our foodstuffs are there — our wagons, seen only briefly since the Wilderness fight, catch up to us and we are again able to prepare food properly. We sleep and eat behind the hill, and move into the trenches for duty. Our target practice during the winter is now resumed, only this time the targets are live. We believe we are doing great damage; we know the Yankees are, every day sees a dozen from the regiment taken to the rear with wounds. Just as we are comfortable — we have been here six days — Bratton's

Brigade gets orders to move. There is grumbling at the thought that we will have to do this all over again, but as it turns out we needn't have worried. We are marched away from the line, as Elliott's Brigade moves into the works we built with both blood and sweat, and put in a deep ravine near a bridge. Nominally we are guarding the bridge; actually we are being given a breather, like a horse that has been worked too hard. The nearest Yankees are more than a mile away and several thousand of our troops are between us and them. We breathe deeply for the first time in weeks, and doze off regularly, basking in the hot sunlight. Our only complaint is that there is not much to eat — not even abandoned crops to glean.

Four days of this and we are moved back to our line, replacing Elliott's Brigade. The entire month of July is spent moving in and out of the line, and a system emerges: We spend eight days in our trenches, then are moved somewhat to the rear, out of immediate danger, for two days. We trade fire with Yankees who halfheartedly probe our position — it is, after all, plain to see, we are all right in front of each other here. They just keep hoping we have walked away, and every now and then send a patrol over to find out. They do it at night, because they dare not show a handful of uniform du`ring daylight. Our best shots are on the line and waiting for them during the day.

We face more deviltry here in the form of mortars, which we had so far in the war managed to avoid. They throw a shell high into the air, so that it drops steeply down. With a mortar they can put shell into our deep trenches, trenches that regular artillery can't reach. But it is very difficult for them to hit anything with a mortar. We learn to keep an eye out when they are in use: Often you can see the shell go up, slow, and then come down. If it does not seem to be going down, but does seem to be getting bigger, it is coming right at you. Or so it is said. I have not observed this, but I have observed flurries of activity along the line when clusters of men realized a mortar shell was coming at least near them.

We burrow into the sides of our trenches. using logs to keep them from collapsing. We are now, McClure observes, more like burrowing prairie dogs than we are humans, right down to keeping one person constantly on the alert for danger in every little cluster of dirty soldiers.

It is impossible to keep clean in the trenches, and we beg our officers to find us a site near water every time we leave. Washing the sandy soil off our clothing and bodies and out of our hair is our greatest pleasure now.

We spend July on the Petersburg line. Near the end of the month there is another alarm — the enemy seems to be getting ready for a thrust on the other side of the James, opposite Drewry's Bluff, and we are rushed to Petersburg and driven aboard a train, which rapidly carries us to Rice's Station. From there we march across the James to Fussill's Mill. We go into line, dig a hasty ditch in the sand, and await the enemy, but nothing happens.

CHAPTER TWENTY

We have been losing men in this new, inconclusive kind of dirt war, and the next batch of replacements includes my brother John. I am stunned — he is and looks a mere child, and he speaks and believes the kind of childishness the rest of us left behind at the first battlefield of Manassas, when war was revealed to us not as a glorious event but as men with their bodies torn open, lying in the rain, stinking.

"Where are the Yankees, brother William?" he asks, all smiles and sparkling grey Coleman eyes, running up to get a brotherly embrace. I knock him to the ground instead and sit on his chest, to his astonishment and the rest of the company's amusement.

"They are very close," I hiss at him. "Why did you come? Were you conscripted? I told Mother to keep you home. Why?"

His face scrunches up; I know the look. He is getting ready to cry.

"I did not wait," he said. I am calculating; the fool has timed it so he arrived in Richmond the day after his 18th birthday. He had that birthday on the train.

"Does Mother even know you are here?" I thunder at him. He shakes his head.

"I left her a letter," he said.

The enormity of this is weighing me down. It is difficult enough staying alive; now I must try to teach John how to do it, and fast.

He is not alone. Other youngsters, those we remember as mere schoolboys when the war started, joined him on this trip and are now being issued weapons.

We move again — Field's entire division has gotten a reputation somehow, and we find ourselves called upon to move from spot to spot along the huge line of works that stretches from south of Petersburg to north of Richmond — more trenches than we have men to occupy. Lee's solution is to put the bulk of the Army of Northern Virginia in front of Meade's main force, then occupy critical strong points elsewhere in the line. If Meade makes a move that could mean there's a thrust coming, Lee shifts forces to meet it. Field's Division is usually that force.

I get another jolt when the supply train from Richmond meets us at our new bivouac: Some of the teamsters are children, local Home Guard units. One boy tells me he is 12 years old. His grandfather, who looks to be around 60, is handling the wagon behind his. Both have what could be a uniform on. The boy is proud, but all he can do is drive the mules. He is too frail to help unload the wagon's heavy boxes and barrels. The old man is grim and tells us we'd better not spend too long fussing over food: The Yankees are moving, they're doing it faster than we are, and they're heading for a section of line that is empty.

That same word reaches Field moments later, and we are startled by the arrival of two regiments of cavalry, one of which is a South Carolina unit — 4th South Carolina Cavalry. We are ordered to climb up with the cavalrymen — one infantryman on each stirrup, and the horses stagger northward, triple loaded. The rest of the division begins marching in our dust, driven on by the urgency that clearly has a grip on the officers; we leave them behind. I made sure John was on the same horse as me — we cling to each other's arms across the bony back of the scrawny cavalryman as we jolt and lurch forward into another emergency.

"Can you move this damned saber?" I ask the cavalryman.

"Where do you suggest I put it?" he snaps back, and turns to glare at me.

"Andrew Jackson Montour," I tell him. "You've come back to the Sixth Regiment."

"Oh, Lord," A.J. says. "William Coleman, how are you?"

"Two Colemans," I correct him. "Say hello to John. You remember John? He was in school when you dragged me off to war. In fact I was cursing you for recruiting him. I thought you were running the Sixth Regiment Reserves?"

"Not any more," A.J. says. "Father wanted me to stay, but I got away."

A.J. turns to look directly at me; it's a new A.J., a trim version with the baby fat boiled away by hard wear.

"The Fourth Cavalry was the state's pet cavalry unit," A.J. says. "Every politician's son and planter's son in the state who was afraid to actually fight joined up, because the Fourth hadn't left the state and hadn't done any fighting in the entire war. They had 16 companies in the Fourth, and every company had 120 men."

"How did that appeal to you?" I ask.

"It didn't," he says. "But this winter Lee ordered them to send the Fourth to Virginia. When that happened, the planters sons and politicians sons set up a howl — quietly, of course, lest they be accused of cowardice. They chopped the regiment up — 80 men from each company would go to Virginia, the other 40 would stay home. What a fracas! When they looked around they were short, and those picked to stay home wouldn't budge. It had been impossible to get into the Fourth, but all of a sudden they were looking for volunteers. I got in there in the gap between them looking for volunteers and Father finding out they were going to Virginia."

"He wasn't that concerned about you getting shot in 1861," I point out.

"He's still not concerned about that," A.J. says, with his face twisting up. "He's concerned about how things look. I lost the election for the Sixth and went home in what he considers disgrace. Running the Reserve seemed to him to be a respectable thing to do. Joining the Fourth and hobnobbing with the fainthearted sons of South Carolina's first families seemed to him to be a respectable thing to do, and one he could use for the bank. But to actually go back to the war as a common trooper — that's what's got him mad."

We bounce and jolt awhile in silence.

"A.J.," I say. "Do you know why I joined the Sixth?"

He laughs.

"Because you didn't know any better, just like all of us," he says.

"No," I say, and I tell him about the petticoat. He frowns.

"That's not the worst of it — that's just me, and to tell you the truth I'm glad I'm part of all this, no matter what happens. But petticoats weren't the worst of it — your father used his power at the bank to force people to join your company." And I tell him about the Michael Moore mortgage and how Moore had joined up but his father had exploited the family.

"I was afraid of this — people have dropped hints back in Chester about people who joined, and why they joined. We'll have to fix this, Coleman — I'll make it really clear to him that Moore's widow is going to be taken care of, out of his personal pocket if necessary. And there's going to be much to talk about when this is over and we're home again. But now — to Hell with my father and all those like him, who wouldn't last a week out here. There's a war to win. And it's coming up right now."

He stopped the horse and John and I catapult off.

"Coleman!" A.J. calls. I stop and turn. "Congratulations on your marriage!" He doffed his battered hat in a mock cavalier bow, and galloped off, with the other troopers, back toward our marching division, now visible as a dust cloud against the blue summer sky.

We are on the west side of a low, and we run up and over the top. There's a line of trenches partway down the slope. Off on the other side of the valley we can see blue, moving blue, with patches of color that will be regimental flags when they come out of the heat haze. We run into the trenches, but when we try to form up the officers spread us out — we are three to five yards apart, and the cavalry now rolling along the hill behind us take their infantrymen farther north, to occupy more of the works. The blue on the other side of the shallow valley suddenly looms up, and firing starts, without any need for orders.

They have so far to go, and they move so slowly. The fire seems to surprise them — there's that hesitation, and some commotion, but then they come on again, in good order. They are advancing in echelon, from our right to our left — as they are arriving at a section of line they apparently expected to be empty, they simply face the line and move forward. Had they all come at once they might have overwhelmed us, but they are coming as brigades. Our position is wonderful — we have a clear field of fire for almost a thousand yards, and as each brigade gets closer it comes into range of more and more rifles up and down the line. Our target practice pays off, as we are much more effective at this than we would have been last year. John and I fire at the right oblique, at a brigade that gets to within 200 yards, then crumbles and staggers back. Then we fire directly ahead, at a brigade coming right at us. It disintegrates 150 yards out. Then we fire at the left oblique, and this brigade gets so close to the line that our oblique fire is lost. They lower bayonets for the final push into our line — and then the rest of Field's Division hurls itself over the hill, shrieking and flinging themselves into the trench and catching the Yankees who come over the top on their bayonets. The Yankee brigade is wrecked and staggers back, taking losses all the way.

Some of the Yankees have huddled in a gully about 200 yards out, hiding from the terrible enfilade fire that has cut down their comrades every step back across the shallow valley. Bratton quickly orders the Sixth to fix bayonets and move out. Our artillery finally arrives and begins throwing shells into the enemy on the far hill, to keep their heads down.

We advance in very loose formation — the officers have less control over us, but they need less control, we know what is expected. The Yankees in the gully are done, we simply come into the gully at each end and round them up.

They are black.

This is the first time we've seen black Yankee soldiers, although we of course have heard about them. We run them across the field — we are getting no fire from either side, of course, the Yankees not wanting to hit their own men. It is an odd sensation to feel safe in front of Yankee guns.

We run them up over the hill and behind the crest, and consider what will happen now.

"They'll be shot," someone suggests. "That's what the government said to do — kill them all, any black man in a uniform."

"No they won't," somebody else answered. "The government said they'd be returned to servitude. Not killed."

"What about the ones who are free?" I ask. That stumps some of them.

Tom Wright is nearby, studying the prisoners as they sit awaiting whatever fate brings them.

"Wright, what do you say?" I ask.

He looks as solemn as I've ever seen him look.

"Jeff Davis didn't tell me what to do with these men, so I don't know," Tom says. That brings smiles to some faces. "But let's look at this. Coleman, what are you doing here?"

"Defending my home," I answer immediately.

"So am I," Tom says. "So are the rest of us. We're fighting Yankees who threaten our homes. So far it's been white Yankees. Now it's black Yankees."

"What's the difference?"

There's a pause, and then he adds, "Nobody ever killed a white Yankee prisoner."

There is some restlessness, and clearly some of the fellows are about to expound on the difference between white men and black men. Other noises indicate that elbows are going into ribs and toes are being stepped on by those who don't want to hear that kind of talk — at least in front of Tom Wright, who has the respect of just about everyone. Not that Tom doesn't know what some of them think — it is impossible to be a black man in the South and not be aware. But he's not done.

Tom goes over to one of the prisoners, a sergeant.

"Why are you fighting us?" he asks the man. The sergeant looks puzzled.

"Freedom," he says.

"Whose?" Tom asks.

"Mine. Yours," the sergeant says.

"But I'm already free," Tom tells him. The man's face screws up into a big question mark. "You havin' trouble with that?"

"I wasn't ready for that," the sergeant admits.

"You think on it," Tom tells him. He starts to walk away, then whirls and fires another question.

"You ever kill any white prisoners?" he asks.

The man shakes his head.

"You think about it?" he persists.

He nods his head, and speaks.

"If I ever found the man who sold my wife and kids away from me, I'd kill him," the sergeant says. "Wouldn't matter if he was a prisoner or not, I'd kill him. Or try to."

"What about these men," Tom asks. "What about Coleman there. You kill him?"

The man looks at me, then back at Tom.

"On the field, yes, I'd kill him. Or try to. But not after."

Tom nodded at him, looked at me, looked at the others from the Sixth who were standing in mesmerized silence, then walked away. The black sergeant folded his arms and looked around.

The prisoners were sent up the line after that, back to wherever it is prisoners of war are sent. We never found out what happened to them. We heard other regiments shot black prisoners. We didn't.

We take trains back to Petersburg, and are constantly on the move as August becomes September, but there is not much fighting, just much movement. Late in September we are rushed back north to Rice's Station and then hurried toward Battery Harrison, which had been taken by the enemy. This is serious, because the battery had commanded a sizable piece of the line southwest of Richmond; it's a key point, and with the Yankees in control of it they are in a position to make one short lunge forward and be in Richmond. That will mean keeping more troops in front of them — and leaving fewer troops for other parts of the line. That's the way even the rank and file understand the situation, and of course it means hot work for the infantry.

We arrived to find the Yankees putting the final touches on the reconstruction of the battery — throwing up works on the open side toward us and converting it into a fortress. It is a formidable work, but the plan proposed is to hurl two divisions on the fort. Our role will involve the fort itself, rather than the Yankee line on either side. Two brigades, concentrated, will rush from a ravine that is close to the new works. Anderson's Brigade is to form in the ravine and wait for us. We are to move from our post to the right, closer to the river, and get behind them. Both brigades will then go forward, with the rest of the line. Our special orders are that if Anderson's Brigade or any parts of it are stopped, we are to go right over them and hurl ourselves on the works as quickly as possible, to take it with the bayonet.

McClure and I try to prepare John and the other new recruits for the madness that is to come.

"Don't stop to load. Don't even stop to shoot unless you are ordered, but do your loading on the move or on the ground if we get bogged down, but let's not let that happen. Stay with the rest of us. The only way we're going to survive this is to get across that open ground in a hurry and get among them with the bayonet."

"Don't look at their faces when you use the bayonet," McClure tells them. "Look where you're striking and don't hesitate. And don't stop when you've put one down, look for the next one — look for friends who need help."

John is white faced and big-eyed; none of the fighting we've done in the weeks since he got here has been at close quarters.

"If they run, keep them running," I chime in. "No matter what you think, keep killing them until the officers tell us to stop. Kill them unless they are surrendering."

Boredom has always been a big part of our life as soldiers, and time always seems to move at a crawl. That day, with the attack set for 2 p.m., seemed to fly on wings. Before we knew it — before, really, we were ready — we saw Anderson's regiments moving forward toward the ravine, where they will have shelter from the firing that has already started.

We start to our left, marching simply by the flank as if we were on a road. We are in ugly ground, with thickets and little gullies, and moving by the flank is the easiest way. We lose sight of everything else. Suddenly the order comes to move at the double quick, and without halting are given the order to march by the right flank — it hurls us into a ragged line of battle, and we emerge from the thickets into the open and see what the rush was about. Anderson's men didn't stop in the ravine, for some reason they kept on going. McClure looks back at me. I slide sideways in my file closer position until I'm behind John — not where I'm exactly supposed to be, but pretty soon that won't matter as much as watching out for John.

We hit the ravine and it's clear why Anderson's men didn't stop; the enemy built a small redoubt on the left that commanded part of the ravine. There are also artillery shells bursting over our heads, sending red-hot fragments of iron down on us. Those men were not protected like the generals thought they'd be, and they'd simply kept moving, preferring to die somewhere else. We are now taking fire from that redoubt, but Bratton has seen the problem. One of our regiments — it turns out to be the Palmetto Sharpshooters — is on the right and somewhat behind the rest of the brigade, left in the thickets when we changed direction. Bratton halts them, sorts them out, and moves them across our rear to take the redoubt. We can see nothing ahead of us but the uproar as Anderson's regiments are torn to pieces — they are moving ahead of everyone else, and are getting fire from much more of the Yankee line than just the part in front of them. They stagger, halt, and disintegrate. We are close on their heels — we managed to close the gap. Officers give commands to switch from a line of battle to "by the right of companies to the front," to let the fleeing men pass through us, but there is too much noise, and only a few companies execute the maneuver. Anderson's men hit our battle line, first staggering it and then tearing it apart as they force their way through. Fear is on them like a stench. We keep moving forward, trying to mass ourselves for the lunge up the parapet that now looms ahead of us like a wall. Under the rattling of the muskets there's a sickening sound — the slap, slap, slap of Minie balls hitting flesh. Screams, the smell of blood — we are under their guns now, though, and taking only musket fire, not artillery. We gather ourselves under the parapet, ready for the desperate scramble — and the center of our line begins to fade away. The colors have been shot down, and every man who picks them up is shot. In seconds we change — it is impossible to say what has happened, but we know the parapet can't be taken. We also know that if we start back across the open ground, we'll die.

There's an outburst of yells and firing from our rear, and we see that the Sharpshooters have taken the redoubt and are driving the enemy out the other end. At the same time it looks like brigades on either side of us have stopped in their advance, but are exchanging fire with the enemy in their front. We start back across the field toward the gully.

John has survived, with a scratch — a ball plowed a shallow furrow along his right forearm when he raised his musket to fire. I stay close to him and look for McClure, who turns up, limping, as we skitter like crabs back across the dying ground. Before we reach the shelter of the thickets, Bratton halts us — much resentment, we are still taking fire. He forms those of us who are still taking orders into a rough line — we are kneeling and lying down — and we fire at the parapet, giving the Palmetto Sharpshooters some protection as they get out of the redoubt. Then it is over and the battlefield is silent except for the calls of the wounded.

We call the roll. Out of 1,200 or so men in the brigade, more than 100 are dead on the field and 300 more are wounded, some of them, also, on the field and headed for capture. Two of the young fellows who came up from Chester with John are gone, their fate uncertain. And our flag has been left on the field — just left, because when the time came to leave, nobody realized that the last man to pick it up had also been shot down.

My heart is like lead. The assault might have succeeded, save for an error in assessment. Or maybe it wasn't an error, maybe the generals knew that gully wasn't much protection, but though the assault had to be made anyway.

"Did you notice?" McClure asks, hobbling over the fire where John and I are trying to cook some pork.

"Notice what?" John asks.

"Those were black troops in the fort."

There seems little to say about that, except that I was surprised he had time to take note of it. Now he looks surprised.

"There was lots of time, we were at the foot of the works for an hour," he says.

"An hour? We were there less than a minute!' I answer.

He glares at me.

"Well, it felt like an hour," he finally says.

That ends it, except I'm thinking about Anderson's men taking fire in that gully, and wondering how long it seemed to them. I fall asleep thinking about time.

My recollection
of the War of Secession
or the War Between the States

By Miss Hanna H. Coleman

In 1864 we were very busy working, for the soldier rations were
getting scarce, and new clothes something to dream of. Nearly every one wore home-made shoes, and knit their own stockings, and
made their own hats out of Palmetto corn shucks, or any thing that
could be plaited; one shape was the gun boat, I had one, that was
quite becoming. home spun dresses were all the rage, they were
quite pretty, particularly those made with a polonaise, the polonaise was trimmed with a large cord, and large wooden buttons,
covered with the homespun; we all wore hoop skirts in those days
of course we could not buy them, but the negroes would make and
sell sets of white oak splints, 5 pieces being used in a skirt, the
top piece was perhaps 1-2 yards long, the bottom piece quite long,
but when they were run in a skirt, they were just the thing, somewhat stiff, but hanging beautifully under a heavy homespun skirt.
I did not have a homespun dress though I wanted one very much, nor
did I wear home knit stockings, I could save my store stockings by
not wearing any at home; my mother bought me a pair of shoes for
.50 that had run the blockade. We were still feeding the soldiers,
and a hospital in an empty ware house, near the depot, was always
filled with the sick and wounded; there was no regular surgeon or
M.D. in attendance; sometimes Dr. Pride, or Dr. DaVega, who kept
a drug store, or any visiting Dr. was called in, to prescribe or
dress wounds.
    Our town too, was filled with refugees, from Charleston, Savan-
nah, and other places that had fallen into the hands of the Yankees, some of the refugees did noble work for the soldiers. One a
Miss C. from Charleston lived next to us, in fact she almost lived
with us, she took tea with us every evening. We gave her real tea
to drink for quite a while, then we had milk and hot water, for the
store tea was giving out. One evening I nearly exploded, when she
asked my mother for another cup of beautiful hot water, Miss C. was
a noble Christian woman.
    About that time a soldier came to our house, sunburned, freck-
led, thin and ragged he had been a prisoner at Johnston's Island.
He was a boy almost, and a preacher, he had bought some grey goods
in Richmond, and was trying to get a suit of clothes made. My moth-

er, Mrs. Martha Mobley and Miss Crain volunteered to make them, if he got them cut, which he did. After his clothes were made and he put them on, he looked so genteel and was so grateful, this soldier was from Tennessee, and is now the great Dr. W. H. Whitsitt, president of the Richmond College, and for years president of the Baptist Theological Seminary, in Louisville, Ky. He never forgot the kindness and sometimes comes to see us.

In May Alan Kennedy was killed at Drury Bluff, the day the news came of his death, his sister lay dying:- About this time my Uncle John Kennedy and his son Henry volunteered, Henry was with Gen. Joe Wheeler so, all of my relatives were in the army, and so few came back.

The body of Gen. John Dunovant was brought home for burial, he was killed, shot in the head while leading his men, in a skirmish, the body was taken to the Episcopal church, a severe storm came up in the afternoon, and, it remained in the church all night. there was a flag draped over the coffin lid, I thought of the old song: "They brought my soldier back to me, and the knot of ribbon blue, But the ghastly wound on his brow was hid, by the flag draped over the coffin lid."

In '64 the war cloud was very dark and lowering, and men in authority wore care worn faces; our forces were completely hemmed in by the foe. In this year the Privateer Jeff Davis was lost off the Florida coast, this vessel had done fine work for the Confederacy, running the blockade, and bringing ammunition and supplies to our army, it was a terror to the Northern Navy, having had many fights with their different vessels, and sinking several of them, in a severe storm, this rebel boat was driven upon the Florida reefs and sunken. Dr. William Babcock was a surgeon on the boat, while the boat was sinking he rescued a pet parrot; and brought Polly home with him. Our ports blockaded, our boys were hungry and ragged but still very brave. Tecumsah Sherman, had commenced his march through Georgia, burning and killing as he went. Atlanta had fallen, and on this horde of house burners came to S. C. where were no men to oppose them, only an army of defenseless women and children. The negroes behaved nobly in those days, they sided with the South, and assisted in hiding and burying the valuables of their owners sometimes they were tortured by the Yankees and made to tell where they were concealed, but seldom told without cruelty. When the Savannah river was crossed and Sherman was in S. C. the devastation commenced in reality: One of the Northern officers, maybe Sherman himself, remarked, if a "Buzzard were to fly from the sea to Columbia, it would have to take it's rations with it," nothing was left, but the chimneys, marking the places of the once happy homes, and a crowd of homeless women and hungry little children.

In Feb. 1865, Columbia fell. Gen. Wade Hampton, and, his men, who had been watching and harassing Sherman, retreated as the Northern army and burned the bridge over the Congaree river: The Capitol of S.C. was in possession of the foe. Sherman's men immediately sacked the city, and set it on fire. From house to house, they went, these men, in the blue uniform of the U.S., with lighted torch. sometimes it was applied to the bed of a sick person, what matter, it was a rebel! I knew a lady with a baby a day or so old, the torch was applied to the bed curtains, her sister put it out, only to have it applied again, she was finally taken from the burning house on a mattress. There were dozens of such cases. One wife took a father, 95 years old out, and sat by his side, in the rain and darkness in a field as his life ebbed away. The yard of the Lunatic Asylum was crowded with women and children, the house itself was full of those who had gone there for protection, thinking, who would molest or war, on God's afflicted, but insane inmates had to be taken out, and, hurried to the Catholic Convent, their screams and shrieks adding to the horrors of the night.

Many homeless refugees came to Chester, living as best they could, in box cars, or any place that sheltered them. The medical, and commissary stores too, were brought here, to be kept from the Northern Army. Some of Wheeler's cavalry were scouring the country, getting mules and horses, to take th places of the worn out animals of the army. I hear many passed for that cavalry, that had never seen the plucky little Joe Wheeler. I remember my Grand-father had a favorite horse, he, my grand-father, was a very old man, and, he used this beautiful animal himself, the horses and mules from the plantation had been brought to town for protection, and this supposed cavalry took them. When they took my Grandfather's riding horse, Grand-ma, with the tears in her eyes, begged them not to take it, and though she had just fed the men, their hearts were of stone, and the last we saw of the horse, was, as she was led away, very reluctantly on her part.

One contemptible feature of Sherman's army was, to destroy historic places: In Columbia after trying to demolish the State House, they took the bronze palmetto tree, that bore the names of the South Carolinian's who fought in Mexico, and tried to break it, fortunately the bronze resisted, but they bent, and twisted, and almost ruined it. When they passed through Camden S. C., they burned the head quarters of Cornwallis, the British officer, that had been kept with such care since the Revolutionary war. In passing through Lancaster Sherman burned the Court house, with many valuable papers, he put the Confederate prisoners he had captured along his route in the jail, and set the building on fire, the prisoners were not removed until the floor above them was burning, they were then taken out, to be shot, but as they filed out, expecting instant death, a rapid firing was heard near by, and thinking Gen. Wade Hampton's Cavalry were upon them, they released the prisoners. Mr. McCarley now living in Winnsboro was one of them.

When Sherman neared this place, he burned the home of Mrs. Ed. Mobley, she was a tiny little woman, with several children, the Yankees put fire in a closet upstairs, and soon the house was a mass of flames. She and the children stood under a tree and watched the burning house, an officer approached, and asked her why she didn't cry, she told him, she wanted him to see how a Southern woman, could bear such cruelty: the officer told her she was a brave woman, and ordered his men to save something for her, but it was too late, and the piano was all that was saved from the handsome home. There were several who lived near here, who left with their families, and valuables trying to get to the mountains of N. C., hut when Sherman turned in the direction of Hanging Rock, he ran upon the wagon train and took everything of any value from them. Kate Mobley had on her Mother's wedding ring, one of the men made her take it off, and give it to him, though she cried and told him her mother was dead.

The Northern army came as far as Woodward church some 6 Or 7 miles from town, and spies were seen lurking around our streets. I remember the day we expected Sherman. Every horse and mule had been taken away, and hidden in the woods, Wheelers men had raided the bar rooms and taken barrels of whiskey into the streets, and emptied them in the gutters, to prevent a repetition of Columbia's horrors. There were several false alarms of the advance of the Yankee army. Once the rumor was spread, Sherman has come! but it was a company or so of our cavalry, who had been out reconnoitering, and were dashing up Columbia St. around by the Baptist Church with shouts and yells. When the last soldier had gone and we, women and children, with two or three old men were left, I commenced losing my bravery. We had buried our jewelry and silver, some had put on extra clothes to save them. I wore my usual clothing, for I thought I could run better if it came to close quarters, in my usual outfit, but, as we waited, with aching hearts, Lo! the news that the army had gone by the way of Hanging Rock, so as to act with Stoneman's Cavalry, which was on this side of Charlotte, N. C., and, from getting between the Confederate forces, Johnstone being in N.

C. and the Cavalry in S. C, my spirits immediately took an upward bound.

Stoneman was trying to capture the Naval stores and Post Office Dept., that was being rushed South from Norfolk, and Richmond, and to try and capture our Cavalry, fortunately his, and Sherman's men got very little farther for Gen. Lee capitulated.

There were car loads upon car loads of Naval stores brought here, and destroyed at Rocky Creek some 3 miles from town, cannon and shell were exploded and shot thrown into the stream, they were destroyed to keep the enemy from getting them, for, the Confederacy was drawing to a close, and the boys in grey were soon to lay down their arms, not conquered, but out-numbered. Most of the most valuable documents of the Confederacy were destroyed near Fort Mill, and at this place Commissary stores that our poor soldiers would so gladly have used were opened, and, taken by any one who wished. A car load of supplies was standing near the white house, below here, a lady told me, not long since as a school girl, at Purity Church, she, with other children went up there, and got their aprons full of sugar.

Chester
February 9, 1865

My dearest Husband,

I hope this finds you safe and well. Your safety is constantly on my mind. Every time they unload dead and wounded soldiers from the train and take them into the hospitals here, my heart almost stops. I am so afraid that one of them will be you.

We are sore beset. Chester is awash in people who have fled from Sherman's armies, which we hear are now coming our way. They are said to be near Columbia. We have people from everywhere he has been clustered here and in Yorkville, and the talk among everyone is where on earth we shall go if the Yankees come here. The only ones who don't seem to care are some clever men who have been making money all during the war — blockade runner captains, some contractors. They are taking their ease here and waiting for the end they say will not be far away. They all have money — gold and silver and letters of credit from banks in Bermuda and South America. Several have approached me about buying some of the properties that have been taken by the bank.

Since you have not seen fit to do so, I have confronted Mr. Mantour regarding his ruination of Lt. Moore and his family. He at first denied the coercion, but finally "acknowledged the corn." He has begged me to remain silent, for these are dangerous and ugly times. I have chosen to remain silent and await your return to decide how we might arrange things.

Your mother has opened her house to wounded soldiers. That was an exceptionally kind thing for her to do, but it may also turn out to be a very practical thing to do. A house used to shelter the wounded is not likely to be desecrated by other soldiers. William, the stories we hear — Yankees stealing everything they can steal. Wheeler's men kill them when they can, but then Wheeler's men are no better than thieves themselves. Our civil authorities can do nothing, and we have what seem to be little more than bands of pirates and marauders rampaging across an increasingly lawless landscape. Those who are sheltering here are well aware of the dangers they face whenever they move — we will probably be able to make our fortune after the war simply by digging under foundations and barns and gathering all the silver and jewelry so desperately hidden here.

"After the war." What a lovely sound that has. But William, "after the war" will have no meaning for me unless you are here. Surely you can come home now? Clearly this will not go on much longer and we need you — I need you! — here in Chester to protect us. What point is there in staying? Others from your army have come home and they tell us you are starving, that the Yankees are just waiting for good weather to crush you. Our western armies are finished, scattered before the wind like chaff. This war is lost and you must consider that your first duty is now to us, not to a government that is happy to bleed you death in the name of a cause that has been lost.

William, you must come home. We are in great and terrible danger here.

Yr obt. Wife,
Elizabeth

Near Petersburg
March 10, 1865

My dearest Elizabeth,

How wonderful to hear from you, even though I fear I must disappoint your hopes. It is impossible for any man who would look himself in the mirror for the rest of his life to leave this army now. Thank God this Regiment and this Brigade are filled with men who know their duty — Bratton says we are the biggest regiment in the army now, and the biggest brigade.

It is not a question now of winning or losing, it is a question of staying the course and seeing it through properly. The Providence that has seen me through four years of war without a scratch will surely continue to look over me. So, no, Elizabeth, I will not return home until released from my duty here.

As for Lt. Moore's property and Mr. Mantour's perfidy, I do not know what you mean by "arranging things." The only arrangement possible is that Mantour return that property to Moore's heirs. Perhaps you did not know: I met A.J. on the battlefield and in the middle of the oddest horseback ride you can imagine we talked about this. He is furious with his father and told me he'd be writing to him immediately to insist that Moore's widow receive money either from the bank or from the Mantour family.

I think A.J. intends to make things right in a great many ways at the bank. I think all of us who come home from this war will not have much truck with the way things were before — we have seen too much of life and death to be overly fastidious about how things get set right, but get set right they will.

Sometimes my life before this war seems something lived by a stranger. I can't believe I labored at a bank and wore a cravat.

Elizabeth, be patient. Things are indeed pointing toward an end, but we must finish this in a way that brings honor to the entire enterprise. Think of those who have died and shed blood — they died not knowing their cause was lost. We owe it to them to keep going.

Your loving Husband,
William

CHAPTER TWENTY-ONE

We trudge out of the Petersburg trenches long before dawn, skulking away quietly so the Yankees won't hear us. We are hungry — we've been hungry for quite a while — but we are on the move, with the sacred earth of Virginia drying and dropping off our shoes after the warm April sun comes up. We are out of the deadly trenches.

It feels good to be on the move, good to be moving away from the white sand and sniping and the smell of death. It is good to be moving away from the rotting corpse of John Vickers, hanging in the abatis in front of our trench in such full view of the enemy that recovering his body, even on the darkest night, was impossible.

It was the Sixth South Carolina's bad luck to be in the trenches at one of the points that was only yards away from the blue troops. We sat there, day after day, while Vickers rotted. What could we write home to Chester? Not the whole truth. We wrote in February to his mother, telling the poor woman that her final sacrifice had been made and her 16-year-old son, the third of her sons to die in the war, had been killed in honorable combat.

We didn't tell her he'd fallen for a Yankee trick, trying to sneak out in front of the trenches to investigate a plump haversack that appeared between the lines one cold, bright morning. He'd been told to ignore it; he'd been told it was a trap; but nobody could sit on him day and night and the boy was still growing and hungry and it hurt him worse to be hungry than some of the rest of us who'd been hungry before. We parched our corn, boiled it in water and made do; he snuck away and tried to crawl to that haversack and of course they were waiting for him, they let him put his hand on it before sending a Minie ball crashing into his leg.

He shrieked once, and the whole company was up on the firing step and peering under the head log in seconds.

"Sweet Jesus," Willie McClure said.

Vickers hunkered down, as best he could, while the scum in the opposite trenches kicked up dirt with deliberately aimed shots that fell all around him, but did not hit him.

"Hungry, Reb?" came the call. "He'p youself." Then they laughed.

Vickers spent some time wrapping his leg with a piece of his shirt, then he looked back at us, eyes huge in the twilight.

"Boy, when we shoot, you try to come," I yelled. The company began popping away at the head log on the Yankee side, trying to keep their heads down. Vickers began to move, and Yankees farther down the line, not under our fire, opened up on him, sending him sprawling in the mud with another wound. The rest of the Sixth was now up on the line to find out what was going on; it took only a glance to figure it out, and they began a steady, rolling fire. Vickers was game; he heard the firing, looked back at us again and began crawling.

The abatis was the problem. He'd gone out through a hole, but that hole was in such a position that it would be death to try it on the way back. He had to climb over at another spot, and of course, when he did, the Yankees poured it in and caught him with an arm and a leg over a branch. He shuddered as the heavy bullets hit, and started to fall back, but got hung up on the sharpened points.

The Yankees cheered, and we screamed with rage and fired like wild men, but it did no good. The boy was dead, and there he hung, blond hair waving in the wind for days while the crows came in the day and the rats came in the night and the boy disintegrated in front of our eyes.

They were big rats. They were eating better than us.

So when Grant finally breaks our line south of Petersburg, we are relieved, even though we suspect the end is near. If we are going to die, better in a field or a forest than a muddy trench in Petersburg where the rats will eat our flesh and friends will lie to our family about our fate.

The Rev. Ichabod Barak McCausland came to me before dawn, while we were getting ready to leave in response to the urgent word that had come down through the commands. McCausland was gaunt and big-eyed — some sort of affliction was on him but he, like others, was still present and doing his duty. He amended that duty from time to time to include performing whatever function was needed, including clerk work and hospital work. He was spending a lot of time in field hospitals.

For once he did not begin the conversation with a Bible verse he considered appropriate.

"Coleman, it would appear we are done, and it escapes me what this was all about," he said. "The blood, the hardship, the strife — for what?"

I of course had no answer either. It seemed to me our chances to affect destiny had slipped away from us, but I wasn't sure how that quite fit into McCausland Calvinist theology, so I merely shook my head.

He looked right at me, eyes burning from deep in their sockets.

"Ichabod. Do you know what Ichabod means in Hebrew? It depends on the translation. It means either 'Where is the glory?' or "no glory." And 'Barak,' Coleman, do you want to know the possibilities there? 'Barak' means either 'thunder; or 'in vain.' Sometimes I think my parents were that rarest of all creatures, Calvinists with a sense of humor."

He sat down heavily on the parapet of the trench.

"Which were we, Coleman? Thunder or in vain? Or is it the same thing? And which did God want us to be?"

These are weighty issues. I finally grasped exactly what he meant — we have always had a feeling that we could have made a difference had things been arranged slightly differently than they were. First Manassas, Chickamauga, Wauhatchie, Fort Sanders, the assault that never happened in the Wilderness after Jenkins and Longstreet were struck down, and the terrible slaughter at Fort Harrison — always the Sixth was not quite able to change fate, or was not used to try to change fate. I am surprised that a Calvinist preacher is so affected by these things, but there is little I can do about him or us. But I am moved by his despondency.

"We are not yet whipped," I told him. "Always there is hope."

He simply looked at me with what I assume is reproach.

Dawn breaks as we leave Petersburg behind. We spend the first day marching through farmland that grows less and less desolate the farther we move away from the trenches. By the third day, we are on ground not touched by fighting. We begin to dare hope we might get something to eat from the farms we are passing, even though not much but cabbage and greens could be growing now. Cabbage and greens sound wonderful. Clearly, many of these people put something away during harvest season; the fields are tended and the stubble shows where corn had been growing. But the doors are all closed. When the surviving remnant of the Aaron Burr Mess gets permission from Col. Steedman to try our luck at one particularly prosperous looking house, no one will answer. We spotted the old farmer between his barn and his house and asked him if he had anything to spare.

"Go away!" he roared. "Damned soldiers! What you coming' here for? Who asked you? Take your thieving hands off my land!"

Four years before, probably, he'd been one of the ones cheering us on when we headed north for Manassas. They couldn't do enough for us then. They piled on more food than we could carry, poured milk into our canteens, had their daughters serve us hot turkey and beef along the roads we marched. Now we, who had been their sons and brothers and sweethearts, had become "just soldiers, stay away, they're dirty."

And so we are. Well clad, in this fourth year of the war. Well shod. Very well equipped. Very well trained. But very dirty and very, very hungry.

I hold the old man while we empty his root cellar, taking every scrap of food. Old potatoes, a basket of dried-up apples: Commissary Sergeant William Coleman is again doing his duty by the 353 men who remain in the Sixth Regiment.

Except that John Bratton rides up partway through our "requisitioning" and made us share it with all 1,500 men in the brigade. No comment about what we are doing, merely brief instructions to make it go as far as it can go.

We march on down the road, a long line of lean men in grey uniforms, chewing on bits of apple or potato and listening to the sound of gunfire behind us, to our right, and to our left. The regiment ahead of us suddenly breaks into a trot and we can see puffs of dirt kicking up in the road; they are under fire. Steedman halts us short of where they became visible to the enemy. We sink to the ground, glad for a rest; let the officers sort it out.

The long column is stalled. From our rear comes a group of horsemen, riding furiously, and suddenly Lee is there in the road next to us, asking what the problem is. The old man is frustrated. His face remains still, but his body gives him away. He twists in the saddle as his aides explain that the Yankees have come within range of the road. This, with most of the army still to cross the dangerous spot.

"Who will rid me of this vexation?" he asks nobody in particular. He looks our way. "What troops are those?"

"The Sixth South Carolina, General," Steedman responds, with a slight bow. He pauses, then adds, "At your service."

"The Sixth South Carolina — Bloody Pines? Yes." He slaps his horse with his hat, riding up and down in front of us until we are all on our feet.

"Will you help me? Will you help me?" he asks. "I want those people suppressed." He points with his hat to the left of the road, where the sound of firing can clearly be heard. His eyes flash. "Will the Sixth help me, one more time? We need this road, we need to get to Farmville and then into the mountains."

What choice do we have? There is never any choice with Lee. He asks, and we feel the pull of duty. It is stronger than gravity, and holds us to the army with as much force.

Tom Wright pulls his drum out of the one wagon we have left and beats the long roll, and we fall in, one company after another, fixing bayonets without being told. Parson McCausland gets out his Bible and began reading and praying, high squeaking voice barely audible over the clanking and rustling of the regiment getting itself ready for just one more fight. McCausland moves to the head of the column. Steedman gets off his horse and gives it to one of Lee's staff officers to hold until the fight is over or he is dead, whichever comes first.

We march up the road by the left flank. When we break out of the woods into a field, we see immediately what had happened: A Yankee regiment had pushed into a point of woods that came within 300 yards of the field, and from cover they are banging away at the road.

Steedman ignores the bullets kicking up dust, marching us up the road until the entire regiment is out in the open.

"By the left flank! March!" he roars, and we change formation into a battle line; the colors move out in front at the double quick, and that fast, we are ready and on the move toward the wood line. Steedman runs down the line until he reaches the colors, put himself ahead of them, and away we go.

The woods get closer and we can see men, blue uniforms, white faces, in the underbrush. The wind blows the white smoke from their guns down on us; men began falling. Steedman waits until we are only 70 yards from the woods.

"Halt!" he roars, and the long line slams to a halt. He scurries through to the rear, pulling the flag bearer with him.

"Ready," he screams, and the muskets come up to the ready position.

"Aim!" he shrieks, and we do, finding targets as best we can in the dark woods ahead of us, just as Winder and Jenkins and Bratton had taught us.

"Fire!" Steedman screams, and a sheet of flame reached out toward the Yankees. You could hear the Minie balls thwacking off the tree trunks.

"Arms port," he roars, and both ranks come to arms port "Forward," Steedman commands, and the long line springs forward and the wild, mournful banshee wail of our battle cry rolls ahead of us, echoing through the trees.

There is almost no return fire from the woods. We are on them in seconds, leveling our bayonets as we hit the wood line and giving them no time to form or think or do anything except take a quick look at those bayonets and then run.

It is a new regiment, mostly recruits, many of them foreigners who jabber at us in an unknown language when we take them prisoner. They break, running through the pine scrub toward the top of a hill, and we take off howling off after them, the Demon Rebs they'd heard about from veterans ever since their first day, the attacking Greybacks they thought had had the sand beat out of them by this late date. We show them their error, pushing again through pine boughs red with the blood of our enemies.

We break up going through the wood lot. When we emerge into the open on the far side, atop a hill, we see a sight that turns the warm day cold as ice. The far side of the field, maybe 400 yards away, is covered with blue infantry, with wagons, with limbered batteries, all moving west, parallel to our line of march. There are thousands of them, an enormous force — and they are south of us, not north, and moving as fast across country on little farm roads and fields as we'd been moving down a pretty good road. We are quietly aghast, for any private in the ranks knows enough to grasp that Yankees south of us, this deep in Virginia, is wrong.

Steedman positions the colors — our old silk colors, sent to us by Bratton's wife after we lost the new colors at Fort Harrison. We have a new flag, the white flag with the battle flag in the corner, but today Steedman chose the first flag we blooded. The men fall into line as they come out into the open. We watch as the shattered Yankee regiment straggles across the field to the safety of the huge blue mass in the distance, and listen as the Yankee army jeers the retreating men for breaking in the face of rabble like us.

Then they start forming battle lines to come after us and brush us out of the way. We see from the flags and from some of the officers, who are identifiable even at this distance, that we face a brigade from what had been Hancock's II Corps, volunteers who had re-enlisted after their first term of service had expired. They have been formed into an entire brigade of Veteran Volunteer regiments. This would not be a raw regiment coming at us, it would be the best the Yankee army could put in the field. They are all men who believe in their cause, as we believe in ours.

I am feeling faint — I have not been right since we took that old man's food, and I wonder if some of the mold on the potatoes has made me sick.

We just watch, and when they are fairly well formed at the bottom of the hill, Steedman motions to Tom Wright, who beats the long roll. The men, who had been standing in a loose line, dress ranks, slowly, lit up brilliantly by golden sunlight. And I think I see Michael Moore — and Fred Babcock. Surely he is dead. So is Henry McElduff, but there he is, taking his place in line. And J.R. Peay — guess he wasn't killed at Frazier's Farm.

"Sweet Pea!" I call out, and he smiles and waves at me and points at the Yankees. Major Hall comes up behind him and waves to me as well, and finally Tom Farrar. McClure comes to me, concern on his face.

"What are you doing?" he asks. "What about Sweet Pea?" I just shake my head and move into line.

Parson McCausland had been standing behind the line, reading from the Bible. He now stops, and very deliberately closes the Book. He takes it to Tom.

"Wright, I'll trade you, now, for that which you have been holding for me," McCausland said. Tom nods his black face and takes the Bible from McCausland. Then he takes off his knapsack, opens it, and pulls out a long piece of bone, which he gives to the parson. McCausland goes over to the pile of Enfields we'd taken from captured Yankees, gets a rifle and a cartridge box and a cap box, and outfits himself as a fighting man.

McCausland turns to me, in the line of file closers.

"Been reading in Judges," McCausland says. Then he walks off, like a great skinny bird.

McCausland goes to the colors, where Steedman is waiting wistfully to see if anyone is sending a regiment or maybe a corps to his support. The colors are posted in the middle of our line, in the front rank. The parson strides up to Steedman.

"Colonel, with your permission? I would like to see to the spiritual needs of the men," he says, blue eyes glinting brightly through a squint.

Steedman, still looking to the rear for some sign of help, nods, thinking McCausland is going to pray or something; he had done it before. I wonder how he'll make his screechy little voice heard down the length of the line of battle, swollen as it is by the arrival of the dead. I am also surprised McCausland did not comment on this odd phenomenon, surely of interest to a man of the cloth. Resurrection? Now? Is this the end of times?

Bony old Parson McCausland takes off his hat and sets it on the ground, as he does before he prays, and walks out in front of the colors. But instead of turning to face us, he keeps on walking a bit, then stands facing the Yankees. They are just about ready, overlapping our line by a hundred yards on each side, and about 200 yards away, already within easy range. They watch, curious to see what this long-haired old man is doing. It is very quiet. The outcome is clear to all of us, on both sides; we have all done this before. Without support, we'll be outflanked and rolled off that hill in minutes.

We are still in a line of battle, but most of the men are kneeling and sitting, heads hanging low, just waiting. McCausland walks down the hill toward the Yankees, then stands and glares at them, until every eye is on him.

He takes his Enfield and lifts it high above his head with his left hand. In his right, he takes his piece of bone — the jawbone of a huge Army mule — and lifts it up where everyone can see. He shakes his Enfield and he shakes his mule bone. His long white hair and flowing beard and his long brown coat blow in the warm breeze, and he stands there in the golden sunlight like an Old Testament figure come to life, taunting the Yankees with the jawbone of an ass and offering, without saying a word, to slay 1,000 before the sun sets. As Samson did in Judges, Book 15.

The hair stands up on the back of my neck.

There is a pause, then a low growl starts among the men. Tom Wright beats the long roll again, and we are all on our feet and screaming, screaming, screaming and throwing hats up in the air and stomping up and down and waving our guns at the Yanks and raging at them to come on, end it, come on. Tears are streaming down my face and for the first time in four years, I want to fight, I want to storm down that hill with these brave men. No more abstractions, no more finding something clever to do, no more thinking. My blood screams and reason leaves me.

From across the little valley comes a roar, and 2,000 of Hancock's veterans, who had been assembled to kill us, begin to cheer and throw their hats in the air and wave their guns. And when their officers go among them, slapping them with flat of their swords and waving pistols around to try to restore order, the men knock some of them down. They finally get one regiment straightened out, giving them the order "Ready! Aim! Fire!" and the men jeer and point their guns straight up in the air and fire. And then one blue regiment after another does the same, sending crashing volleys into the sky while their officers rage.

Steedman is bawling like a baby, but he manages to give the orders for us to aim and fire, and we send a volley — into the sky. Steedman takes one last wistful look in our rear and, seeing no relief, orders us to the rear by the right of companies, and we march back into the woods to the cheers of the Yankees.

Parson McCausland truly saved our bacon, because if we had stayed there we'd have been swept from the hill. But by defying them and then leaving, they suspected a trap, and kept their distance. Salute us, yes; trust us not to trick them, no, not yet. We'd bloodied their noses too many times.

McCausland, not Steedman, leads us back to the road, where an ashen-faced group of officers waited to be told what the tremendous volleys had been about. When Steedman tells Lee that a vast host is south of us and moving fast, Lee's shoulders slump.

Longstreet is there by then, and Lee asks him a question I can't hear.

"Not yet, not yet," Longstreet says quietly, looking west to where we should soon see the Blue Ridge.

We reform in the road and began marching west again. Steedman passes down word that our destination is Appomattox Court House, where a supply train is waiting with rations. About then I look around for Sweet Peay, can't find him and pass out.

CHAPTER TWENTY-TWO

There are no rations at Appomattox the next day, but there are Yankees. More than enough. We put out pickets and wait, for a day. After a time, without much being said, we come to understand that we are going to surrender. Bratton forms us up.

"It is over and you're going home," he tells us. "We will go down to the Yankee army, stack arms, turn in our colors, draw rations and start for South Carolina."

"Which colors?" someone asks. The question starts a flurry of conversation among the field officers. Most of the regiments have more than one flag; a quiet consensus is reached that each regiment will turn in whichever flag it chooses, and hide the other. For the Sixth, the decision is easy: the old silk 12-star flag that has been with us since the fall of 1861 is going home to South Carolina.

We call the roll one last time, and join the weary men marching over the hill toward the village. There we find the Yankee army drawn up and waiting for us, and it is an odd feeling to be walking in the open in front of them. I keep expecting to hear the muskets.

I am still not feeling well, and get permission to ride in our regimental wagon.

One by one the regiments march into the village, stack arms, strip off their accouterments, and place their furled colors on the stacks, just as if we were going into bivouac. But this is the last time.

There is a flurry as we come up to take our turn; one of the federal officers recognizes McCausland from his jawbone-of-a-mule glory. This officer, however, is an arrogant twit who has figured out that while the Reverend is the same, the flag is not. Where, he wants to know, is our "other" flag, the one we used the other day? He reminds me of Major Brett, the strutting peacock from Beauregard's staff we began this war with. Is there no end to men like these?

Despite our officers' protests that they don't understand, a platoon of Yankees is sent among us to open knapsacks and search for the pale flag. They are not successful until they reach Tom Wright, who had been given custody of the colors — the man least likely to be searched or questioned. Yankees are thorough, however, and I watch with dismay as they go through his knapsack. There is suddenly a flurry of blue around him, but then the sergeant in charge of the search details calls out "Still nothing. Search the wagon."

Four Yankee soldiers come over to the wagon and make a big show of pawing through boxes and checking the three of us who are inside. One of them comes over to me and opens my jacket; he trips and comes down on top of me and I feel him poking around. He scrambles up, eyes twinkling.

"Now just hush," he whispers. He moves away, calling out "Nothing, nothing but sick Confederates and lice."

I look down and see a corner of our flag peeking out from under my jacket.

We are allowed to move on after that, and a funny thing happens. Every Yankee regiment comes to "shoulder arms" when we pass.

All is not well, however. When we arrive at the spot where we are to be paroled, Tom Wright is taken away by the officer I believe truly must be Major Brett's brother, and put with other black

Confederate soldiers. Apparently he is told he does not need to sign a parole, and he is wildly indignant. It will come to nothing in the end: Our field officers have been given signed paroles and need only to fill in the names of the men in their commands. Steedman will fill out one for Tom Wright and we will get it to him. To our consternation, however, when the paroles are filled out and we move out — still as a brigade, even without weapons — Tom Wright is not among us.

Bratton urges us to stay together for the march back to South Carolina. Apparently we do, but I know little of this. Whatever is wrong with me is taking hold, and I spend much of the trip in a stupor. I am told we commandeered an entire train for part of the trip, but have no clear recollection of any such thing. I have fuzzy recollections of Willie helping me and talking at me, but that's all. What I do remember next is my mind coming clear as my brother John, McClure and I walk into the front door of Mother's house, with a grown-up Hanna shrieking with joy, Mother crying like a baby and my wife Elizabeth running to find out what was wrong.

WILLIAM'S EPILOGUE

A.J. is preening again, as best he can in his emaciated condition, wearing his old tattered uniform one last time while waiting for Willie McClure and me to come downstairs and join him in a glass of wine. Yes, wine. A case of Malaga wine, hidden in a weedy corner down at the railroad yard. Elizabeth brought us a bottle, saying that we deserve a toast to launch our new lives.

Elizabeth and I have had a tremendous row about Montour and the Moore farm. She wished for me to accept Montour's offer of the land — that he would give it to me and I would then be silent about the dishonorable thing he did four years ago. "I don't see that happening," I told both him and Elizabeth. The land includes the Great Falls on the Catawba River — it must go to Michael Moore's widow. A.J. and I believe we can convince the Widow Moore to allow us to start a mill there — we can put men from the Sixth Regiment and all the other regiments to work, and Moore's family will profit from the enterprise. We have plans for a lumber mill and a cotton mill — lumber to rebuild all that has been destroyed, and cotton to get our economy going again.

"You could own all that," Elizabeth says.

"I do not wish to own all that, I wish to see an injustice addressed," I tell her. We simply do not see this issue the same, and it upsets me tremendously. But it will have to wait. It has waited for the last two weeks, since we got here, and it can wait a bit longer.

I am not going to think about how a bottle of wine survived this chaos, I'm just going to enjoy it. She says her friend McDonald gave it to her.

I have looked over this wartime journal of mine one last time; this is the last page in the last chapter. It is time for a new journal, the one that details how we move forward now after having lost a nation. I have put my latest writings with the ones I'd sent home to Sarah Wright for safekeeping. Sarah is downstairs, waiting impatiently for me to finish it, so she can take it to her farm and hide it. She and Tom will keep it safe — when Tom shows up. He has not yet done so. He just disappeared after the surrender.

There are reports that Yankees are on the way, to be a garrison force in Chester. There will probably be no trouble, but just in case, I am letting Sarah hold the journal. The Yankees will not search a black family's home. It will not occur to them that there is anything of value there. It's probably a lot safer than the vault in A.J.'s bank — not that anyone will be looking there for anything of value, either. The bank holds a lot of land, but all its liquid assets were in Confederate bonds.

It looks like everything is going downhill. Lincoln's assassination means we face retribution, not reconciliation. But I am myself reconciled. We fought to create a nation, and we failed. It would not have been a perfect nation, but neither were the 13 colonies perfect when they created the United States. They started out with the blemish of slavery. It is now purged, for all of us, by torrents of blood. I think it could have been done otherwise, but we will never know.

It's an odd thing. I feel like "independence" is a fine and noble concept, but it's not really why I fought. Southern independence might have been the end result, if the outcome had been in our favor, but it's not the real answer. I have looked back on this journal for some kind of an answer, and I feel it lies with the parson on the road to Appomattox. I was eager to fight, with my brothers, because we had become brothers, and for no other reason. We were soldiers, and brothers, and The Cause was ourselves.

I feel the hair going up on the back of my neck and I sense that, finally, after four long years, my thoughts and my feelings are in perfect harmony. Politicians evoke causes, dreamers create visions of the future, but soldiers fight for each other, not for causes or visions. I know that in the future, when I pass other men from the Sixth Regiment or Bratton's Brigade or the Army of Northern Virginia — or a Yankee soldier, for that matter — we will look at each other and know things about each other that those who stayed behind can never know or understand. Duty, and pride, and honor, and brotherhood — words that can't be understood until they are lived. We lived them, and the understanding is our prize.

I have no idea what the future holds, but I am satisfied with my small role in what is now our Southern history. I am proud of who I am — William Coleman, former Confederate soldier — and I hope I do right by my brothers in the years to come.

My recollection
of the War of Secession
or the War Between the States

By Miss Hanna H. Coleman

The 9th of April 1865 Gen Lee surrendered at Appomattox, and Gen. Johnstone at Greensboro, N.C. on the 26th. It was brave in Lee to surrender to save the lives his men, for there was no way of reinforcing his handful of worn out soldiers; while Grant had a horde of foreigners to swell his army, that were offered large pay to fight on the Northern side.- Many of our boys came home without taking the oath of allegiance. The rail roads were torn up, so our Southern boys came the best they could, and so many found their homes gone, and their loved ones in destitution. There were no floating banners and the fife and drum were silent.

The last of April, and in May our Chester boys came, my brother William had broken down, and fainted by the wayside. Our town was filled with soldiers trying to get home, crowds would go marching through, very different in appearance to what they were when they went away, now there were no guns, and often, no shoes, and many ragged uniforms;- Wheelers Cavalry seemed to be every where.- They had fought and now they helped themselves to whatever they saw, in the line of commissary stores.-

In the cellar of a store occupied by Mr. Gunhouse there were a quantity of medical and Commissary stores packed away. A man by the name of McDonald knew of it, he was a Charlestonian, had not been in the army but ran the blockade, and was helping himself to whatever he could get.- In this cellar was a cask of wine of Colchicum, he, McDonald marked it malaga wine, and the soldiers seeing it drank of it, it was a deadly poison, a few drops being a dose. Willie McClure heard of it, and invited Col. Montour, my brother William and others of his friends to take a glass of it, thinking it was malaga wine, my brother being sick did not want to go, but did go, and though he only took a sip of it, he died, just two weeks after he came home. Willie McClure died the same night he took the poison, Col. Montour the next evening, and my brother the next morning.

It was in the early morning he died and the mockingbirds were singing in the hedge near the window, I never hear the song of that bird now, after so many years, without it's bringing back that sad morning. My Mother was crushed, and ever afterward was sad. No one knows how many of the soldiers died from the effects of the poison; it is said they sank and died all along the road side, for days afterward.-

I remember when the funeral of my brother was being preached. Hoods Brigade was passing through Chester up the street, past our house, they came shouting and hurrahing. Before the gate the hearse was standing, and the street filled with carriages. My Cousin, Col. William Lewis, went out, and asked them to be quiet, that a brother soldier lay dead in the house, and although hundreds seemed to pass after the request, not a sound was heard, but the tramp, tramp of their footsteps.

Postscript by the author

I lived in South Carolina for two years. New friends, sensing my fascination with history, directed me to a dog-eared, faded, type-written essay by "Hanna Hemphill Coleman" in the public library in Chester. OK, a girl's recollection of the Civil War with a lot of emphasis on her brother, William . Since she was, some time after the war, writing about the Sixth South Carolina, and I was one of a group of living historians breathing life back into the regiment, I read it closely.

Bill Watson

I got to the part where she described her brother's accidental death by poison, a death that came after he'd survived four years of war. It mentally knocked the breath out of me. It was a story that had to be told. And eventually, I did, constructing a story line around that dog-eared treasure of an essay, the real history of the Sixth South Carolina, my own imagination, and hard-won knowledge of what soldier life was like.

Imagine my surprise, late in 2010, when William Coleman's real-world great-great niece, Jane Slaton, contacted me. Imagine my delight when she and her daughter, Maggie Harshbarger, agreed to illustrate a new edition of the book. And imagine my fascination when they told me there was no "Hanna Hemphill Coleman." Just when I thought I'd walked the line between truth and fiction, it moved.

So now we have drawings worthy of Alfred Bellard or any other soldier who drew what he saw during the war. We have two photos of the real William Coleman. We have a new mystery. And we have an instinctive move by Jane and Maggie to re-establish for you the line between truth and fiction: Given complete freedom to pick what they wanted to illustrate, they chose incidents that are "real," confirmed in family lore. That, for me, is a perfect ending for you, the reader.

— Bill Watson

Postscript from the family

In 2003 my son had a college writing assignment to see if he could discover why his ancestors came to America. I gave him what little information we had on early generations, and out of curiosity did an online search for my great grandfather, John Kennedy Coleman. I knew he was from Chester, SC and that he joined the Confederacy when he was 17 and was at Appomattox Court House when he was 18. I had a copy of his Civil War diary, but on visits to a few Civil War battlefields I had learned nothing about him. Then up popped a Web site with a collection of 50 Civil War letters in the Pearce Museum at Navarro College in Corsicana, TX. There were 47 letters written by William Coleman and 3 written by his brother John Kennedy Coleman.

Jane Slaton

I read through this information with growing excitement. When growing up my family would often visit our great aunts and an uncle who lived in the house their father, John Kennedy Coleman, had built in Asheville, North Carolina. We were told stories of "Uncle Willie," John's older brother, whose portrait hung in the parlor. He was William Coleman, who fought all through the Civil War and died tragically two weeks after returning home. I raced to find my copy of the diary and sat down to read the synopsis of the letters and the diary together. In growing wonder the letters told some of the same stories that were in the diary. Pay dirt.

I track family stories, sometimes with obsessive fervor, and other times with a more relaxed hope. Each new discovery comes with a sense of excitement at putting together bits of the everyday past. My love is not the long list of who begat who, but any stories or tales that give a feel for what people's lives were like.

I have been lucky in my search. Some family members were pack rats and some were writers.

Maggie Harshberger

Every now and then I return to the Internet and put in a family name to see if any new information has surfaced. Imagine my surprise when I put in William Coleman's name in 2010 and up came a book called "Brother William's War," written as a fictionalized story about the experiences of William Coleman, a soldier in the Sixth South Carolina from Chester, SC. I hunted through the list of soldiers in the Sixth South Carolina from Chester to make sure there wasn't another William Coleman. When the only William Coleman I could find was "my" William, I tracked down the author.

It turned out that this William (Watson) was a writer, a lover of history and enjoyed Civil War re-enactments. An essay in the Chester, South Carolina, library attributed to Hanna Hemphill Coleman, a sister of William Coleman, had sparked his imagination, and he was off on an adventure mixing what he knew of William from the essay, stories and facts from the Sixth and info about Chester into a fictional story based on our "Uncle Willy."

When William Watson contacted me to see if there were any artist in the family who would be interested in doing some illustrations for the book, my daughter, Maggie, and I, who express ourselves more through pictorial work than the written word, were happy to jump on board.

The real William was a store clerk, not a bank clerk. He never married, but did have a number of girl friends and met someone during the war that he thought was special. He traveled as far as Texas before the war and made a number of visits to an uncle's home in Mississippi. Most of the books in the Coleman library were marked as belonging to William Coleman. He played the violin and guitar. During the war a friend wrote that listening to him play and sing "Mary of Argyle" was heavenly. He was connected to the commissary department for most of the war, but was a private from start to finish. His father died when William was 16, and he became the father to his younger siblings, with a strong influence from his grandfather, John Kennedy, who lived in Chester. William was the beloved oldest son and looked up to by his brother John, who chose to join William's regiment when he entered the war. (John diary is on-line though a site set up by the University of South Carolina.) The events written about in the essay are true.

The lovely part of fiction is that you are not trying to write an exact history, but give a feel for the people and the time. I think William Watson has done a great job of telling a story and using bits and pieces of the real William to bring it to life.

— Jane Z. Slaton

RESEARCH SOURCES

"My recollection of the War of Secession or the War Between the States", By Miss Hanna H. Coleman, unpublished manuscript, Chester Free Public Library, Chester, S.C., date of writing unknown.

Address of Maj. Thomas W. Woodward, delivered before the Survivors' Association of the Sixth Regiment, South Carolina Volunteers, at Chester, S.C., on 9th August, 1883, "Fort Sumter to Dranesville." Published at the Presbyterian Publishing House, Columbia, S.C., 1883

"The Sixth South Carolina Regiment," an address by J.L. Cokers to the Survivors' Association of the Sixth Regiment, South Carolina Volunteers, July, 1887, Chester, S.C. Unpublished, handwritten manuscript provided by Scott Coleman, Chester, S.C.

"History of the Sixth S.C.V. Infantry," Col. J.H. Rion, Winnsboro, S.C.

Speech of Capt. Butler P. Alston, delivered at the reunion of the Survivors of the Sixth Regiment of South Carolina Volunteers, Chester, S.C., August 15th, 1878.

"Brigadier General Micah Jenkins, C.S.A. -- Prince of Edisto," By James S. Swisher, Rockbridge Publishing Company, Berryville, Va. 1996

Special thanks to Scott Coleman of Chester, S.C., without whom this book would not exist, and to Manning Williams of Charleston, for an unforgettable insight.

Those who wish for more may visit the graves of the real William Coleman and Willie McClure, and others of the Sixth, in Evergreen Cemetery in Chester, S.C. Also buried there are more than 55 of the unknown soldiers who died on trains detained in Chester are also buried. On display in Chester's town square is a Parrott gun, one of four found buried beneath the parking lot of a local church after the war by men who, unlike the William in our story, were not reconciled to the outcome. And yes, Hanna's essay is still carefully filed away in Chester's public library.

William Coleman, 1861. This may
be the uniform of the Chester militia.
Those of you who are interested in
material culture details -- you know
who you are -- note: Jane Slaton
reports that according to family lore,
the dark trim came from his sister
Catherine's hat.